Theo Sundermeier

The Individual and Community
in African Traditional Religions

D1524083

Beiträge zur Missionswissenschaft und Interkulturellen Theologie

herausgegeben von

Theo Sundermeier und Dieter Becker

Band 6

LIT

Theo Sundermeier

The Individual and Community
in African Traditional Religions

LIT

Die Deutsche Bibliothek – CIP-Einheitsaufnahme

Sundermeier, Theo
The Individual and Community in African Traditional Religions /
Theo Sundermeier . – Hamburg : LIT, 1998
  (Beiträge zur Missionswissenschaft und interkulturellen Theologie ; 6 .)
  ISBN 3-89473-937-1

NE: GT

© LIT VERLAG
  Grindelberg 15a 20144 Hamburg Tel. 040–44 64 46 Fax 040–44 14 22

Distributed in North America by:

Transaction Publishers
New Brunswick (U.S.A.) and London (U.K.)

Transaction Publishers
Rutgers University
35 Berrue Circle
Piscataway, NJ 08854

Tel.: (732) 445 – 2280
Fax: (732) 445 – 3138
for orders (U.S. only):
toll free 888-999-6778

Table of contents

INTRODUCTION: "PRIMITIVE" RELIGIONS?

1. In less fast-moving times, it used to be a rare privilege to encounter people from other cultural and language backgrounds. Now, however, this has become a common thing for many people in the North, due to the spread of tourism, contacts with migrant workers, international business relations or personal experience of overseas aid work. And although such encounters with the South may have lost the attraction of the exotic and be more a matter of course, they sometimes leave us with mixed feelings. While attracted to what is new and different, we may still find some things hard to understand – not just an unfamiliar language but also people's reactions, and their ways of thinking and expressing themselves.

This book is intended for those living in Europeanised societies, traditionally called the West and now frequently (because of its economic power) the North. It seeks to increase understanding and sympathy for Africans. If you do not know anything about the person you are talking to, misunderstandings will arise. Cultural differences raise barriers to understanding and only knowledge can help disperse bewilderment. In encountering Africans we may indeed recognise or discover something familiar in things that at first sight seem strange.

The following pages will not provide a full picture of the cultures, societies and religions of sub-Saharan Africa, but will concentrate on their image of humankind. The traditional religions of Africa are 'human' in the deepest sense, because they focus on people. The way earlier researchers portrayed them – as 'primitive', 'barbaric' and so on – is one of the greatest misunderstandings of former generations, and can only be explained by the arrogance of the Western attitude to mission. Blind to its own weaknesses, it portrayed other cultures as inferior in order to justify colonialist adventures and claims to sovereignty. Even though unqualified faith in 'Western' civilisation and 'humane' technological progress is no longer possible today, many still admit to thinking that world history revolves around the Western concept of freedom. A. Rüstow represented this point of view in his wide-ranging attempt at a 'perspective on the present'. To his mind, freedom is a profoundly 'humanist' concept without which everything would become relative. Then the "history of the Botocudo, the Zulu Kaffirs, or any other people", would be "just as interesting, important and 'immediate to God' as Western history".[1] Yet in my conviction that is precisely what they are.

African cultures are cultures in the full sense of the word.[2] I share the opinion of the social anthropologist, M. Fortes, that there is no belief and no custom in primitive societies which does not have its equivalent in our civilisation.[3] With regard to traditional religions, we must go a stage further: they are the matrix of all religions. It would be wrong to identify them all with 'magic', in order to distinguish them from the 'higher' religions of Asia and Europe. This is why these two terms will not be used. The undeniable distinction between traditional and world religions will be left to the closing chapter, which will describe how they relate to each other and what this means in terms of religious history.

2. First we must attempt to define traditional religions, and examine whether they can be grouped together at all. A short look at the history of research may help to situate them. One influential writer was Sir James Frazer (1851–1941), a pioneering anthropologist and historian of religion. In his opinion 'primitive peoples' were closely attached to 'magical thought'. By this he understood a primitive, preliminary stage of coping technically with the world, built on faulty reasoning. C. Lévy-Bruhl (1857–1939) likewise spoke of a 'primitive way of thinking', which he described as 'pre-logical'. Even though he actually revoked this expression at the end of his life, once uttered it did not fail to have an effect.[4]

It was a real step forward for research into traditional religions when E. B. Tylor (1832–1917) coined the broad term 'animism'. He was convinced

---

[1] A. Rüstow, Ortsbestimmung der Gegenwart: eine universal-geschichtliche Kulturkritik, vol. 2, 1964, p. 12.

[2] Cf. T. I. van Baaren, 1964.

[3] M. Fortes, 1967, p. 101.

[4] On this subject, cf. F. Gölz, 1963.

that animism could be seen as the first stage of 'educating the world', a process extending over centuries. Of course enormous progress separated us from the animists' world of perception. Yet 'survivals' of earlier cultural stages were to be found even in our societies. They appeared childish to us today, Tylor declared, because they originated in the kind of humanity constituting the infancy of the human race.

With this outlook, Tylor proved himself to be a child of the Enlightenment, and a devotee of positivism as represented by Auguste Comte (1798–1857) and Herbert Spencer (1820–1903), who applied evolutionary theory to society. In accordance with Comte's 'three-stage theory', which stated that the development of the human mind progressed from the theological to the metaphysical and abstract, and finally to the 'positive' (practical) stage, Tylor divided human beings into three categories: savage, barbarian and civilised. The transition from one stage to another was slow, those (Westerners) who had reached the last stage of technological progress having to lead the others to this climax of development. Tylor hereby introduced the contemporary theory of evolution into anthropological research. While Tylor's younger contemporaries showed that his theories could not be proven from religious sources, the evolution model has not been outgrown. It is still thriving in the form of social Darwinism.

What does the evolution model say, and why must it be rejected? It makes three basic assumptions concerning development: 1. Development follows the same pattern everywhere. 2. While the same dynamic speed of development cannot be perceived everywhere, progress basically comes step by step, not in jumps. 3. Movement is always from the lower to the higher level. This model is as untenable in historical terms as the animism theory. We have no proof that religion developed out of the magic stage, nor that belief in souls and spirits led up to belief in a 'high God' or that 'taboos' are preliminary forms of sacral experience.

Without doubt, religions are subject to transformation. The history of religion is full of changes, but they are based on another, multi-dimensional dynamic, not the law of development from the lower to the higher. Tylor and his spiritual successors saw their Western cultural values as absolutes. With

3

the break-up of the colonial empires and with insight into the questionable nature of the 'achievements' of modern times, we have a better appreciation today of the value of other cultures, patterns of conduct and mindsets. In our global society, we need the knowledge and insights of those who have not only survived under extreme environmental conditions, but who have remained truly human in their common life and given it a cultural form that can only be admired.

3. Let us now turn to the peoples of sub-Saharan Africa. They are not culturally homogeneous, yet the differences between the ethnic groups are slighter than between them and the Arabic-speaking peoples of northern Africa. There is no single, all-inclusive name for their religions. *Naturreligionen* ('nature religions', a term widely used in German), is factually wrong. While the non-judgemental designations, 'culture of non-literate peoples' and 'tribal religions', express important elements of traditional religions, they emphasise only a single aspect. For example, it is very difficult to describe the religions to which many millions of people belong (e. g. the Yoruba in Nigeria) as still 'tribal'. Nevertheless, the majority of people with whom we are concerned here are influenced ethnically, socially and religiously by what must be described as 'small-scale societies'. While they are breaking down nowadays and integrating into larger political entities, religious symbols, i. e. the social forms of religious expression, are still meaningful in the new urban or state structure.

4. Religions are not conditioned exclusively by society. Yet the interdependence of society and religion is so great that we must list the most important characteristics of small-scale societies. Otherwise, the framework of religious and symbolic interpretation will not be clear; it will be difficult to make sense of the transition from small-scale to large-scale societies, and the effect this has on forms of religious expression. What the religious change looks like, and how the symbols and modes of thought are integrated into the overarching, world-wide religious systems must be left to the final chapter.

Here are some characteristics of small-scale societies.[5]

• The unity and clear delimitation of a territory signifies a restriction on the number of people with whom each individual comes into contact. The smaller the area, the less the opportunity for many contacts. The few contacts they have are organised more intensively. While external activities are restricted, life in the community is protected and safe.

• The limited space entails economic interdependence. The smaller the society, the more self-contained it is. Members are highly dependent upon each other and close economic co-operation is necessary. Mutual dependence receives symbolic expression in the actual or perceived unity of the people, whose origin is traced back to one ancestor.

• The size of the territory available to a society not only determines the intensity of communication, it causes cultural equality. People speak the same language, manufacture the same tools, go out together to hunt, and develop a culture permitting few variations. A single cultural pattern runs through the whole fabric of life.

• The society lives from continuity. Breaks and deviations would endanger its existence. The range of decisions to be taken is limited; controlled by ultimately conservative behaviour patterns, life is based on precedent and tradition.

• The unity and limitation of space are reflected in the perception of time. Life is focussed on the present, precisely because it is determined by past events. The past, represented by the ancestors, covers a limited time-span, which may reach back over two or three hundred years, but normally covers only two to three generations. The time-span is also determined by the size of the space available, and the necessity of legitimising present life.

• There is only room for one religion in this space. Choosing between different religions is out of the question. Religion and society are in such close symbiosis that they can be distinguished, but not separated. Religion de-

---

[5]   In the following I rely on the work of Godfrey and Monica Wilson, based on their observations in Central Africa, and published for the first time in 1945. In 1971, M. Wilson returned to this subject, modifying her views. Cf. also T. Sundermeier, 1974.

termines the ritual and social aspects of life. It has no validity beyond the territory and the people, and there is no attempt to extend its influence beyond these boundaries. The question of its truth does not arise, because it is part of reality in that society. What counts is its power. In other words, traditional religions are non-missionary and tolerant in their relations with other religions, but intolerant towards deviations in behaviour in the area they control.

- The form and structure of authority is not defined by the dimensions of the land or the society, but it is possible to make distinctions regarding administrative and political functions as the people grows in size. The large West African peoples differ considerably from the smaller Bantu peoples of southern Africa. It is obvious that an expansion of territory will have a decisive effect on the perceived value and sacral dignity of leadership roles, while not greatly disturbing the way the society views and understands humankind.

A final question needs to be answered. Can we examine religions in Africa with a view to finding a image of humankind common to them all? Are not the differences so great that plausible results can only be achieved by inadmissible reductionism? There is no question that for every example cited you will be able to find another one contradicting it. It is certainly one thing to start from the primary experience of the southern Bantu and Khoisan peoples, as I do here, having lived among them for eleven years, and another to adopt the perspective of West African or eastern Sudanese (Nilotic) ethnic groups. However, I am convinced that the result will not be basically different. The more deeply you enter into African spirituality, and understand the ethnic and social basis for the way Africans cope with the world, the more – it seems to me – you are justified in talking of African religion in the singular, as does D. Zahan, whose special field was the Bambara of Mali.[6] Even if I do not share this view, the structural similarity never ceases to amaze me.

---

[6] Cf. D. Zahan, 1979, p. 4: "Africans are no more divided than are Muslims or Christians".

One basic structure runs through all African religions, the creation of symbols around people, as we will see below. This is an element clearly distinguishing them from Indian and Chinese religions with their symbols based on cosmology. It is this basic pattern which entitles us to examine these religions with regard to their image of humankind.

Because of the multiplicity of peoples and ethnic groups, and also the richness of African religions and cultures, I have adopted an approach based on examples. In each case, one example will be discussed in detail and its full significance explored. References to others will be kept to a minimum, even though I have tried to keep the frame of reference broad enough to include examples from different parts of Africa. An examination of basic concepts will make it easier to bring out all subsequent aspects of African religions and cultures. The footnotes and bibliography indicate material for further study.

I dedicate this book to our children, who were born in Africa, so that they do not completely forget the land of their birth and its warm-hearted people, their early friends and playmates.

I. AFRICAN CONSCIOUSNESS

Anyone encountering Africans will find they are passionate lovers of life. They are not influenced by the philosophy of Plato, who questioned the phenomenological world and gave real ontological value only to the invisible. They are not influenced by the philosophy of Descartes, who put a distance between thinking human beings *(res cogitans)* and the world *(res extensa)*. This led to the domination of nature and animals, which were held in such contempt that in the end the cry of an animal was not valued more highly than the noise of a machine.[7] Africans turn to this world in order to experience their wholeness. The African understanding of reality can, in fact, only be described in terms of the phenomena of this world. The world does not consist of these phenomena, they point to the world. They are in themselves transparent, and transcend themselves. They do not point to something else, but reveal themselves. Perception is therefore not of a reality lying beyond the material world, but of one which reveals itself in it. Africans are strongly convinced of the reality of the powerful spiritual world, approaching it in religion with respect and awe, yet the wellspring of life lies in the given material world. The external is decisive, the real thing, because everything to do with people and their earthly life has its place here, in this world. Body and soul cannot be separated, and so perception proceeds from the external to the internal. If Goethe captured the traditional Western experience of reality in the couplet:

> "Denn das ist der Natur Gehalt,
> dass aussen gilt, was innen galt".[8]

then it should be reversed for Africa: the content of nature is that the inside is determined by the outside.

---

[7] On this difference, cf. A. Köberle, Descartes und die Folgen: ein Weltbild in der Krise. EZW-Texte, 1984; C. Link, Subjektivität und Wahrheit: Die Grundlegung der neuzeitlichen Metaphysik durch Descartes, 1978.

In their relations to their environment, people are not influenced by spirit as the true, imperishable, essential part of themselves; instead, their spirit is formed and changed by what the body and the outside world conveys to it. While the external and the internal are intimately related, the external is always accorded priority. This is because we participate in the world only through our body; our spirit is ultimately material rather than immaterial, and cannot be imagined as detached from matter. The invisible world of the spirits is not perceived through the spirit but always materially, even in ecstasy. The spiritual world only becomes real when it impinges on the body and is perceived through it. The following anecdote will illustrate this point. Once we were reading Luther's 'Of the freedom of a Christian' in a theological seminar. The African students spontaneously and violently opposed Luther's claim that appearances and outward signs are not important. Even Jesus' saying that it is what comes out a person that makes him or her unclean, and not what goes in (Mark 7: 15, 20), was not understood as a devaluation of outward signs. The interdependence of the external and the internal is part of being human. Because the external takes priority, our clothes, food and the things around us are significant. Clothes make people in Africa too, in the village, in public life and at church. Clothes and external appearance are not simply the expression of an inner attitude, or marks of belonging to specific groups. By adopting the 'outward signs' of others, we gain an identity; convictions, ideologies and beliefs are internalised. Anybody who wants to understand African humanity must overcome the crude dichotomy of body and soul which places the internal over the external. If we fail to appreciate the multi-facetted African view of body and soul as being mutually interdependent we will seriously misjudge the ritual and ethics of Africans, along with their entire religious and social behaviour.

---

[8] Cf. G. van der Leeuw, 1976, p. 523.

1. Body and soul

What is the connection between body and soul? Different African peoples give different answers to this question, and distinguish three, four or even five different factors, in order to define the nature and being of a person.[9] The corresponding concepts can hardly be rendered correctly in European languages. The Ashanti, a matrilineal people in Ghana, distinguish between *mogya* (blood) and *ntoro* (spirit). These are not clearly defined physical substances, but more like social relations. Children receive *mogya* from their mothers. This determines their social adherence to the family, the clan and the state. It shapes their status in life. Since there are twelve clans among the Ashanti there is no place in the entire country where a person will not come across family members and be given assistance. Children receive the spiritual side from their father, their personality and character, called *sunsum*. This means their moral qualities, as the father is responsible for ethical standards in matrilineal Ashanti society. In the clan the *ntoro* is something like a group personality, corresponding to the *sunsum*. The *ntoro* links people with their father's line, of which they share the characteristics and forms of conduct (taboos). There is also the *kra*, which comes from God, relating a person to him. An old Ashanti explained its meaning as follows: "The *sunsum* is with you when you go into your wife; then Onyakopon, the Great One (= God) comes, takes something from his *kra*, and blesses your union. You give your *sunsum* to the child, not your *kra*. He comes with his *kra*. As the Great One has given you something from his *kra*, so he gives of his *kra* to your child".[10]

---

9   For a survey, cf. E. Dammann, 1963, pp.10ff.

10   For this whole subject, cf. K. A. Busia, 1963, pp.190ff., on this particular topic, p. 197; cf. also G. Parrinder, 1961, pp.113ff.; P. Mercier (in: D. Forde, 1963, p. 227) summarises the Benin Fon's highly complex view of the soul as follows: "The human soul (*se*) has many forms, although its essential unity is insisted upon: there is the *joto*, the soul handed on from the ancestor of whom each living man is the representative, and who is his guardian. The *se*, which strictly speaking is a portion of Mawu, the great *Se* of the world; the *selido*, which is life, feeling, personality, the individual's peculiar properties with which *kpoli*, the destiny revealed by *Fa*, is identified; finally, there is the *ye,*, this is the term most commonly used, and denotes the shadow, the indestructible portion of

11

People are not naturally self-contained and sufficient unto themselves, but are made up of relationships. They can only be described as becoming citizens through their mothers, and belonging to a religious and ethical group through their fathers, while receiving their strength from God. People do not 'have' bodies, souls or spirits – to use inadequate terms – but are defined by them in their deepest involvement with the environment. These are not possessions or property, but a gift. Encountering their 'spirit' does not mean ecountering themselves as thinking persons. In conversation with their 'soul' they are not communing with themselves. These gifts from outside remind people that they are indebted to others, and that they can live only through and with them. Their *sunsum* is linked with that of their father. Children cannot survive if their father's *sunsum* is burdened. If somebody feels guilty towards their 'soul', their guilt is not directed towards themself but towards others. Therefore contrition, the remorse of the heart, is not the appropriate reaction to guilt. Instead, the person who confronts his or her soul, looking into it from outside and in relation to circumstances, has to be cleansed from outside. There is a ritual for cleansing the *ntoro* (*sunsum*). The external cleansing also goes inside, purifying the whole person.

No matter how much we are concerned with the idea of life here and now, it is always mediated life, pointing beyond itself. It points to the group, with which the person shares their name and being, and to God himself, who is present in the same way through the father. A person's life is not confined to the private sphere, but is interwoven with the life of everybody else. The

---

the individual, which, at the time of burial, becomes invisible and leaves the body... The *se* has an individual character, but at death it is reabsorbed into Mawu. The *selido*, however, is peculiar to the individual man. It is his spiritual faculty, the preserver of his identity, the vehicle of his fate; it cannot enter into another man. The *ye*, on the other hand, the man's shadow, returns to earth as *joto*, which is why a child may be the exact image of an ancestor, because the *ye* preserves its bodily form. The soul always returns to earth in the same clan because the gods have guaranteed the fundamental social value which inheres in the clan. And within the clan, by the return of the *ye* in the form of *joto*, the union of the dead and the living is perpetually assured". The various relationships of persons, to their past, present and future, to themselves and to their family and clan, are mirrored in this model of the soul in its diverse aspects. Connections and relationships are all important. This is independent of whether there are ontological overtones in the way the members of the clan see themselves.

life of the whole clan is present in it, as is the life to come. This is why there is no division into sacred and profane. Where there is life, there is transcen-dance. Living always means more than material life, all of which transcends itself. There is a sacramental dimension to life.

Like the Ashanti, the *Karanga* (Shona) in Zimbabwe believe that God, the Creator, is present at the creation of new life, at procreation. "We help each other with the help of God" is what they call the act of procreation.[11] How does that happen? The conjugal sexual act should take place at night, in private but not in darkness, "because the time and place are sanctified". A small fire is lit. "The fire should burn so that the child will be brown (beauti-ful), so that it knows its parents, and is not afraid of the fire (light), and so that we can be seen by the ancestors".[12] The lovers whisper their terms of en-dearment, which are otherwise taboo (the names for the woman contain sex-ual elements). That serves to increase love and fertility, to show the potential child its origin and also to show the ancestors the legitimacy of the child. The fire is lit on the hearth, built of three stones symbolising the woman's womb. It is kindled in a piece of wood lying across the stones. These details speak a special language: the sexual act is more than just physical copulation. The hearth, the lighting of the fire, the fire itself, pronouncing the names – all these 'sacramentalise' the sexual act, increase life, serve fertility, and show that besides the ancestors God himself is involved. Ultimately, it is he who decides whether a human being is conceived or not. The Ashanti say that from him comes the *kra*, which is necessary for life, the *munhu*, the *karanga*. By this they mean the 'spirit' or the 'soul', or in general what makes us hu-man. Animals have life, but no *munhu*.

---

[11] For what follows, cf. H. Aschwanden, 1976, pp.15ff.; for the quotation, cf. op. cit., p. 16.
[12] Op. cit., p. 191.

2. Life

For Africans life is what matters most; preserving life is the real purpose of all religious activity.[13] People share life with the world that surrounds them, the world of animals and plants. Even the world of minerals is included. That can be demonstrated linguistically. In his book, *La Philosophie Bantu-Ruandaise de l'Etre*,[14] A. Kagame interpreted the classification system of Bantu languages as a reflection of the internal bonds between all that exists.

The 12 or 13 word-classes can be divided into four basic categories of the linguistic root NTU, which can be interpreted simply as 'being'. They relate to world phenomena, and indicate different ways of participation in being. First there is humankind, *mu-ntu*, in whom all powers are centred. *Ki-ntu* is the object or thing: to this class belong the 'forces which react to human command.' *Ha-ntu* locates every movement and experience; it is the category of space and time. In contrast, *ku-ntu* covers the 'modality' of being, determining expression, beauty, and particular qualities.

Following Placide Tempels, Kagame interpreted the relations of the categories dynamically, because in Africa 'being' is strength. Also, like Tempels, he fitted this pattern into Thomist ontology, so devising a Bantu philosophy.

In his presentation of the African concept of *lewenskrag*, in which he obviously drew on homeopathic ideas, Tempels brought out the 'sense' and the coherence of the African world-view. His work first appeared in 1945 and opened the eyes of many missionaries and researchers. He inspired a group of African scholars to study other ethnic groups and confirm his own results from the Congo, thus broadening the knowledge base.[15] In my own research,

---

[13] Africa and Christianity, Oxford, 1937, p. 80; quoted in: W. Ringwald, 1952, p. 63.

[14] A. Kagame, 1956.

[15] P. Tempels, 1959, obviously borrowed the Afrikaans term 'lewenskrag' ['vital force'] from B. Ankermann, who modified its meaning in the interpretation of the religion of primitive peoples. B. Ankermann, in: P. D. Chantepie de la Saussaye, Manual of the science of religion; trans. by B. S. Colyer-Ferguson, London, 1891. For the whole of this subject, cf. A. Kagame, 1956. Tempels' interpretation was popularised by J. Jahn,

the comprehensive concept of 'life' has proved appropriate to express the centre of African humanity. It is, however, important to free this concept from the context of Western philosophy, and to understand its characteristically African significance. So what is special about the African concept of life?

Continuity

Life is *one*. It is handed down from parents to children. Every generation is only a link in an infinitely long chain. While in European thought life includes its own end and the knowledge that it has to be shaped individually, Africans have traditionally not been aware of this limitation. No sense of irrevocability and uniqueness determines their ideas about life and how to organise it. Instead, the concepts of continuity and unity bring relief. The life of the individual does not possess an infinite value. Not everyone has to ascribe a distinctive meaning to their life. People know where their lives comes from, and that they are part of a stream of life that has always flowed through their family. The individual is nothing but the recipient of life, and has the duty to pass it on. What is important is not the individual, but the collective – the family, the clan, the whole people.

Death is not repressed. Knowing about death, people do not seek what is special or unique in life, but what is universal, because they know that their life is part of the life of others. Uniqueness, or leaving the mainstream, would endanger life. The effects of this attitude on ethics, art and culture are easy to see, and will be dealt with below. The conservative streak in African culture has its origins here.

When everybody is under an obligation to pass on the life they have received, childlessness is the greatest tragedy. It is seen as failure. When a woman is barren, she can only be cured if she has first confessed her guilt. If a young Sotho in northern South Africa dies without having fathered any children, a glowing piece of wood is inserted into his anus at his traditional

---

1958, especially pp.103ff.; V. Mulago 1968;   cf. also A. Kagame, 1976; J. W. Sempebwa, 1983.

15

funeral: a drastic form of punishment for his 'sin', expressed in an anti-symbol.

In Africa monasticism is unappealing, and the celibacy of the Catholic priesthood was more than once described to me by African students as being against nature, and therefore an act of disobedience to God's commands.

Repetition

If death means the end of everything, it will play a dominating role, with life always moving towards death. This is not the case in Africa. Not that death is not feared. It makes a difference, however, whether life is understood as irretrievable and irreversible, or whether it can be repeated. Repeating life is not called re-incarnation, even though hints of this can be detected among a few West African peoples. At any rate, life is not seen essentially as a cycle involving all creatures, an idea underlying Indian religions.[16] In Africa there is no question of the self having to suffer the burden of bodily and material life in a new form, by way of punishment and purification for wrongdoing. Instead, a new birth is a sign of the continuity of life. The deceased does not re-appear indiscriminately anywhere or in any form; life only continues within the family. Here it can and must be renewed. A hymn of praise goes to a deceased man when he is recognised again in his grandson, and the latter is called 'he has returned' due to this physical similarity (this is the case among the Zaramo in Tanzania and many other peoples). In Ghana, when a widow calls her grandson 'my husband', there is pride and joy in such a form of address. There is also an overtone of confidence in life: it does not end, it carries on. Both of them, grandmother and grandson, take their place in the stream of life. The grandmother says farewell knowing that her life was not in vain; it has reached its goal and will be renewed. Her death will be good, not evil. The grandson, however, knows from his name that he is bound up in the larger community; he is indebted to others, and must act responsibly towards them.

Since in Africa life is exclusively the place in which people become aware of God and encounter him, whether through the ancestors or directly, the experience of living always has a religious hue. The repeatability and continuity of life generate feelings of trust and reliability – for both the old lady and her grandson. Trust is the breath of life.

Communal life

For the Westerner, life means individuality. We know each other as individuals; the development of life is understood as enhancing individuality. Community, being with others, is secondary. For Africans, it is the other way round. Individuals only exist because of the community. "Because we exist, I exist", as John S. Mbiti puts it. The community is the given condition of life. It extends in time beyond the bounds of the present era, backward to the ancestors and forward to future generations.

Individuals exist only in so far as they are members of a group. The future son is born at the same time as his father, just as, seen the other way round, "the birth of the son means the birth of the father".[17] The term 'corporate personality' was coined to express this idea in a Semitic context. It can also be applied in Africa. "Man is family", they say in Tanzania".[18] Only in your father's house are you 'at home'; your own house is a subsidiary branch, a section of your father's house. In the village structure of various tribes this means that the son inhabits a smaller house, a copy of the house of the head of the kraal. After his father's death, the son moves into his father's house and frequently takes over his wives (except his own mother). Then he is regarded as the father of his younger brothers and sisters.

The whole is represented in the individual, and the individual stands for the whole community. 'Nginguzulu' has both meanings: "I am a Zulu", but also, "I am the Zulu people", its representative. In South Africa, according to

---

[16] An opposite view to that of D. Zahan, 1979, p. 6. Cf. further on this question C. U. Manus, 1986; R. Friedli, 1986.
[17] M. Buthelezi, 1976, p. 101; on this whole subject, cf. J. S. Mbiti, 1990.
[18] J. V. Taylor, 1965, p. 78; cf. further J. B. M. Kiwovele, 1980.

17

the Zulu myth, the first ancestor arose out of the reeds, Uhlanga. This was the origin of the Zulu people, which now reproduces itself from generation to generation. Each individual is a part of this whole Ngiluhlanga. To say, "I am an Uhlanga, the one who arose out of the reeds (the 'original root')" is to say, "I belong to the Uhlanga collective, which is created again and again out of itself".[19]

Interdependence

The relationship of the human being to the community goes further than community life. It involves interdependence: people, animals and environment exchange their strength, and are in a relationship of osmosis.[20] This mutual dependence can be perceived and defined physically. It is more than economic interdependence, which controls modern life. The life of individuals, their luck and the jealousy of their companions, their misfortune and the goodwill of others, have an effect on the weal and woe of the community and the fertility of the land. After an unsuccessful hunt they ask where there is discord in the community and try to find out who is the cause of it and, by extension, of the unsuccessful hunt.[21] In the individual's life interdependence takes the form of *participation*. Certain persons share in special powers because of their positions or occupations, but also as members of a group. There is collective participation in special powers (see below, under totemism), in special animals, plants and places. There is not merely a sharing in the life forces of the environment, but also in giving to the community. This is a mutual event, and signifies the profound inner connection between human beings and the world. The separation of subject and object – which Western philosophy since Descartes has striven to overcome, to some extent successfully in existentialism – is not possible in Africa because of the 'law of par-

---

19 G. Asmus, 1983, p. 19f.
20 Thus, I. Tödt, in: Buthelezi, 1976, p. 251.
21 Cf. on this subject the hunting diary of M. Douglas among the Lele in Zaire, in: D. Forde, 1963, pp.17ff.; cf. below, pp.113ff.

ticipation' (Lévy-Bruhl).[22] There is a feeling for life in Africa that is similar to that of existentialism, even if it is at a more vital level and is always found in community, without the overtones of Western individualism. As a deliberate antithesis to Descartes and to existentialism, J. V. Taylor produced the formula; "*Participio ergo sum*" – I participate, therefore I am.[23]

From all this emerges a relationship to the environment which is clearly different from the Western stance of domination. The latter has been justified by appealing to the first chapter of Genesis and has become an essential characteristic of our time, in the form of technological manipulation. The concept of participation does not allow of domination and exploitation of the world, but demands adaptation to the whole. For this consciousness of always being part of the whole Lévy-Bruhl found the rather vague term 'mystical participation'. J. V. Taylor occasionally expressed the idea more aptly as 'consubstantial existence.' The term *analogous participation* is even more precise: it underlines certain laws and is selective. Human beings do not participate equally in all forces and in all beings. Nothing forces them to leave the confines of their own living space and world. This 'integrated world outlook'[24] provides for fullness of life. Good days are the highest goal. Super-man is not the ideal, nor is Faust (the frustrated thinker), or *homo faber* (the practitioner).

Potentiality

This term, used as a description of the African understanding of life, does not mean the Aristotelian distinction between 'possibility' and 'act'. It does not aim at defining life in the sense of our ideal of personality, which selects a form of identity from various individually limited possibilities. It means the internal potential of life to grow, the ideal being the harmonious balance of all forces. So threats to life are felt especially strongly. Weakness

---

[22] This is what Lévy-Bruhl called the primal feeling for life, even if his interpretation was based on inappropriate premises. Cf. on this subject, T. I. van Baaren, 1964, pp.17ff.

[23] J. V. Taylor, 1963, p. 50.

[24] H. W. Turner, 1967, vol. 2., p. 357.

and illness are perceived in Africa as dying, and in various languages are so characterised.[25] On the other hand, the meaning of life is felt in the increase of strength. True life becomes a celebration of being. "We will celebrate our being human ... all are welcome where we celebrate .... Anyone who refuses to celebrate is a sinner ... Whoever celebrates with us is a neighbour. Together we are healed, blessed and enriched".[26]

Life is one, but the powers of creatures differ. There is a hierarchy of powers. It is reflected in the hierarchical ordering of society and in the association of humans and animals. You may want to interpret the ordering of classes in Bantu languages dynamically, as do Jahn and Kagame, but the hierarchical pyramid of powers is still a fundamental part of the African's world-view. In this respect, Tempels' research findings have not been superseded.

God stands at the pinnacle of powers. He is the source of his own existence, and of that of all other beings; from him come all powers. They include the divinities, the ancestors and the spirits. The scale descends to plants and animals. Human beings are in the middle of this pyramid. They know what it is all about. They are compelled to adapt their lives to these powers, and at the same time to use them for the well-being of the community. As part of the cosmos of powers, they must take care to multiply, so that the community is not diminished. Like a child growing up, or a tree trunk becoming stronger year by year, the human being is destined to constantly increase life. If grandparents have seen a steady stream of grandchildren on their laps, they will not have lived in vain; after a fulfilled life, their death will be a good end.

---

[25] "This craving for power is the driving force in the life of African religion. It has its origin not in logical reflection, but in a feeling of incapacity and in an obstinate desire to overcome it... Man is weak, and what he needs is increased strength... The absorbing question for him is how to acquire some of this power so that it may serve for his own salvation or that of the group for which he is responsible". D. Westermann, Africa and Christianity, Oxford, 1937, p. 84; quoted in E. W. Smith, 1961, pp.28–29.

[26] This is how a Sotho from southern Africa described the meaning of community. Quoted in T. Sundermeier, 1975b, p. 123.

3. The Word

There is good life and bad life, but life is ambivalent. "For Africans, life has many meanings in this existence and is unstable on all levels, including blessing, honour, etc., until they become one with their ancestors in the great company of the unlimited stability of existence" (Judah Kiwovele).[27] The ambivalence lies rooted in the possibility of misusing the powers of the world and using them against people, without their perceiving where the negative influence comes from. You have a certain amount of safety in the family, says Kiwovele, because life is unambiguous in a circumscribed space, and the static hierarchical order contributes to the stability. "Without the stability of the hierarchy, there is no stability of life for the individual", who remains "devoid of a meaningful life".[28]

Though this remark is correct, it does not take into account the fact that threats and ambivalence can be found in the family, since jealousy and anger occur everywhere. You need reassurance in the family too. In the midst of growth and transience, life everywhere must be wrested from ambiguity. Also, the group as a whole is exposed to the many facets of the world which cause anxiety. The group has to find order in the primeval forest, the hazards of the wide-open spaces must be limited by boundary stones, and rivers must be prevented from flooding. In the undergrowth of the forest you need paths, in the endless savannah landmarks from which to get your bearings. You need clear directions, if *one* of the many dangers becomes life-threatening – apparently without reason. But what gives rise to the inner certainty without which life cannot go on? What helps people penetrate to the unequivocal meaning of life, and 'a place to feel at home'?[29]

Western anthropologists would refer at this point to the nature of human language. Language marks out human beings. Only in language can they tell

---

[27] J. B. M. Kiwovele, in: H. Bettscheider, 1978, p. 89.

[28] Op. cit., p. 90.

[29] Cf. the book of the same name by F. B. Welbourn and B. A. Ogot, 1966.

the truth or give clear definitions. Religion and language are closely linked, because faith lives from the fact that truth is put into words.

In the African context, the nature of language is an essential aspect of human life. The word does not become the key to unlock existence because of its rational and external nature, but because of its power. The power of words in Africa was acknowledged by Léopold Senghor. There is no word without consequences. Naming things is not only a rational, aesthetic, artistic or even creative act. A name reveals what is always there. In this way, it releases power. Ambiguity is clarified when something is named; ambivalence becomes certainty. The word is effective because it participates in reality.

Nummo is the word, the name of the creative principle and son of God for the Dogon in Mali. "The *Nummo*", says the sage Ogotemmêli, "who is water and heat, enters the body in the water one drinks and communicates his heat to the bile and the liver. The life-force, which is the bearer of the Word, which *is* the Word, leaves the mouth in the form of breath, or water vapour, which is water and is Word".[30] Every word uttered comes from the depths, from the innermost being of people. For the Dogon that is the liver. In primeval times, according to the myth, the first word ever spoken was uttered before a woman's reproductive organs. The word brings fertility; it enables life. "Issuing from a woman's sexual part", said Ogotemmêli, "the word enters another organ, namely the ear". So the word belongs to the sexual act. The good word penetrates a woman through the ear and produces fertility as a water-word, by mixing with the waters of the womb. Something of that primeval word still clings to the words uttered now. "All good words, whether spoken by the mouths of men or women, enter the bodies of all women, and prepare them for future mating and childbirth". Bad words have a negative effect. They spoil the germ of life, they spoil the woman – evil can be 'smelled'. "Bad words enters by the ear and pass into the throat, the liver, and finally the womb. The unpleasant smell of the female sexual parts comes from the bad words heard by the ear".[31]

---

[30] M. Griaule, 1973, p. 138.

[31] Op. cit., pp.139.

The bad word also influences men in their sexuality. It makes them 'go cold'. The good word, uttered in daylight, produces life; the dark word, shouted at night, destroys the peace of humanity, the calm of the village, the harmony of the world. It cuts through the harmonious play of forces. It must be resisted.

The word accompanies people in everything that they do. The hymn of praise, the worksong, the funeral chant, the proverb, the mythical narrative – they all name things and give them their being. The word of the smith can kill. His word of blessing, when he forges the plough or hardens the spear, brings success: "May the seeds sprout and bear fruit... may shield and spear go to war and be victorious over the enemy – may they return with blessing and riches".[32] After battle, the warriors of the Chagga in Tanzania bring the smith a cow as a thanks-offering. The Chagga recognise the office of the teacher-elder, who has to preserve and communicate their traditional teaching. He is also the circumciser. Both functions belong together since, "Whoever has power over blood, also has power over the word". "A person who possesses this power penetrates deeply, very deeply, into human life. The strength of the tribe is sealed in the word and in blood. Word and blood belong together; the one cannot exist without the other". (P. Njau)[33]

To this day, one of the most powerful threats for an African is: "Just wait – you'll see what will happen". A father can talk this way to his son if he refuses to obey; the pastor to his colleague if he senses jealousy; a brother to another brother if they do not get on. The menace lies in what is left unspoken, the dark hint, and this will disturb and haunt the one so addressed. All the uncertainties of life loom up. Words can hold such threats at bay. If, among the Okavanga in Namibia, a child dies before the father has given it a ritual name, it will just be covered with earth and not buried with the customary ceremony. Naming creates social acceptance and opens the way to the joys of life. The word overcomes ambivalence, and sums up the situation.

---

[32] This is how P. Njau in Tanzania handed down the words of the elders (according to C. Reisach, 1981, p. 63).
[33] Op. cit., p. 11.

23

As it brings life, so the word produces death. E. E. Evans-Pritchard met a man among the Nuer of the Sudan who appeared unusually downcast and unhappy. His story was strange enough. He had been away from his village for a long time. When the news reached his family that he was dead, all the preparations were made for mourning, and he was buried in his absence. But one fine day he re-appeared in his village. He was now called *'joagh in tegh'*, the 'living ghost'. "He lives in our village, but we no longer count him as a member, since he is dead. The funeral rituals have been held for him".[34]

He had been declared dead. The word had cut through the uncertainty of the situation. It had taken on a public form through the ritual, and a new situation had been officially created. It could not be reversed. Everybody submitted to it.

4. Space and time

Space and time are linked together in the closest possible way in traditional religions, and in many languages are the identical word (e. g. *oruveze*, Otjiherero). Time is experienced spatially, because it is not an abstract, autonomous unit of measurement. It is determined by human action and organised according to the spatial, visible course of natural events, the rising and setting of the sun. Temporal distance is given as the distance between spaces. The crossing of spatial distance allows time to happen. In their acts, people create time. Whether there is passage of time without human activity is an unimportant question. It is the human being who gives everything 'weight', and therefore 'being'. A friend of mine, who was a missionary in the Transvaal, South Africa, had brought workers to a church building site and then drove on to another workplace. When he came back after some time, he found the workers still sitting by the fire, chatting. When he furiously inquired what they had been doing the whole time, they replied, "We are creating time!"

---

[34]   E. E. Evans-Pritchard, 1967, pp.152f.

In his thesis on the eschatology of the New Testament, John S. Mbiti recognised the significance of the concept of time for African religions, and highlighted its special role. Even if his findings cannot be generalised, he rightly drew attention to the essential element.[35] According to the African understanding, time does not grow into the future, but into the past. The Bantu languages have little scope for making distinctions with regard to the future, but there are numerous shades of meaning to indicate times past. Time is determined by human act. There is the time of fetching water, the time for drinking, the time when the cattle come home, the time when they are driven into the enclosure. Life is ordered according to these tasks, and time is named accordingly. When major events take place, people happily take their bearings from similar events in the past, and name the years after them, to the annoyance of historically minded Europeans wanting to establish the correct date. The special event has occurred, they should not be too worried about when. I myself witnessed what happened when an assembly of the elders of the Mbanderu in Namibia realised that they could only name the most recent years in 'European' style, i. e. give them numbers. Recollecting the most important events of those years, they renamed them in association with notable events, in the manner of their fathers.[36]

When the irreversibility of time is characteristic of a world-view, as in the West, youth has to be highly treasured as a unique period of awakening and freshness. In contrast, where it is human acts that count, and fill time, seniority is treasured. In Africa youth is a stage on the way to the more important things ahead. As the annual rings give a tree trunk strength, so the years bring wisdom and prestige. The counsel of the elders carries weight. This process of growth is not brought to an end by death, but is reconstituted by it. The prestige of the dead lives on in the ancestors. People gain greater dignity as they grow into the past, into the Zamani period, as Mbiti calls it.

---

[35] J. S. Mbiti, 1974, pp.18ff. This analysis does not apply to the Khoisan languages, for example. Similarly with other languages.
[36] H. Vedder, 1934, pp.150ff.; T. Sundermeier, 1977, pp.177f.

The Akan recognise clear divisions in the week. However, for the majority of ethnic groups the week is not divided, nor is the year. Yet chaos does not prevail. The year is regulated by the course of nature, by seed-time and harvest. Above all, it is divided by the ritual celebration of festivals. Festivities heighten time; they activate it through bringing back the past. If the Herero get the impression that the *okuruuo*, their 'ancestral fire', has become 'tired' and lost its power, they assemble at the graves of their ancestors, and rekindle the flames. The time of the ancestors becomes the present through this 'pilgrimage' and feast; more precisely, the present is projected back into the time of the ancestors, and thus empowered. The ritual, while referring to the past, speaks to people *now*. The present is meant to be the fullness of time. Festivities are times of abundance and central events; never is time so forgotten as in African celebrations.

An outlook on life focussed on the present and empowered from the past also reflects their concept of space: tribal territory is the centre of the world. Many peoples call themselves 'humans' in an exclusive sense. This term is not applied to other groups with the same significance. Creation myths seldom speak of the origins of humanity as such, but refer to the ancestors of one people, or royal family. Even when it is known that the ancestors have migrated here from other areas, people point out the place, the cave, the rock or the reed, from which the first human beings emerged, within or around the present tribal land. If this land is the centre of the world, then the paramount chief's kraal, the royal seat, is the centre of the land, and every house is a centre in itself. The chief of the kraal lives in the midst of them all, sometimes represented by a central pole in the hut of the main house.

The land has a mythical quality. It is sanctified as the ancestors' place of origin, by their great deeds, their history and their graves. Its dignity is that of the indigenous inhabitants, and vice versa. Whoever reduces the land, endangers their life. Land was never private property in Africa. It always belonged to the community. Only the king or chief could dispose of it, distributing it as a loan. It was one of the Europeans' biggest mistakes to believe they could buy land. In African eyes their gifts, and money, were no more than acknowledgement of the sovereignty of the chief, who gave the land as a loan and regarded the Europeans as his subjects, but without full rights. The uprisings against the colonial powers, even separatist movements within the church in Africa were deeply rooted in the land question.[37] Here is a small example of how strongly Africans felt about property rights. In 1888 the Rhenish Mission sold to the colonial regime the land and buildings of their teacher training college and seminary for pastors, the Augustineum in Okahandja, in what was then known as South West Africa. Because they did so without consulting Maharero, the Paramount Chief, he protested, closed the churches, and forbade them to ring their bells.[38]

The science of animal behaviour has shown that having a fixed habitat is just as much a primary need for the fertility of animals as their grazing and reproductive instincts, possibly even the decisive factor. Sometimes the 'homing instinct', the 'desire for a home' is regarded as the strongest, unalterable driving force of humankind.[39] 'Home' does not simply mean land as a source of livelihood, it means organised space, separation from the unorganised, from the chaos of the steppe or primeval forest. The 'architecture' of a Herero encampment in Namibia provides a clear example of this order.

When the Herero want to build a house, they look for an evenly shaped post and set it up. It is called *ondunde*, the holder. The centre of the house and encampment, it represents the chief, in whom the life of the ancestors is concentrated, and who is the connection between past, present and future generations. A circle is drawn around the post, saplings are driven into the ground, and bound to the top of the post. Twigs are woven in between, and daubed with a paste made of mud, cow-dung and urine. The man who is going to live in the house surrounds himself with the 'powers' of animals with which he has entered into the closest symbiosis.

---

[37] B. Sundkler, 1964, pp.38ff.; T. Sundermeier, 1973, pp.184f., 254f.; W. E. Mühlmann, 1964, pp.107ff. For the special law relating to ownership of land among the Kikuyu, cf. L. S. Leakey, 1952, pp.15ff.

[38] Cf. The chronicle of the Okahandja Station, Archives of the Evangelical Lutheran Church in Windhoek, Namibia.

[39] Cf. W. Jetter, 1978, p. 98 A. For the ethological problem, cf. R. Ardrey, 1966.

Everything in the house follows a set pattern. The door opens to the West. An invisible line between the post and the door divides the house into two halves, right and left, North and South. On the right-hand side (as seen from the post) sleep the man and his chief wife. On the wall, directly above the bed, which in the past included the hide the bridegroom tanned during their wedding night, are displayed the man's kirri and hunting equipment. The left-hand side is the woman's side; here the milk calabashes and other utensils are stored. At the back, where it is darkest, 'mementoes' of the deceased chiefs are preserved. That is the actual 'place of the ancestors'. The implements for religious ceremonies conducted at the ancestors' fire are also kept there. The Herero cannot explain why the place of the ancestors is in the background, but the Zulu, who build their houses similarly, know why. The ancestors love the darkness, they say, because for them it is 'light'.

Outside the door, between the door and the cattle compound, is the ancestors' hearth. Morning and evening, when the cows come home, the fire is ritually kindled, because the ancestors come with the cattle. The division into left and right, into strong and weak sides, continues in the circular layout of the whole village. Every hut, each with the door facing the cattle kraal, follows the arrangements of the principal house. Every house is a reflection of a higher order, a microcosm of the world.

Two principles can be recognised in the structure: the circle with its central dynamic, and the East-West axis. The circle marks out the boundaries and binds things together. It is the most profound symbol of life and security. The village is centred around the ancestral fire and the cattle compound, the house around the *ondunde*. Every circle points to the whole foundation of life, showing where life is dependent, what it is dependent upon, and how to find access to it. The ancestors came from the East, it is said. The East is a mythical home, since their ancestors actually came from the North, something of which the Herero are fully aware.

Right and left reflect the duality of life, the weak and the strong sides. That is why women live on the right side of the house, because they need strength of their husband. The sons of the chief are strong themselves, and can live on the left. If the chief dies, the post will be ripped out and the encampment abandoned. On the right side of the old encampment, i. e. to the North or the East, a new one will be built. If cattle go missing, they are always looked for in the West, because the Herero have found that they are only lost on this side. The polarity of the sexes and of life is expressed in this structure, as is also the opposition and unity of the sacred and the profane. This is difficult for an outsider to understand: for wherever the ancestors are, life is generally carried on normally. Yet there are certain taboos around centres which are looked on as *zera*, or holy. There are certain prohibitions regarding the cattle compound, the ancestral fire and the principal house. The 'sacred' structures the encampment, the living space, but not so that it is set apart. On the contrary, it forms the centre and opens up the 'profane' space, in which all can move freely. It creates this space and protects it through its 'strength'. Everyday things, such as cooking, slaughtering, etc., are put on the left side, the weaker side of the encampment. Among other peoples, the women also live on the lefthand side. Cows are milked by women in the cattle compound. Part of the first milking is always given to the chief for 'tasting'; in his absence it is poured over the central post, after which everybody can drink some of the milk. Ritual liberates daily life – the sacred enables the profane.[40]

Like time, space is not an autonomous measure, but is defined by the activity of human beings and given quality by their lives. The polarity of human life – its duality, right and left, above and below, weak and strong, which find concentrated expression in human sexuality – is the basic principle by which people wrest their living space from chaos, and give it shape. This does not mean that the world becomes an object for human use in the Cartesian sense: it highlights the fact that all living beings are manifestly interrelated. That essentially includes the relationship to the 'transcendent', to use a Western concept. Africans would not call it that, however; for them it is 'extended world'.

---

[40] For further details, cf. T. Sundermeier, 1977c, pp.136ff. For the structure of the Zulu house, cf. G. Asmus, 1939, pp.15ff.

5. Analogous participation

The idea of 'vital participation', according to which "every manifestation of Bantu life reflects this interaction of being on one another" (V. Mulago),[41] has been treated in the history of religion under the heading of *dynamism*. It goes back to the famous letter of a missionary called R. H. Codrington (published by H. Müller in 1878) drawing attention to the phenomenon of belief in power known as *mana* among the Melanesians. J. G. Frazer attempted to give the use of these forces a definite order. He discovered three laws of sorcery: 'homeopathy', 'sympathetic' or 'contagious' magic, and 'imitative magic'. Tempels fell back upon the idea of dynamism, which then had some effect on research in social anthropology.[42] Yet this approach was unsatisfactory in that power was interpreted as *impersonal power* (by analogy with electricity) used for magical manipulation, in contrast to religious activity, which was seen as always resulting from a personal relationship. This is a false distinction. Codrington himself had realised that *mana* is "always linked with a person, through whom it is channelled".[43] *Mana*, the life power, must not be understood as the ground of all being – nor as NTU, as in Jahn's interpretation – but as an elementary experience of reality in dealing with things. There is no basis for a theoretical distinction between magic and religion and this is not supported in African religions. Distinctions between powers

---

[41] V. Mulago, 1968, p. 148.

[42] P. Tempels, 1959, pp.45ff. Cf. V. Mulago, 1968, pp.156f. To the dynamic explanatory model belong also the descriptions of African religions by E. Dammann, 1963, E. W. Smith, 1961, and also the phenomenology of religion of G. van der Leeuw, 1955. Among the older works in the history of religion, the following should be mentioned: J. G. Frazer, The Golden Bough. A Study in Magic and Religion, London, 1922, pp.48ff.; K. Beth, Religion und Magie, ein religionsgeschichtlicher Beitrag zur psychologischen Grundlagen der religiösen Prinzipienlehre, Leipzig, 2nd ed. 1927.

[43] He wrote this in 1891; cf. van Baaren, 1964, p. 106. On this problem, cf. E. E. Evans-Pritchard, in: J. Middleton, 1967, p. 4. "The Zanda would reject... the idea of magic as universal power as expressed in the concepts of mana in Polynesia and waken and orenda in North America", and he adds: "I do not wish to state that these forces are conceived of as impersonal by the natives themselves, but that they have been described as such by ethnographers and theoretical writers such as Marett, Preuss, Hubert and Mauss, Durkheim and others".

should not be interpreted as an ontological stratification, since, according to the African world-view, all power, whether it is of the ancestors, people, animals, or plants, derives from one source, God himself, and is always exercised through people. It is only a question of contact, of channelling, of how and to what degree a person participates in the powers, whether as an individual or as a group.

If power is bound up with people and is only effective personally, i. e. through people, whose anger, hatred, jealousy and faith are conditions of its effectiveness, then its application certainly has to do with religion. But then there also has to be an order by which the powers operate. After all, arbitrariness is not a feature of any religion, not even of African religions, however much Western authors may talk of (black) magic and (primitive) witchcraft with regard to African religion and medicine.[44]

The problem that we have here can best be clarified on the example of African medicine. A statement by a South African Zulu may serve to introduce it: "The power is just there in the medicines, doing nothing. It is just there. Then a man comes, seeking this kind of *imithi* which can do the thing which he is planning. He sees it. He keeps quiet, just remembering the place where he saw it. When he is alone, he returns, taking with him his hoe and his bag. He digs, removing the medicine. When he has finished digging, he puts the medicine in his bag. He returns home. He uses the medicine in the way that he is used to. That is the description of how the power of *imithi* is used by *inyanga yemithi* (literally specialist in *imithi*, i. e. herbalist)".[45]

What do herbalists (traditionally called medicine-men) look for? They do not refer to the book of nature as doctors normally consult their books after establishing the diagnosis, in order to prescribe the appropriate medicine. They do not take just any medicine. They watch out for something specific. Then they discover it. Let us take a simple example. A woman has a breast

---

[44] L. Mair, 1969 (cf. the suggestive German title, 'Magie im schwarzen Erdteil' ['Magic in the Black Region of the Earth']. Mair should not be included in this category, because she writes her work on 'Magic' exclusively from the point of view of social anthropology.

[45] A.-I. Berglund, 1975, p. 256.

complaint. The herbalist sees the breast-shaped fruit of the papaya. When he or she breaks off a leaf from a double-stemmed tree – the female stem has larger fruit than the male – a white juice comes out of the stalk. Something natural has been found with a certain relationship to the part of the body of the patient. There is an analogy here. Herbalists activate passive power into kinetic energy, for good or ill, depending on their intention. They can activate 'vital participation' on recognising the analogy that binds things together. I should like to call this bond 'analogous unity'. It is what gives the African world-view coherence.[46]

Plato was the first to introduce the idea of analogy into philosophy. In *The Timaeus* he says: "... they [earth and fire] need a bond between them which shall join them both. The best of bonds is that which makes itself and those which it binds as complete a unity as possible: and the nature of analogy is to accomplish this most perfectly".[47]

According to Plato, analogy is a principle of cosmic structure which orders the heavens and the earth, the world of people and the world of the transcendent, by binding them together. Even a fleeting glimpse into the world of the Dogon in Mali, in which every detail of village and house structure is a model of the mythical realities,[48] shows that this principle also applies in Africa. The difference is that it is understood dynamically and put to real use in magic and medicine. Its significance is not limited to poetry, philosophy, mythology or theology, as it is in Western tradition. The real problem is whether we can go beyond the bald statement of significance as such, and identify the laws of construction of analogies. From my many years of living among the southern Bantu and Khoisan-speaking Africans, after many discussions with healers and religious leaders, and after going through the literature on the subject, I have formulated the following seven rules. Admittedly, this is a typically European attempt to identify and systematise the use of analogy. Africans deal with it intuitively. I have also put it to the

---

[46] For a detailed treatment of the whole subject, cf. T. Sundermeier, 1973.
[47] The Timaeus 31a.
[48] Cf. M. Griaule in: D. Forde (ed.), 1963, pp.83ff.

test myself, going out in search of possible medicines for certain illnesses. One of my informants, a former well-known herbalist, reacted with great astonishment. "How do you, a white man, have this knowledge? I thought that this was my own secret, which I had never before told anyone!"

I will start with the most general and well-known analogies, using my own terminology.

1. The *functional analogy*. It is known in biology as morphological analogy, and states that things which have the same function are related to each other. Taboos and specific cultural ways of behaviour are most easily explained by it. In traditional Africa, for example, the slaughtering of animals is not simply a secular matter for the purpose of supplying food, it is a ritual and social occasion. Certain parts of the cattle are given to certain people: men get the eyes, so as to see better when hunting. A soup is made from the hooves for the herdboys so that their feet can be made stronger. The women are not allowed to eat the tongues, lest their own tongues become too 'sharp'. The eldest son of the house gets the front legs, because he must give the lead to others. The master of the house gets the hind legs, because the whole house rests on him. Among the Herero, the sexual organs and the surrounding parts can only be eaten by men who were circumcised together. This increases their virility. Mothers receive the back, which strengthens their backs in pregnancy.[49]

2. The *homeological analogy*. Its significance is known from homeopathy, and was used by Frazer to explain 'the primitive consciousness'. He understood it as the fundamental principle of 'magic'. In Africa things which are similar in form and colour have an analogous power relationship to each other. Red earth can stand for the menstrual flow, as can molten red iron. Therefore a woman who has no regular periods is, if possible, given medicine by the smith. Often it will be a sufficient remedy if she goes and watches him

---

[49] For the way the meat is distributed, cf. T. Sundermeier, 1977, pp.153f.; G. Lienhardt, 1967, pp.23ff.

at work. A smith will only ply his trade when the moon is waxing. When the moon is waning, he has no strength and his work would be worth little. A pregnant woman, by contrast, will avoid being near a smith. That could cause a haemorrhage and induce a miscarriage.

Everything resembling male or female forms has a bearing on sexuality. White powder kept in a phallus-shaped container represents semen and is given to an impotent man (Ndembu in Zambia). Jugs and containers used by women in the rituals surrounding a wedding have a similarly appropriate form, symbolising the womb and vagina (Karanga of Zimbabwe).[50]

The Khoisan languages use this analogy for their gender system, to classify the world around; everything long and thin is masculine; everything round is feminine; only those things defying classification are neuter.

The homeological analogy lies at the root of most African symbol formation. Among the Herero, if a boy is born within the settlement, the midwife cries out: "A bow! A bow!" In the case of a girl, she cries: "An onion! An onion!" The Herero explained this custom to me by reference to the future work of the new-born child. A boy will go out hunting, a girl will gather onions! Unaware of the almost archetypal sexual symbolism to be found in all cultures, they were unconsciously using it.

Naming things is a part of the analogous unity. In many cases, it makes the analogy effective in the first place. The word fixes what the eye sees or whatever sentiments arise. In ritual, fire is kindled preferably by twisting sticks. The stick lying on the ground is called the 'woman'; the upright stick, the 'man'. In this way fire becomes a symbol of life, enhancing fertility. In the case of certain grasses or herbs for medicine or magic, naming them is often the crucial factor, otherwise they might be used at random.[51]

3. The law of *taking a part for the whole* includes those special features of African medicine and magic which Frazer called 'contagious' or 'sympa-

---

[50] Cf. the illustrations and widely varying shades of meaning in H. Aschwanden, 1976, pp.176ff.

[51] Cf. on this subject the wealth of material in G. Asmus, 1939. pp.101ff.; V. W. Turner, 1967.

thetic' magic. His interpretation has been widely accepted as enlightening, but it gets in the way of proper understanding. This law of forming analogies is one of the most elementary laws of communication, and underlies all jurisprudence. Without it, there could be no communication of binding political transactions. The flag represents a people; the crown, authority; a post in the centre of a house in the Herero village, the chief; part of the quarry, the claim to the whole animal; part of the body of the defeated enemy, complete victory; walking on part of the land means laying claim to the whole land. Hairs from a dead person indicate their nearness; nail-clippings and sand from footprints not only keep alive the memory of the dead, but can also be used for harmful magic.

4. *Condensation.* Various homogeneous and heterogeneous elements which form an analogy themselves are condensed to form a new analogy. In this way, one and the same element can be used for different, and often contradictory, analogies. The colour red has seven different meanings in the rituals of the Ndembu in Zambia, which can be established by the particular connection: the blood of animals, the blood of a woman giving birth, menstrual blood, the blood of a murderer or of the murdered person, the blood of circumcision. Blood indicates power. It also stands for bad semen, because good semen is white. Red blood can stand for good as well as evil, because it is assigned to various analogies, which then condense into a new symbol.

5. *Displacement.* This law often makes it difficult to recognise and understand the actual analogy. It seems that the function is to obscure the meaning, so that the underlying secret will not be perceived by everyone. According to this law of analogy, non-essentials are moved to the centre; the essential point is touched upon only casually, or remains completely unspoken. The law of displacement would appear to destroy the analogy. It seems like a hoax, and is sometimes also understood by Africans as such. At funerals, for example, in various peoples the body is carried out of the back of the hut, which often has to be broken open. Afterwards, this opening is closed up. The spirit is not supposed to find the entrance to the house again (actually,

this ritual involves an inverse analogy, see below). The Herero used to tear down the house of the chief after his death, but today – for financial and other reasons – they only move the main entrance a few inches.

The following example seems to illustrate displacement, even if a new symbol was created out of it. In olden times, among the Herero, the chief had to guard the ancestral fire. This task was delegated to the woman of the house, who in her turn employed a young girl. The first Europeans saw only this final development, comparing it with the institution of the vestal virgins in Ancient Rome; the result was a profound misunderstanding.[52]

The law of displacement is mainly employed in symbolic gestures. A homeological analogy, for example, would be obscene and inappropriate outside of fertility rituals.

6. The *inverse analogy*. For Europeans, this is the most baffling way of creating analogies. The paradoxical nature of African thought seemingly becomes apparent here. Yet the fact that these are true analogies has something to do with the wholeness of African thought, in which the complementarity of all life guarantees balance. There is no place here for dualism; instead opposites are held in tension. Only when right and left, East and West, good and its opposing force, are coordinated with each other is the equilibrium achieved – a well-ordered relationship, even of opposing forces. Beauty is realised through beautiful herbs, but also through the opposite, through evil-smelling or ugly plants. Indeed, sometimes this analogy is even more effective. A plant with particularly ugly flowers will help the lover to become more attractive.[53] Needles and spear points, which are usually avoided because they attract the spear of the enemy, are especially favoured wear for diviners and medicine-men; in their case they have the opposite effect, protecting against invisible arrows with hostile intent.

The law of inversion underlies symbol formation in death and mourning. This can be seen not only in all mourning rituals in Africa, but also in other

---

[52] Cf. T. Sundermeier, 1977c, pp.150ff.

[53] A.-I. Berglund, 1975, p. 354.

cultures, in Europe as much as in India. The ritual walk is normally executed clock-wise, but now takes the opposite direction. The corpse is carried out of the back door, and at the grave everything is done with the left hand (which is otherwise considered 'dirty'). What would be highly unlucky in normal circumstances, is now called for; the grave-diggers must, as far as possible, be naked (at least this used to be the case among the Zulu). In the Independent Zulu churches, the pastors turn their collars round so that the button is at the front.

The reason why this analogy is so important is to be found in the history of religion. The double negative is the strongest affirmative. You defend yourself against death by doing the opposite of what you want to achieve. The same goes for witchcraft in all cultures.[54] In this field, the imagination seems to know no bounds. The law of inverse analogy indicates that there is method in the apparent absurdities.

7. The law of *dramatisation*. A thought seeks verbal form; an analogy requires physical, total representation. The power of participation lies in things themselves. It is the individual who must discover the analogy and make use of the corresponding powers. That happens by dramatisation. The analogy will be transformed into movement. Ritual is enacted analogy. Every repeated gesture or action in which the analogous behaviour becomes visible, is ultimately a ritual. It synchronises the powers of nature and of human beings.[55] Through it, people may participate in the power play revealed by the analogy. Ritual releases power for the well-being or harm of the individual or community. It is both instrumental and expressive.

The laws of analogy formation correspond in general to the laws of the dream world.[56] This is not so surprising if you consider the fact that the dream has the same reality in Africa as daytime experience; dreaming is "the

---

[54] G. Parrinder, 1963, has emphasised the large measure of agreement between practitioneers of magic in Africa and in England; cf. further L. Mair, 1969.
[55] Behaviourism has also drawn attention to this. Cf. A. Portmann, 1950, p. 392.
[56] S. Freud, The Interpretation of Dreams, London, 1953.

meeting-point between the powers of the ego and the cosmos".[57] Therefore it seems absolutely natural that the laws of dreams also play a role in the cognitive process, and that they provide the foundation for coping with reality. This is also the reason why analogy formation is found everywhere in African cultures, and why Africans intuitively understand it. Finally, this is the reason why Westerners, for whom the same dream laws apply, can find African symbols meaningful, even if they interpret things differently.

6. Forming symbols

Symbol and reality

Analogical unity is the formal principle of coping with the world. Analogies are condensed into a unity in the symbol, making reality transparent enough to handle. Symbols help to articulate it. "The symbol makes you think", says Paul Ricoeur.[58] It unfolds reality in such a way that it communicates reality. Indeed, there is no other reality than that accessible in the symbol. The symbol lives from unity, even when it is directed at the partial. It does not cry out from within reality, but emanates reality in such a way that participation becomes possible. It comes from the whole and unfolds it before us. The 'whole' is the world around, of which the invisible world is an essential part. Dream reality, ancestors and spirits, and ultimately the all-embracing world of God are not something from another world; they are always immanent and making things happen in this life. Symbols always contain something of them, sometimes strongly, sometimes faintly.

Reality precedes thought and perception. Thought does not create reality, it confronts it. It can only comprehend reality symbolically, because there is no other mode of communication that is both expressive and instrumental. Because human beings are themselves part of the life that runs through eve-

---

[57] P. Bjerres, in: W. Kemper, Der Traum und seine Be-Deutung, 1995, p. 97.

[58] P. Ricoeur, 1971, pp.404f.

38

rything, they are also part of the reality revealed in symbols. Therefore they must be present in the symbol itself. The world is not the object communicating itself to the subject, because the subject was never separated from the object. In African thought the symbol does not bring together two realities, as the Greek origin of the term suggests (*symballein* = to throw together, to connect); it does not add anything, but makes the segment of reality so accessible that the connection with the whole does not get lost in the detail. "Everything is symbol", says the sage Ogotemmêli.[59] You have to go in search of reality and track it down. It is always 'there', in space and time, for 'being' is always expressed in Bantu languages as 'being there'.[60] Consciousness follows experience, and becomes language with the symbolic naming of given interrelatedness.

Symbol should not be confused with allegory. The law of analogy prohibits this. Allegory links up things which do not belong together, adding something to reality. Symbols, on the other hand, make visible the powers which belong together, and participate in each other.[61] Nor should a symbol be confused with a sign. Signs are one-directional, unmistakable. Symbols condense several aspects which are not fully explainable. Interpretation can change, without the previous interpretation losing its validity, even when its significance decreases. Different interpretations are not mutually exclusive. They have to be understood as supplementary, since each interpretation embraces only one level of meaning, be it social (as in social anthropology), legal, psychological or religious. Synchronising these levels is the essential task of the symbol.

Symbols relate to the actual world and always have a material side; they can be heard, felt and imagined. Because of their sensory character, they speak to the emotional nature of human beings. They are satisfying; that is

---

[59] M. Griaule, 1973

[60] A. Kagame, 1956, pp.125ff.

[61] H. Rücker rightly refers to this difference in his dissertation (Bochum University, 1982), without however giving enough attention to the principle of analogy. I refer to this work in detail, because it discusses thoroughly and convincingly the epistemologi-

why it is in their nature to be accepted. They have to resonate with the feelings and values of the group and individual. The recipient is part of the symbol. If the symbol is not accepted, it is not valid. Whatever the herbalists do, their explanations must be intelligible and acceptable to those seeking help, otherwise their medicines will not work.

This aspect cannot be emphasised enough in intercultural encounter, missionary work, conventional medical care, and development aid work. If there is no symbolic equivalent of what comes as 'new' from the North, i. e. no inner acceptance, the message will fall on deaf ears, the symbolic religious actions will be incomprehensible and international aid will be in vain.

Not only the recipient, also the interpreter forms a constituent part of the symbol. Because symbols make you think, they must be articulated. They cry out for an expert to interpret them. Interpretation – in word or ritual – is the principal way of activating symbols. Symbols need an interpreter, somebody to conduct the rites, a diviner, a priest.

According to the Freudian understanding, only that which is repressed is symbolised; symbols serve to veil meaning. That does not apply to the African understanding of symbols, which reveal that which is latent and make purposeful action possible. They are not only retrospective, but also prospective. In my research among the Mbanderu in Namibia, I came across a number of symbolic acts designed to shape the future of the people, for good or ill.[62] The symbolic acts of herbalists, for example, uncover hidden tensions, and give new vitality to the group and to the individual; by contrast, the sorcerer uses the power of symbols in order to destroy life.

Body symbolism

Just as symbols live from the unity of the visible and the invisible, so they embrace the realms of dreams and poetry. After everything that we have

---

cal implications of the African concept of symbols. For what follows, cf. in detail T. Sundermeier, 1975, pp.155ff.

40

said about the laws of analogy, this cannot be otherwise. Human beings discover symbols in the world and within themselves. Symbols relate to people and at the same time stem from them. Situated on the borderline between the conscious and the unconscious, they are the means of leading people into the world, the world having its own relationship to people. This reciprocity is essential to analogous participation.

With this we have arrived at the secret of African symbolism. Human beings are the source, origin, and reference point of symbols.[63] They experience the world around them as full of powers which have a relationship to them and their bodies. They experience nature personally. The body is the model according to which nature is understood and symbolically interpreted. It is the great treasure-house from which one analogy after another is taken and condensed into a large spectrum of symbols with which people can identify. Everything can symbolise the body, and conversely the body can symbolise everything else.[64] Because society and religion have only one aim, to serve the ends of life, human life in community here and now, the symbol must relate to, and stem from, what is human. Otherwise it would only be a sign, not a symbol.

It has been pointed out that Africans see themselves as 'the centre of their world', and in their language name the outside world after their body (a tree has a foot, its twigs are arms, and leaves are called ears). But it does not follow that Africans are 'egocentric',[65] and their religion 'anthropocentric',[66] in a pejorative sense. Africans are just incorrigible lovers of life, and only this life can be the 'meeting-point with God', as Manes Buthelezi once put it.[67]

---

[62] Cf. T. Sundermeier, 1977c; K. Schlosser, 1949.

[63] Cf. V. W. Turner, 1967, p. 90.

[64] M. Douglas, 1970, p. 146; cf. M. L. Swantz, 1979, pp.51, 301f.

[65] D. Westermann, 1937, p. 159.

[66] In the words of W. Ringwald, 1952, pp.120f. V. Mulago also calls African religions "essentially anthropo-centric", 1971, p. 166.

[67] M. Buthelezi, 1976.

We must clarify what has been said with practical examples, and see how people explore the world and assimilate it in symbols relevant to themselves. The word the Ndembu in Zambia use for symbols is *chinjikikilu*, which derives from the verb *ku-jikijila*, 'to mark out a track'. In an unknown area they carve a sign in the bark of a tree, or break off a branch, so that somebody following can find the way. The symbol is the signpost which shows the way through virgin territory. It helps you to get your bearings, bringing order into the world. Another term used in this connection comes from the verb *ku-solola*, 'to make visible'. The verb refers to the *musoli* tree. Certain animals crave its young shoots and fruits. They leave their hiding place to feast on the fruits of the tree. The tree makes the animals 'visible', so that the hunters can easily track them down. Hunters are given medicine from this tree to attract wild animals. Similarly, if an infertile woman is given this medicine it "will make children visible".[68] It is dispensed in a special ritual, which serves to reconcile people since it brings out everything they have hidden in their hearts. It brings the truth to light. The place where important rituals are conducted is called by a derivative of this concept: *chisoli* or *isolo*. The place of ritual is hierophanous, i. e. it reveals the sacred mystery. It turns private concerns into public ones, thereby giving them social status.[69]

African symbol formation can be clearly shown in four areas: village architecture, sacrifice, body symbolism, and medicine.

Among the Dogon of Mali, for example, every detail of the *village layout*, the house and household utensils points beyond itself. The village is in the shape of the human body, as are the individual houses.[70] The centre of the large house is the 'stomach space', that is the cooking place, three store rooms, the goat shed, and the main room. It is flanked by the entrance and another stable. On both sides of the entrance and at the corners of one of the rooms there are four conical towers, each with a dome on top. On closer in-

---

[68] V. W. Turner, 1967, p. 49.

[69] Op. cit., p. 50. Ogotemmêli uses for 'symbol' a composite word, which means literally 'word of this low world'. Griaule, 1973

[70] Op. cit., p. 95. For what follows, cf. Griaule, 1963, pp.97f.

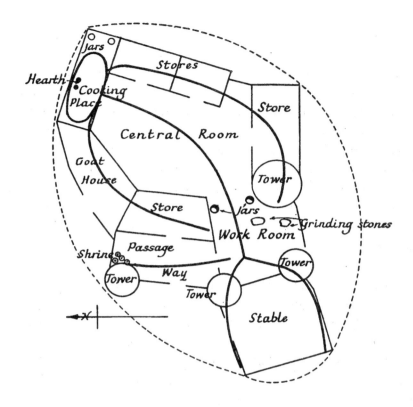

The anthropomorphic dwelling compound of the Dogon in Mali (taken from D. Forde (ed.), African Worlds. Studies in the Cosmological Ideas and Social Values of African Worlds, London, New York, Toronto, 1954, p. 98)

spection you can see the outline of a man lying on his right side. The cooking area forms his head; his eyes are the stones on which the hearth is built. The torso is formed by the main room, the arms by the irregularly placed store rooms, the chest by two jars of water placed at the entrance to the main room, and the legs by the stable. A narrow passageway (the penis) leads to a workroom where water jars and grindstones are kept. Fresh maize cobs are ground here so that a white liquid is extracted (semen), which is poured onto the ancestors' shrine, to the left of the entrance.

43

The bridegroom will spend his wedding night lying on his right side; he will also be buried in the same position when he is committed again to the earth. The house is surrounded by an invisible oval line, the placenta, from which every space and living creature originated over the ages.

We can pass over the cosmological dimensions, which are especially pronounced among the Dogon. Only the anthropomorphic form of the house is of interest here. People have created their homes in their own image, and in so doing emphasised what is important to them – fertility. Building a house is not merely a routine or, at best, an aesthetic act. It is the construction of life itself. The things with which people surround themselves have an influence upon them. The powers of the world can be channelled in such a way that they show and mediate what people want to preserve – the power of the creator, of procreation.

Even if few ethnic groups charge every detail of house and compound with as much symbolism as the Dogon, certain basic elements are found everywhere. Part of this is the division of the room into right and left, which reflects the two sides of the human body, a symbol of the polarity of life. People have two arms and hands, there are two sexes, the path of the sun is determined by sunrise and sunset, there is day and night, heaven and earth. The whole always embraces both poles. They cannot be separated. The basic experience of people with their bodies is maintained in all these relations. The left-hand side is the woman's, on which she carries her baby; the right-hand side is the man's, where he carries a bow and arrow. It is the strong side. These basic divisions are common in the planning of villages, houses and royal palaces (Nyoro, Zulu, Herero, Swazi, to name but a few). The left side is usually regarded as unlucky, foreboding evil. The right side is the lucky one. This idea is likewise rooted in the religious world-view. The simple arrangement of the room reflects the world of the ancestors. According to the Zulu, they live the other way round to us. What is right, is left in their world. Black people have 'white' ancestors. The ancestors love the dark, while people live in the light and avoid the night. They work during the day; the ancestors at night. The ancestors like cattle bile, it is the 'food of the gods', which is why people like to hang up gall-bladders over the entrance to their huts. In dealings with the ancestors, right and left are reversed. At funerals, everything that is normally done with the right hand is done with the left, and on the left-hand side.

The expressive symbolism of body and space has a transcendent dimension; it conveys religious experiences. When the Dinka in the Sudan slaughter an ox,[71] the meat is distributed to the community at a sacrificial feast. The clan deity receives the highest part, the hump, this piece of flesh being first laid at the foot of the altar, and then eaten by the family who made the sacrifice. The old people of the village (taking precedence over the others) receive the head. The people from the cattle kraal are entitled to the flanks. The young girls from the lineage of the sacrificer receive the left foreleg; the men, the right one. The older men of the lineage and the older sons receive the member and genitals, while the middle sons and all the wives of the sacrificer, as well as the guests, are served the middle parts of the beast. The younger sons (they come 'last') get the base of the tail and the tail itself. While all full and half brothers receive the left hind leg, the right one is distributed among the mother's family. In sacrifice, humans and cattle are interchangeable, the one standing for the other. The social order of the community is symbolically reproduced in the sacrifice, in which the whole range of hierarchical nuances is observed; it is renewed by the sacrifice and reinforced by the distribution of meat. Everybody has a fixed place in society, and is symbolically present in the sacrificial animal. His or her position is openly validated. Society finds its identity again in the beast, and is renewed through the common meal.

Colour symbolism

The basic colours of African symbol formation are those of the human body and its secretions, red, white and black. Red is for blood, white for a mother's milk and a man's semen, and black, by contrast, is dirt, a person's shadow and the grave in which the dead are laid. Occasionally black is associated with skin colour, but that is possible only where black has a positive significance, which is very exceptional.

All other variants can be derived from this basic meaning. The connotations for the recipient of the symbols, the ritual use and the total cultic context are decisive factors in establishing meaning. Elements of the latter may appear contradictory, but they must be understood as complementary in the light of the law of inverse analogy.

Since white stands for semen, it can symbolise fertility, manliness, health and life. Mother's milk makes the suckling happy, so white can stand for joy. Like water, white is clear and transparent. Nothing secret or dangerous is hidden behind this colour, so it stands for honesty, for everything visible. It has the character of revelation.

White is also the colour of the ancestors, who have greater power than the living. Yet black can also be their colour, since the grave is black. The sacrifice of black animals is often connected with the cult of the ancestors although, among the Herero in Namibia, this only arose relatively recently. Black can stand for strength and power, although mainly in a negative sense. The power of witches and sorcerers is expressed by the colour black, since witches work by night. Black, therefore, often stands for evil, for bad luck, illness and death. It indicates uncleanliness.

Red has an ambivalent character, more so than black or white. Being the colour of the blood of a menstruating woman or a murder victim, it has a negative ring. It shows infertility, death and suffering. On the other hand, blood has power: people are only born when the red blood of the woman and the white semen of the man come together (according to the understanding of many African peoples). Therefore red stands for fertility. A person comes from the blood of the mother, red shows the family link. Such colour symbolism points to the values and categories of a society. P. H. Bartle came across this problem among the Ashanti, where it had not been observed pre-

---

[71] For what follows, cf. G. Lienhardt, 1967, pp.23f. Similarly among the Herero, T. Sundermeier, 1977c. pp.162ff.

viously. On the basis of colour differences he ventured to analyse and interpret the entire religious and social structure of the Ashanti people.[72]

Colours also have an *emotional* side. They indicate heat and cold. The heat in the human body indicates anger, whether the latter is justified or not. Angry people do things that are not good. Anger is the psychological precondition for the power of the sorcerer. Heat is dangerous; rightly or wrongly, it stirs the body to sexual longings. The colour for anger and sexual 'fever' is red. The angry person has red eyes. Hot blood indicates great potency. By contrast, white indicates the coolness of water. To be cool means to act thoughtfully, level-headedly and wisely. Coolness symbolises self-control. The cool person is pure, hiding nothing, and living in peace. The sorcerer has no power over such a person. Coolness stands for healing and new birth.

Medicines

The field in which analogies are cumulatively condensed into effective symbols is that of medicines. In the treatment of an illness, the most important thing is not always or exclusively the actual medicines, it is treatment in a socio-religious environment. That means the imparting of healing by symbols befitting the origin and the symptoms of the illness in question. This is why traditional healers rely mainly on symbols. Once the symbol required has been identified, the next step is to find the medium for the symbol.[73] The symptoms of the illness determine the symbol that is used. The symbol reflects the symptoms, which in turn influence the choice of medicine.. Life comes from within, evil from without. So healing must also come from outside. The symbol shows the way. The relation to the human body is obvious.

---

[72] For this whole subject, cf. V. W. Turner, 1967, pp.59ff.; M. L. Swantz, 1979, pp.247ff., 432. The examples are taken from Bantu culture. The colour symbolism of the West African Dogon (M. Griaule, 1963, pp.79f.) is more complicated. Possibly other influences are at work here, e. g. from Islam. The change that Islam has produced in a Bantu society and its symbolism has been shown by M. L. Swantz, 1979. For the changes that Christianity has worked on the symbolism of colour, cf. B. Sundkler, 1964, pp.234ff.; V. W. Turner, 1968. For the Ashanti, cf. P. H. Bartle, 1983.

[73] A.-I. Berglund, 1975. Cf. especially, R. F. Thompson, 1973.

All five human senses come into play. The type of medicine and its special qualities are important, and likewise its taste, colour and smell. Occasionally the symbolic link to the illness is established only by the place where the medicine was found. The medicine, which always consists of different objects, is in itself an accumulation of analogies, in which the vessel used, the place of treatment and the point in time increase its symbolic value, and hence its healing power. Even if there are hardly any limits to the imagination of herbalists, they will never act arbitrarily. Their success is for the most part founded on their gifts of observation. The more analogies they discover, the more effectively they can help. "Among the Bamba on the upper Ogowe, all the inhabitants of the village must eat together of the flesh of the antelope *osibi*, before they occupy a village. This animal grazes only at night. During the day, it lies still, either sleeping or chewing its cud. This habit has led the Africans to see in this animal a symbol of stability. When all the villagers eat the flesh together, they acquire its stability, no-one will desert the village, and the group will be preserved undisturbed".[74]

One of my students, a herbalist, told me how he treated a splitting headache. Into a pot of boiling water he threw all kinds of pointed objects, pineneedles, thorn twigs, knives, forks, sewing needles and more besides. He healed impotence, on the other hand, by using medicines from plants with a straight root or strong stems. Zulus consider baldness to be a sign of infertility: "Hair is like life. If there is no life on the head, then there is no life in the thing of men. (The word *imphilo* was used to describe the life of the hair on the head and the life of the male member). This medicine is called *amakhambhi*. This sickness in men is treated with medicines from gardens with much life (*imphilo*)".[75]

In rituals and fixed patterns of symbols the objects representing the male and female make up the symbol only when they are together, but the two elements are not usually brought together in medicine. The polarity of the

---

[74] D. Westermann, 1937, pp.199f.
[75] A.-I. Berglund, 1975, pp.355f.

48

sexes neutralises their power. Double-stemmed papaya plants were growing in a friend's garden. The gardener, a Zulu, advised him to root them out: "Do you want your wife to be barren?".[76]

7. Participatory thinking

African consciousness lives from the law of relationships and analogous participation. Accordingly, its mode of thinking is especially discursive and seems to contrast in every respect with Western linear, 'directed thought' (C. G. Jung). Years ago L. Abegg drew attention to a difference in thinking between Europeans and Asians.[77] She calls the East Asian way of thinking 'encircling or embracing thinking'. That also applies in Africa. For the Westerner, the law of causality and identity is valid everywhere and in the same way. A always equals A, and B always equals B. The same causes produce the same effects. There is a straightforward process of thought, corresponding to the law of identity, which produces precise results. A leads straight to B. Even if hindered or interrupted on this path, you never lose sight of it. Analogous thinking means approaching from different angles. Since what is in front of you is not simply an object, but you already participate in it, you have to approach it from various angles. Like an animal stalking its prey you slowly circle around the goal, drawing nearer all the time. Access becomes easier through movement and the goal becomes clearer through your taking thought. Europeans either arrive at the goal or not. Africans cannot miss it – it is reached not coolly and directly, but peripatetically. They come near and do not need to touch the goal. This too is rooted in the participatory mood. The other person must take the last step forward and come to meet their partner. That shows whether he or she wants to participate or not. In this way, neither loses face if they want to separate.

In practice it appears that you do not say exactly what you want from someone; you circle round the subject, and leave it to the other person to

---

[76] On double symbols, cf. M. L. Swantz, 1979, pp.283ff.
[77] L. Abegg, 1949, pp.46ff.

guess what it is all about. If he or she speaks up, this shows an inner readiness to enter into a relationship with you, and to fulfil your desire as far as possible. The simple answer, '*mba zuwa*' in Otjiherero ('I have heard'), contains a 'promise' of help, without specifying the time and form it will take. In Nama (Namibia) a distinction is made between two forms of making a request, that of a dog, and that of a European. In the first, you beg wordlessly, just with signs. In the second, you go straight to the point. The first form establishes relationships, and protects both the supplicant as well as the person addressed. It makes it possible for them to separate without the community or the connection being destroyed. A direct request and a negative response sever the connection. Both partners lose face.

Because of the laws of causality, the Westerner can say exactly how something happened, but the African is interested in *why* it happened. The former's attitude to life is mainly mechanistic and materialistic. The latter's is personal and is interested in (human) relationships.

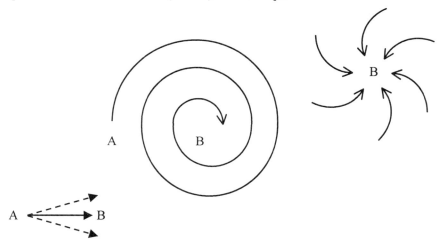

Of course, the contrast should not be taken too far, because it is quite clear that Western thinking can also be discursive, and circular,[78] just as Africans operate very well

---

[78] C. G. Jung, Psychological Types, London, 1923 (rev. ed., 1971).

in a secular, goal-orientated space. Nevertheless, this difference has led to many misunder-standings in intercultural encounters. In their book, *Die Weissen denken zu viel* (The Whites think too much), P. Parin, F. D. Morgenthaler, and Y. G. Parin-Matthéy describe a case of illness: Abinu had two toes amputated. An evil spell had caused an abscess on one. At that time, he was living abroad and was exposed to his enemies. Concerning a similar complaint on the other toe, which had broken out when he was still living under the pro-tection of his family, he was of the opinion: "No, that was something different. It was an infection". The doctors commented: "It was clear where the symbolic and the logical ways of thinking, the magical and scientific world-views, clashed with each other".[79] They asso-ciate symbolic thinking with the pre-Oedipal phase, which in the Oedipal phase yields to logical, abstract thinking, though it is not completely superseded, and can be drawn upon in certain circumstances. I consider this position to be wrong and to hinder the approach to a true understanding. It also displays an unacceptable lapse into an obsolete colonial anthro-pology, and exposes the prejudices of social Darwinism which would see the Africans as being at the childhood stage of humanity.

In both answers, Abinu follows the same way of thinking. He gives an answer to the question, "Why?" in both cases. This does not exclude the search for a (mechanical) origin for the illness. The why-question goes deeper, because it includes the question of meaning and names the circumstances of life. In the first answer, Abinu describes, for those who can hear, his loneliness, his fears and the dangers during his stay abroad; maybe he hints at ethical failings. In the second answer, however, he wants to say that his life and that of his family were all right, that there were no misdoings, and that the peace had not been dis-turbed. In this case, there can only be a 'mechanical' cause of his illness, and no personal reason. It is the respective situations and the spiritual and physical conditions arising from them which make different answers necessary. It makes a very big difference whether you are living at home and in peace, or exposed to dangers abroad. How differently we partici-pate in the world, and how differently the world affects us!

This dimension cannot be included in the question asked by the Western doctor and his academic, medical answer. For the African, however, it is crucial.

To summarise: in Africa symbols link the past to the present; they link people to their environment, of which they are a part, and transform them. Symbols are mirrors of real life, mirrors of people in society and the cosmos. The symbol, which points beyond itself, involving many layers of meaning which cannot be grasped rationally, is the point of contact with 'transcen-

---

[79] P. Parin, et al., 1971, p. 31.

dence', the channel for the powers of the other world, which in Africa is so close and so immanent. It has the character of an event. Symbols make Africans aware of themselves, and of the world in which they have a part. To pick up a phrase of Paul Tillich, human beings symbolise "that which is their ultimate concern", in terms and ideas which are taken from their own bodies, "their own being".[80]

---

[80] P. Tillich, Systematic Theology, vol. I, London, 1953, p. 270.

II. RITUALS

The word must be spoken, the symbol brought to life. Analogy imposes dramatisation. The movement must be repeated, because a lone event is fleeting and dangerous. Just as the symbol is constant and only its interpretation changes with the observer, the movement must be constantly repeated, so that it can unfold its indwelling force and convey the feelings, convictions and values it contains. Individuals may celebrate the various phases of their lives; ritual, however, can only be performed within a group. It is, by definition, communal. It converts latent power into kinetic energy.

Ritual is possibly older than religious contemplation, as A. R. Radcliffe-Brown assumed; in any case it is a constitutive part of religion. Just as there is no community which does not enhance its social behaviour through ritual, we know of no religion which has not expressed itself in appropriate ritual. Ritual calls forth emotions which the group believes are essential for its own continued existence and the well-being of the individual; it stabilises and channels them. In this respect it has a controlling function.[81]

Scholars have not always appreciated the significance of rituals. Frazer treated them as a branch of 'magic', and Freud saw in them neurotic compulsive acts, regulating repressed desires. Compulsive repetition can have a therapeutic significance, but still remains pathological. Freud believed that, like religion, ritual was an act of sublimation with cultural elements.

Emile Durkheim introduced a change of direction into research by examining rituals on the basis of their significance for society; he concluded that they were a kind of school for a people, in which it expressed its innermost convictions. Society reconstituted itself continually in its rituals. Structuralism and the British school of social anthropology have confirmed and modified these discoveries.

The basic significance of rituals for communal life has recently been confirmed by behaviourism. Rituals are basic constants of anthropology. Even animals have rituals. They have a protective function. Dangers are overcome, helpful behaviour is internalised, so that it can be handed on to the next generation. Rituals consolidate the 'pecking order';, they

---

[81] Cf. A. R. Radcliffe-Brown, 1952, p. 157.

ensure that the victor does not destroy the opponent in a struggle and that the status of those of higher rank is respected. Rituals make communal life possible.[82]

The term 'ritual' or 'rite' comes from the Indo-Germanic word *ṛta*, which means 'order', or 'regulated behaviour'. The unordered world is dangerous, because it is chaotic. Anyone who builds a house knows how uncomfortable the process can be. It is only when there are paths, trees and a garden that life there becomes possible and it is now 'home'. Rituals are ways of ordering the world and making it manageable. They hold chaos in check and ward off accidents. To describe them exclusively as the correct behaviour towards a holy power, as repetitions of powerful acts (G. van der Leeuw),[83] is limiting and misleading. As in the case of symbols, the meaning of rituals has many dimensions. What would be complex to express analytically, because events extend into different levels, is grounded and synchronised in ritual. Ritual has to be interpreted on several levels if we want to understand it. At least six dimensions can be distinguished:

1. The social function is emphasised by social anthropology. It includes the dimension of social psychology, but should not neglect the dimension of individual psychology, as we shall later see in the case of mourning rites. The whole gamut of mourning, fear, aggression, identity, joy and ecstasy are activated by ritual.

2. The expressive, poetic dimension is included in the above. Rituals are impressive, artificial 'happenings', which shape the aesthetics of a society and its culture. They shake people out of their routine and make them creative. They exalt the everyday and strengthen life through celebration. Body painting, tattooing, the shape of masks and the dances themselves combine exceptional beauty with powerful expression. They satisfy aesthetic feelings and make it possible for knowledge to be passed on and conduct to be learned.

---

[82] Cf. A. Portmann, 1950, pp.358ff. For the theological reception of research into rituals, cf. R. Grainger, 1974; W. Jetter, 1978.

[83] G. van der Leeuw, 1956, para. 48.

3. Rituals possess a cognitive, educational function. They reveal and rehearse the values which form the basis of society. Knowledge of primeval times, memories of historical events, information about daily life and ethical standards are passed on visually, orally and in actions, so that they are internalised through imitation and participation.

4. Rituals are ways of structuring space. They divide it into sacred and secular – even if only on a temporary basis. They give the earth a reassuring structure.

5. Since they have a public character, they possess a legal dimension. Through ritual the new status of an individual is recognised. It covers inheritance and property rights, as well as wrongful behaviour. Ritual sees to it that (uncodified) law is respected.

6. The religious dimension need not be present everywhere in the same way, even though it is the most comprehensive. It penetrates the others and gives them their essential nature and depth. The origin of life – the ancestors, God – are recalled in colours, in clothing, in special equipment, in songs and hymns of praise, in myths and in the use of medicines. Rituals make the invisible visible, and strengthen people who are dependent on them to live in the here-and-now in harmony with all powers and creatures. Ritual becomes the "central act of preserving and fashioning life".[84]

1. Rites of passage

People can only exist in community. They become persons through their fellow human beings, as we have seen. Despite the strongly levelling character of African social life and culture, everyone does not occupy the same rank in society. On the contrary, the more closely knit the community, the more tightly it is structured. In a small African society, nobody has the same status. There is a firm hierarchy. African, like Indian, society must be described as essentially hierarchical.[85]

---

[84] A. Kirchgässner, 1959, p. 278.
[85] Cf. L. M. Dumont, Homo hierarchicus, Chicago, 1980.

The principle of seniority possesses the greatest power of differentiation and highest degree of universality. It is age which distinguishes people from each other and defines the various areas of inferiority and superiority. Nobody possesses the same rank; equality among siblings and equality for women do not exist. The oldest son occupies the first place after the head of the family. Being closest to his father, and his potential successor, he is an intermediary between his father and younger brothers and sisters, just as his father communicates with the ancestors. In matrilineal societies, the wife's eldest brother occupies the highest social and juridical position, above the husband, who occupies the same position of superiority in the family of his younger sister. The principal wife, the first to be married and thus the 'eldest' in social terms, enjoys the highest status among the wives. This is expressed in the fact that she lives in the house on the right-hand side of the chief house, or even in the chief house itself. On the left-hand side, or further away to the right, lives the second wife, and so on (this is the pattern in the circular villages among the Bantu). Status is visible in the arrangement of the houses or rooms occupied. Yet this is not the only way; rituals respect and reinforce status in various ways, especially mourning rituals.

Seniority means a higher position, more respect, greater power. The person grows into this position. Respect grows with age. In the first place, it is of no importance whether he or she is cleverer or wiser than the younger generation. Even senile old people enjoy full honour. Respect for age is compensation for the lower position and deprivations they suffered in their youth. The old harvest the fruits of life, for which they previously had to struggle. Now they can receive from children and grandchildren what they previously owed to parents and grandparents – service, obedience and respect.

We can easily imagine the crises affecting the small-scale African society and what personal tragedies it gives rise to – far exceeding the normal generational conflicts which are known in all societies – when in modern times school education and qualifications count for more than seniority. The older generation, which no longer has the chance to benefit from education, are doubly cheated, because they are forced to occupy a subordinate role in their old age, just as they were in their youth.

The stages of seniority differ from society to society. The Kikuyu in Kenya, with their close bonds in an age-structured society, have an especially large number of divisions. Acceptance into the community, which takes place a few weeks after birth, is the first stage, replaced after five years when a boy is able to tend the goats – an important task in Kikuyu society. The 'second birth', which also alters the position of the mother, follows at about the age of nine, with circumcision. The fourth stage turns the boy into a man, ready for marriage. Marriage makes the next stage possible, but he only becomes eligible for membership of the council of elders when his first child is born. The child makes him into a father, a socially acceptable, complete man.[86]

Only in a limited sense does he grow into a higher status 'by himself'. Africans well understand the natural progression of becoming and passing on. They know how to wait and how to adapt to the natural conditions of life; yet everything in Africa still has to be accompanied by rituals and religious observances if it is to follow its normal and regulated course.

Life is endangered life, and never more so than during rites of passage. These are the crisis points of life which affect the whole of society. Nothing can be taken for granted, and this is why things have to be ordered and structured anew, both socially and religiously. The community does not leave the individual alone amid these dangers; it gives support. The acceptance into the new status must receive public and legal recognition.

It was Flame van Gennep who in 1909 coined the expression *rites de passage*, drawing attention to their existence in all cultures. He distinguished three main stages within the individual rites: separation, the transition and introduction to the new status. This basic model can be shown in all rites of passage to this day, even if the individual phases are not always clearly separated, and transitions are fluid. The central statement, however, is the same: the individual is changed by the ritual. He or she receives a new status and occupies a new rank; life takes on a new quality and must be lived in a different way, something others have to respect.

---

[86] Cf. the ordering of stages in W. E. Mühlmann, 1964, pp.112ff.

Birth, adolescence, marriage and death are the fundamental crisis points for all. The dangers which attend birth, for both mother and child, are well known, but the fact that the lives of the other members of the family may also be at risk, because the ancestors have to prove their strength, may be new to us. We are more familiar with the situation where the family are so emotionally affected that they feel obliged to participate. We know how helpless fathers often are at the birth of their first child, and we also know nowadays that their presence at the birth helps the mother and child. According to the African view of life, such a feeling of inner sympathy indicates how closely the powers of life are bound up. With the life of one individual the life of another is equally at risk, and the strength of one must be shared with another. Shared living must become visible, even dramatically, as in the case of the *couvade*. The father-to-be takes to his bed and observes the same food taboos as his wife, and is treated like a woman in labour.

The man is also affected because, until the birth has been successfully completed, he cannot know whether the child is really his, or whether alien 'blood' has been mixed with his wife's blood, which would be most dangerous for them both. If the wife is unable to bear children, this is attributed to secret adultery, and only confession can free her from her guilt and lead to a successful birth. A host of taboos surround birth. All the utensils used at the birth have in some way or another a symbolic meaning, in order to promote a successful birth and to indicate the legitimacy of the child.[87]

Among many peoples, the birth only reaches its conclusion when the child is accepted into the community through ritual. This can be a simple act of 'outdooring', in which the father receives the child from the arms of the midwife, and thereby acknowledges it as his own. Name-giving is another opportunity, in which the naming also represents the presentation of the child to the ancestors. Among pastoral nomadic peoples, the child is presented with a calf on the occasion of these ritual observances, to ensure a future livelihood. Religious, legal and economic aspects form a unity in ritual. For the community, however, it is a welcome opportunity to break out of the hum-

---

[87] Cf. the wealth of material in H. Aschwanden (himself a doctor), 1976, pp.213ff.

drum of everyday events and celebrate the continuation of life. This is a reason for play, for rejoicing and for thanksgiving.

Three rituals will now be examined, each from another people: circumcision, marriage and mourning. In the first case, the symbolism of all observances is prominent; in wedding rituals, the religious and legal aspect; and in burial rituals, coping with mourning through individual psychology. Obviously other aspects are implied in every instance.

2. Circumcision

Among the Ndemu in Zambia[88] the time for circumcision does not necessarily have to coincide with the onset of puberty. The chief has to decide when the ritual will be carried out. He may follow the advice of the elders, who put forward their opinion if the youths become too high-spirited and it seems right to subject them to the hardship of circumcision in order to introduce them into the orderly life of the community.

As soon as it has been decided to carry out the ceremony, a suitable place must be sought and the appropriate medicines gathered. Initiation has to do with maturity, with preparation for the subsequent propagation of the species. That is why all the medicines point towards this end. They include, for example, parts of the *chikoli* tree, whose wood is so hard that it even resists termites and cannot be uprooted by elephants. It means strength. "It stands upright like an erect penis, or a man's strong body".[89] It produces whatever it symbolises. The medicine taken from the *mudyi* tree recalls the ancestor who introduced circumcision and who rested beneath this tree. The fruits of the *musoli* tree attract animals so that they can be easily shot while feeding. Just as it 'makes game visible', so it is said to make the glans of the youths easy to see. The uncircumcised glans is regarded as 'dirty', and only the circumcised one is 'pure'. The *musenga* tree bears much fruit. It stands for fertility and will bring it forth. These four medicines – and many more are collected –

---

[88] For what follows, cf. V. W. Turner, 1967, pp.151ff.
[89] Op. cit., p. 191.

make clear the purpose of circumcision: the novices are initiated into the life of their people, their traditions and ethics (presence of the ancestors, history). The youths are to be healthy, bold and virile. They are purified for life in order to satisfy its real purpose, raising up descendants.

After the medicines are collected, the circumcisers and assistants go off to a camp, in the middle of which stands a *chikoli* tree. They dance around it and sing the following song:

> "I am the lion, who eats on the path.
> You sleep on your back, you look into the sky -
> Nest of the marabout stork where a black kite lays eggs.
> Hole of the mamba where the harmless lizard lays her eggs.
> Novice's mother, you used to revile me,
> Bring me your child that I may mistreat (him).
> Your child has gone
> The son of a chief is like a slave".

The song is full of analogies and allusions to the coming act of circumcision, as were the medicines. The circumciser is compared to the lion, which pounces on its prey. He has to perform the circumcision without hesitation. The lion stands for power, manliness, skill in hunting and chieftaincy. Moreover, the comparison draws attention to the danger involved in circumcision. It can have fatal consequences. In many initiations by circumcision, the act itself is described as being swallowed by a monster,[90] a motif familiar from psychoanalysis. The lion is a recurrent dream symbol, symbolising sexual aggression and anticipating the fear of castration.

The second motif of the song is the tension between the circumciser and the mothers. The children are being torn away from their mothers and introduced into the male community. The mothers are losing their children – and sometimes they do so literally, the strain is so great.

Finally, the song recalls the second stage of the rites of passage, which Turner aptly describes as "between and betwixt": after the children are released from the female society and before they are introduced into the male

---

[90] Cf. in E. Dammann, 1963, p. 181.

society, there is an intermediate stage, where the former order no longer applies. The chief's son is treated like a slave. Tension between the sexes may turn into boisterousness; obscenities, otherwise taboo, may be freely uttered; what is otherwise forbidden is allowed.

In the song the stages of the ritual are described, the participants are prepared for what is to come, and the danger is named and exorcised, with everyone foreshadowing the event.

Meanwhile, the novices have assembled in the house of the chief. They are covered with white paint. White is the colour of the ancestors and of semen. Prayers have been offered for the neophytes at their parent's shrine to the ancestors; they have been placed under the latters' protection. Again the purpose of the ceremony is made known: fertility, purity and peace. Once more prayers are offered for the novices in the house of the chief, mention being made of all those ancestors still remembered, from the most recently deceased to the earliest ones in the dim and distant past. All are intermediaries between the living and God, the source of all life. At stake is the preservation of the whole people, and even of the ancestors themselves. The fate of all is at risk. They must be present, offering protection and help. Their protection against evil magic and witches is sought.

The women who cook for the novices and for the helpers spend the night in an isolated place, not far from the actual place of circumcision. Together with the mothers of the youths, they are subject to certain taboos. They must not have sex, or eat salt (salt is white and refers to the sexual act). Breaking the taboo would weaken the youths, while abstinence strengthens them. Certain kinds of meat are also forbidden, for example the meat of chickens which have a speckled colour, otherwise the young people will catch leprosy. Everything is subject to analogous participation. Nobody lives for themself, and everything that the individual does has an influence upon the group, especially in times of crisis. Each participates in the other and helps to bear the other's lot, ritually and emotionally. The inhabitants of the village are warned to avoid all strife, because the youths' wounds can heal up quickly only where peace reigns. Strife harms the ritual; anger lessens its power.

The youths are not able or allowed to sleep during this night. They are carried on the backs of helpers and those already initiated. Today dancing is allowed, all strife is forgotten, people dance their anger away. What is to come is approached in dancing and play. The lion dance becomes more and more erotic.

The next morning there is another sumptuous meal, at which each mother feeds her own son. Childhood is finally coming to an end. The youths go alone to the place of circumcision, where no other uncircumcised person and no woman may set foot – nor anybody who has been circumcised without ritual on the mission station or in a hospital. Circumcision alone is worth little; it needs the word, the medicine, the community. External circumcision would be only a sign. Through ritual it becomes a sacramental act. It is the total context that makes the sign into an effective symbolic event.

The path to the place of circumcision is surrounded by symbolic signs, and leads through a kind of gate. Here the youths hang up the clothes that they wore as children. They go through the gate naked. The gate is the womb that leads to the new life. Whoever enters here goes towards a new birth.

At the place of circumcision the boys sleep on branches of the *mudyi* tree, as the ancestor did once upon a time. In the middle of the place stands a branch of the *muyombu* tree. There is a special reason for this: it has white wood. If the bark is cut in strips, it rolls up, and the white wood is revealed; i. e. a 'circumcision', because this is the way that the foreskin is rolled back, so that the 'white', i. e. the pure glans is visible. This cutting of the wood is called *kusolola*, 'making visible'.

By the tree of the ancestors there is white maize beer, and all the circumcisers take some of this to pour over a *mudyi* leaf and to hold aloft while praying. The chief circumciser calls upon the ancestors and prays to the first ancestor to look kindly on the ceremony he established so long ago.

During the circumcision that now follows, drums are beaten. They show the parents that the great moment has now arrived. Normally the boys are not allowed to cry out; among the Ndemu they may shout for their father, but not for their mother. The sound of the drums drowns their cries.

62

Speed and safety in cutting count as qualifications for the circumcisers. After the operation, the novice is taken to the ancestors' tree and sprinkled with medicines. The wound is held over a hollowed-out termite hill until the blood ceases to flow. Further treatment with medicine is succeeded by a ritual meal, consisting of beans and white cassava, which the fathers feed their sons.

After the circumcision, initiation into adult society begins, and this lasts about two months. A special camp is set up for the novices, to the south of the former circumcision camp, which henceforth the youths must not enter. Their stay in the camp is divided into three phases. First of all the wounds must heal, which demands intensive medicinal treatment, and includes a ban on various types of food, e. g. eating the flesh of elephants and mice (both have a 'trunk' like the youths before circumcision). Then follows instruction in certain masked dances and rituals. Finally, there is instruction in tribal lore and customs. If a boy dies during circumcision, no legal action is taken against the person in charge of the ceremony. "God alone is responsible", is the response.

During this time the youths wear no clothes. Any food which is not consumed is brought together to a certain place. They must not look upon it any more: in the same way, they have left their childhood behind them. The friendship, even blood brotherhood, which is formed between initiands during this time is called, 'they have eaten uncleanliness together'.

Return to normal life is prepared for by rituals which last two days. The youths receive the flesh of tortoises to eat. "That should strengthen their penises". One of the helpers wraps himself in a blanket. He is called 'old woman'. The novices come to him, as he sits on the ground with his legs spread apart, and mime the sexual act. They also imitate penetration with a small pumpkin in which a hole has been cut.

After this the novice master informs them, "Tomorrow you will return to your mothers. But each of you will be carried into the camp by another helper than before. How your mothers will weep when they see different children on the shoulders of the helpers". The youths are treated with medicine once more, this time on the eye-brows and on the navel. Part of the dried and ground up foreskin has been worked into this medicine. This is known as, 'the body is given back to them'. Coated over and over again with red and white paint, the youths are carried into the parents' camp. Their mothers do not recognise them. Twice more they are carried out of the camp and then back in again, while drums are beaten. Each time the jubilation rises, finally boiling over in an exuberant dance under the *chikoli* tree. A festival is celebrated all through the night. Towards morning the novices' hut is burnt down. From now on the place is avoided like a graveyard. The novices are brought to a river and washed. The kilts that they wore on their way out of the camps are thrown into the river. After their hair is cut, the youths receive from their fathers new clothes which have been bought or made for the occasion.

Back in the parents' camp, each boy performs the dances he has learnt. The best is allowed to show off. The festival is over when the first or second to be circumcised throws a knife at the feet of the circumciser.

Following this, a separate celebration is held within the family. At this point, the initiation as such is over.

The social and religious aspects are closely interwoven in the ritual. The mother-son relation changes; a new relation is forged with the father. The son is no longer the same as he was before circumcision. He takes on new tasks; the purpose of life, procreation within a formal marriage, draws nearer.

The transition from the life of a child to that of an adult does not take place simply in biological terms. The youths are not yet sexually mature. Even if they were, that is not the decisive step. Maturity is reached through death. The youths die ritually, and in the African context that means in real terms. It could be called a 'sacramental death'. It takes place in word and deed. While the novice dies, the community is summoned to strengthen life. A person is not cut off from the community in ritual. On the contrary, the surrounding powers can be used for personal benefit. Which powers are useful, and how they are found and applied is known to the specialists. Even when their application in a particular case is not evident to everyone, the symbol engages the observer. It makes participation possible.

Ritual death is not the death of an individual, but the death of a group. A young person undergoes death in company, and receives new life in company. Old ties are replaced by new ones. Ritual death does not lead to isolation, it binds the community to the ancestors. The novice enters into a new redeeming relationship with them, in the same way as he is linked to the group of adults, because life concerns everybody in the same way.

A final word on the significance of God in this ritual. Mentioned only at one point, on the occasion of the possible death of a novice, God appears to be absent from the rest of the ritual. This is a matter for the ancestors since in all questions of fertility they are reminded of their responsibilities. Among the Xhosa of South Africa, the ancestors are called '*Idhlosi*', and that also means 'semen'. It is only when sudden death puts the ritual in question that people feel confronted by God. In normal life, they only have to deal with him indirectly, unlike with the ancestors . It is not going too far to claim that they are drawn towards God when they sense something going beyond their every-day, practical concerns – the great threat to life.

The wealth of the ritual cannot be described here; indeed, some important aspects will be omitted, e. g. the meaning of dance. However, let us summarise the main points of initiation, with features from the rituals of other peoples, and from female circumcision. To begin with, the tension running through all phases of the rituals, based on polarity, seems a structural principle. There is the tension between young and old; between the childhood home (which structuralism interprets as a secular, unregulated place, even as 'the wild', since nothing is forbidden there and the child is unaware of good and evil), and the circumcision camp, the place of laws and culture; between the sexes, consisting of separation and union; between the present time and the time of myth, which is reenacted and resolved as time stands still; between the sacred and the profane; between what is taboo and what is allowed, which is established by the periodical reversal of order; finally, there is the great tension between life and death which runs through all phases of the ritual. This contradiction is, however, overcome through the initiation into the unity of life and death in the course of the ritual.

The Bakoko of Cameroon express this duality through numbers. Nine is the number which stands for God. Four is the number for a woman (she has only four limbs); five the number for a man. The addition of these two, which plays an important role in circumcision, is the number of life, the number of completeness, the number for God.[91]

1. For the young people, initiation is a major process of separation. The break is so sharp that it has actually been called a second weaning. They leave the parental home. For the first time they have to undergo the hardships of life without the protection of mother or father. This applies to boys, but even more to girls, who must undergo a deep, painful operation without their mothers being present – a foretaste of the pains of childbirth.[92]

The girls and boys are torn away from their environment, which has hitherto meant security or even freedom. Hardly anything is forbidden to African children; they are not aware of wrong-doing; they do not know what 'sacred' and 'taboo' mean. They live beyond good and evil, because they are not called to account for any of their actions.

2. They are led into an extreme situation, in which the previous order no longer applies. The society of the adults with its hierarchy and structure dies for a while. The novices run around naked, they are allowed to steal (in some societies), they are tormented without cause by the adults, and they themselves must torment. They are made fun of and they make fun of others. They are allowed to speak a language that is otherwise forbidden, and learn things that must never be spoken of again. The abolition of order draws them into a no man's land, without a sense of direction, which is the precondition of the new order and the new life. They are, in a way, brought face to face with themselves, their bodies, their situations, which until this time have been un-

---

[91] M. Ntetem, 1983, pp.112f. For the whole subject cf. L. V. Thomas and R. Luneau, 1975, pp.203ff. and 233ff.

[92] P. Hanry writes in Erotisme africain, Paris 1970, p. 174: "Maturity obtained with the mother's assistance has little attraction. Excision seems to play an important role here: a solemn moment which profoundly affects the young girl's psyche is gone through without the mother being present. For the first time in her life, and in exceptional circumstances which at one and the same time affect both her entire personality and her sexual activity, the girl finds herself alone, away from her indulgent mother, and so *quite on her own* assumes responsibilities of an adult woman, and which lead definitively into the world of adults. This aspect is enough to explain the willing acceptance by the girl of the pain of excision". (Quoted by L. V. Thomas & R. Luneau, 1975, p. 227).

known to them. There is no help for them in all this. Courage, perseverance, the strength to endure pain, and their skilfulness are challenged to the utmost. Now the youths and girls realise what they they are capable of. Initiation is a time of war, blood flows; only those who have proved themselves can endure.

3. Concentrating on sex is also a part of the confrontation with their own body, the symbolic centre of the world, as we have seen. The fears of the adolescents are absorbed into the ritual and symbolically reinforced. The dense web of bonding with their mother, then separation, curiosity about the female sex, and fear of losing their sexual organ – this is all lived out. A woman is not just a mother; she can be a dangerous monster who threatens to destroy sexuality. Various rituals display a monster in the form of a woman who eats the young man.[93] Through masks, in dancing and dramatic performances, these fears are acted out, lived out and focussed.

4. Initiation conclusively establishes a person's gender. The latent bisexuality of the youths, which was previously socially acceptable, as shown, for example, by their sleeping with the women, now becomes physically unambiguous. The youth can no longer hide his sex behind his foreskin (which is sometimes regarded as being 'female'), just as the girl loses the (apparent) remnant of her masculinity – her clitoris. In his own eyes, and in the eyes of the community, the youth has now become a man. Both he and the others accept his sexuality. It need no longer be suppressed, but will now be channelled. In the same way, the girl is to be deprived of the possibility of masturbation and her desire for a male strengthened. The Dogon express this mythically as follows: "The 'second soul' is taken away from the novices. The ritual serves to 'integrate the *muntu* into oneself" (M. Ntetem).[94] Among the Bavenda of South Africa this applies whether circumcision takes place or not.

---

[93] Cf. on this subject the myth which is related among the Bavenda in South Africa during initiation rituals: The hero and heroine of the ritual kill each other, and in this way they gain rebirth. Cf. H. A. Stayt, 1968, pp.112f.

[94] Ntetem, 1983, pp.97ff. For further literature on initiation cf. V. Popp, 1969; F. B. Welbourn, 1969.

5. The time of initiation is like school. The young people are introduced to life, they learn the techniques of hunting, how to till the land and how to build houses. They are initiated into tribal lore and ethics. They are also taught sexual techniques. This applies particularly to the initiation of girls. The hardships they undergo are also a way of checking that they are not yet pregnant, and this is a desired side-effect.

6. The ancestors are present. The young people grow closer to them, so to speak, because their status in the society has grown. They have come closer to the real task of life, the continuation of life through children, and in the future they will share in serving the ancestors. Through being initiated into the myths and secret lore of their people, and through dancing the dances of their fathers, they become a part of the religion. They become guilty and from now on need the protection of their forebears and reconciliation with them. It would be wrong to say that they become capable of participating in religion, because that would be to presuppose a division between religion and society; rather, their participation in religion has reached a new stage.

Everything affects the participants in the deepest part of their being, their sexuality. No matter how hard and cruel initiation may be, their innermost emotions are touched. That can be traumatic (as women have reported), but for the most part it raises life to a new level in a creative sense. A second birth has taken place. Life comes only out of death. They have experienced this. The eternal human song of life and death, passing away and resurrection, is played out and experienced here. And God himself is involved, no matter how rarely or directly he is named and called upon. His indirect presence is announced in many ways.

7. Re-integration into society takes place in a double sense. The initiates form their own group (peer-group, regiment, etc.), whose cohesion is shown through many kinds of social links and obligations, ending only in death. The male neophyte can now never be solitary; in all future times of crisis he will be part of a group which shares the same fate, upholding and sustaining him. This community is so close that under certain conditions it has included the women's community (Herero).

Neophytes are integrated into the whole community together. They are accepted as full members, with all rights and duties. In some peoples they receive a new name, e. g. among the Bavenda and Bakoko. By so recognising their new identity, the community makes them part of itself.

In Old Testament times people had to be born again through being accepted into the Covenant.[95] For Africa we should say: quite apart from physical birth, people become people through acceptance. At birth, the infant is accepted by the family; the whole community accepts the young person through initiation.

3. Marriage

In Africa marriage is not the short act of a wedding ceremony between two partners of different sexes, but a longer process of steady bonding between two social groups. The small societies of Africa are centred on the family or, to be more exact, the lineage. In acephalous societies this has an extra significance. The group can only survive if it clings together, defending itself against any loss of members. Every contact with another group is implicitly dangerous. That is why caution is called for when one group forms a link with another one. Slowly the antagonism is dismantled, and through marriage is transformed into friendship. In order to avoid all possible dangers, it is advisable to choose a lineage to which the family is already related, or in contact. Preferential marriages are therefore known all over Africa, whether it be the prescribed marriage of parallel or cross cousins, or the need to stay within a specific totem. The legal system, whether matrilineal or patrilineal, determines the particulars. Where both systems exist side by side within a people, the matrilineal mainly takes priority, because the women's side has jurisdiction in matters of inheritance, whereas the patrilineal determines more the religious level. It is advantageous when a previous marriage is repeated structurally in a new connection. That prevents the fragmentation of the in-

---

[95] K. H. Miskotte, Wenn die Götter schweigen, 2nd ed. 1963, p. 163.

heritance, facilitates family gatherings, and limits the danger of subsequent dissension.

When, for example, among the Herero, the mother belongs to the maternal line (*eanda*) A, and the husband to the maternal line B, the son belongs to the maternal line A, but also to his father's line. If he marries the daughter of his father's sister, his cross cousin, who belongs to the line B through her father, the linkage between the two lines (*omaanda*) A and B is repeated in his marriage.

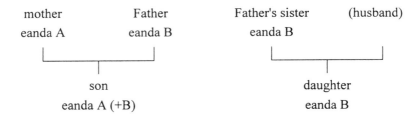

mother	Father	Father's sister	(husband)
eanda A	eanda B	eanda B	
son		daughter	
eanda A (+B)		eanda B	

Since ritual reflects and channels the feelings of the group, it is no wonder that this antagonism influences the marriage rites and all the preparations for them. The people most concerned, the bride and the bridegroom, remain in the background; it is their families and friends who take action. Transactions are carried on through intermediaries, who do not lose face if – as is usual and necessary – they are treated coolly at first and turned away (when a hidden or recognised signal clearly indicates that a second visit is desired). The bringing of presents smoothes the way – they are known as 'mouth-openers'. A second visit allows the acquaintance to grow, and removes feelings of strangeness. Even the shortest way of handling the matter, the (ritual) capture of the bride is known among various peoples. This shows more clearly what is at the heart of the matter: the bride's family cannot allow its potential strength to be diminished by another family. The balance of forces would be appreciably damaged. Marriage is robbery or, in other words, an invasion of the family. Among the Zulu, the bride's father used to say, "You have stabbed me", when he gave his consent to the marriage of his daughter.[96] One family loses part of its fertility, the other family gains. In matrilineal societies, it is the woman's family. This applies also in cases of patrilocal law of residence, because the new-born children remain in the company of the mother's family; the man's family is strengthened in patrilineal association. Presents must restore the damaged relationship of powers. This is at the heart of the *system of bride price*, known throughout the whole of Africa. It has nothing to do with the bride herself. Nowhere in the course of the negotiations is there talk of selling the bride. She cannot be sold, and in many peoples she remains a member of her family after the payment of the bride price. She can return there if, for any reason, the marriage does not work out. However, she cannot take her children back if the bride price has been duly handed over. If that has not happened, the children remain with her.

The system of bride price is not about the bride, it is about her fertility and her children. The children are brought into the husband's family by the exchange of cattle and gifts. The children are 'bought'. The Zulu say, "*Lobolo* produces children".[97] The bridegroom's family receives the fertility of the bride's family. She is under an obligation to bear children, if the bride price ('children's price') has been paid. Since nobody really knows whether the bride is fertile, however, among some peoples only a part is paid at the outset of the marriage, the rest following when a healthy child is born. Bride price debts do not lapse, and must be paid even after the decease of the woman. If the father is too poor, he can promise to hand over the her first daughter to the father-in-law, as compensation. The granddaughter then compensates the family of her mother. She is not regarded as the child of her father's family, but as the child of the family of her maternal grandparents. If, in spite of various warnings, the family of the bridegroom is still slow to pay up, the bride's family has the right to secretly take her back again (among the Xhosa in the Transkei), in order to force the husband to settle the remaining debt. Among the Venda in South Africa, the last payment only takes place when the woman's eldest daughter gets married. The rest of the mother's

---

[96] E. J. Krige, 1965, p. 120.
[97] Quoted by F. P. Bruwer, 1963, p. 71.

bride price is paid with the cattle of the daughter's bride price. The cycle is complete, the woman's fertility returns to her family in the cattle of the granddaughter.

The bride price guarantees children. What happens if the woman is unable to bear children? The first solution is the 'sister marriage'. The bride's family makes another woman available, the bride's sister. No further bride price needs to be paid for her. At most a small gift is handed over out of friendship. The sister has no position in her husband's house, and her children are regarded as her sister's children, for whom the price was paid. She is merely the medium through which her sister has children.

If no sister is available, the niece, the daughter of the bride's brother, takes her place, because the bride price for the brother's wife is paid with the cattle that the sister has brought into the family (among the Venda and Lobedu in South Africa). Among the Lobedu, this principle is even reflected in the form of address. The niece will always address her uncle, the husband of her father's sister, as 'my husband', whether she has married him or not. In any case, according to family tradition he is potentially her husband.

The system of bride price is raised not only by a woman's infertility, but also by the death of the husband. What happens if he dies before a child can be produced? The wife is obliged to bear her husband a child. His death does not relieve her of this obligation, otherwise the price must be handed back. In this case, there is a leviratical marriage. The dead man's younger brother takes his place. Any children born of this association count as the children of the dead man. Among the Xhosa, an outsider can also take the place of the deceased; his children are counted as the children of the dead man, and can inherit his property.

If a man dies before marrying, the family can pay the bride price for a woman to revive its line by bearing children to a member of this man's family or to an outsider. No matter whose children they are, they are counted as the children of the dead man, because the cattle for the bride price came from him. The Sotho say, "The woman is married to a grave". The purpose of such a 'ghost marriage', as Evans-Pritchard[98] calls it, is clear: the son of the family must be given children. The doctrine of the immortality of the soul arouses little interest in Africa. All that counts is the 'immortality' of the family.

A Venda custom shows how appropriate the bride price system is, and how consistently it is applied. If a wealthy woman wants to better her position and increase her standing, she can 'buy' a woman with her cattle. She takes a young woman into her house and ensures that she becomes pregnant and bears children. The children count as hers, and she counts as their 'father'. In this way, the following situation can arise which may appear bizarre, but which is fully understandable according to the system. A woman can be the mother of the children of her husband and is called 'mother' by them; at the same time she is the 'father' of the children of the woman for whom she paid the bride price, and is addressed as 'father' by them. In fact, only the latter children 'belong' to her, because the others belong to the lineage of her husband.

The bride price has an important function in stabilising marriage. Normally, the cattle (or goats and sheep), which the bride brings to her family as compensation for her fertility are used to pay the bride price for the next of her brothers to marry. If the marriage of the sister breaks down and she returns to her parental home, part or the whole of the bride price must be repaid. The brother's marriage is placed at risk, because he must give back the cattle or compensate for them. He – and his whole family – will therefore do everything in their power to save his sister's marriage, and settle the misunderstandings and disputes which have caused the disagreement.

In matrilineal peoples there is only an exchange of gifts at marriage. Among the Ovambo in Namibia, the man gives the bride's family only one beast to thank them for looking after her so far. The children belong to the woman's family. If the man dies, the woman returns with her children (among patrilocal families) to her parents' home, However, she returns poor and brings nothing with her, because the man's property, even what they produced together, goes to the man's family. His brothers will come and take

---

[98] E. E. Evans-Pritchard, 1967, p. 163.

everything with them. From now on it is entirely the responsibility of the widow's family to care for the children.

How does the system of bride price affect the status of women? In its original form she was not a mere commodity. It was only the introduction of money that altered its meaning. Today the parents of the bride regard the money as a return for their work and investment in her education, and as security for their old age. By the use of money, marriage is being reduced to a financial transaction. This is now spreading among those peoples which did not use to have the bride-price system, or where it played only a minor role. The tendency to reduce the significance of marriage to the nuclear family is fostering this development. In the original system the position of the woman was strengthened by the transfer of living property. She was worth something, she represented life. Living property is handled with care. No matter how closely she was integrated into her husband's family, she never became her husband's slave. She still had her original home, her family. They offered her a refuge and back-up which she could employ in any conflict with her husband. If she were the mother of healthy children, she enjoyed a position of respect in the house of her parents-in-law, even after the death of her husband. As a young widow, her place was secure at the side of a man from her husband's family. The bride-price system meant a form of social security.

Marriage is a concern of society to such an extent that many researchers have sought to interpret marriage rituals only in terms of their social significance. They are said to be secular events.[99] That applies to the individual case, but their meaning is restricted if they are not seen as part of the overall world-view. Marriage is more than the union of two young people and also more than the joining of two lineages. Where life and new life are concerned, the ancestors are involved. Two alien groups of ancestors meet in the lineages. That causes the real danger which is more than the mere opposition of two alien social groups. This becomes real in the sexual act. The similarity of the concepts blood – semen – ancestors, and the latent analogies indicate that two groups of ancestors meet in the sex act. The Karanga are very explicit

---

[99] This is the view of H. O. Mönnig, for example, on the rituals of the Pedi.

about this. According to them, a battle takes place. The woman's blood 'devours' the man's semen. Only strong, 'pure' semen can win, i. e. from a man who has the blessing of the fathers in his actions.[100] If alien semen is introduced, i. e. if the woman has previously had sexual intercourse outside marriage, this will make her husband ill. Moreover, she runs into danger herself, she may become barren, suffer a miscarriage, or have a difficult birth. The man, however, also endangers his wife if, during her period, he has sexual intercourse with another woman; this means mixing alien blood with that of his wife. Because he brings together ancestors who do not 'know' each other, this will have an evil outcome.[101]

Physical life is open to transcendence, good conduct is blessed. The union of husband and wife must be legitimate and must not take place in strife, hatred or fear. There can only be peace when the ancestors are 'satisfied'. "When you try to have a child, do so only out of love and with a good intention, otherwise your child will have a bad character. The act of making love is thus made holy, and a couple who have not previously examined their hearts should not come together. A quarrel must be peaceably settled before a child is conceived".[102] In order to achieve this end and to ensure that peace extends even into the invisible world of the ancestors, the marriage preparations must be elaborate and the path to marriage must be long and smoothed with many gifts. Marriage is also a religious institution, and the religious connotations of marriage rituals should not be overlooked.

Marriage rituals consist of two parts: the first is celebrated in the bride's house and marks the introduction of the son-in-law, but above all the departure of the daughter from the family and lineage of her parents. The rituals have different importance, according to whether it is a matrilineal, patrilineal or a 'mixed' society. The second part of the wedding takes place in the hus-

---

[100] Cf. H. Aschwanden, 1976, pp.202ff. For similar reasons, the Sotho have the same idea that only repeated sexual acts can produce enough semen to lead to pregnancy; cf. I. Schapera, 1971, chaps. 1 & 2, especially, pp.189ff.

[101] This could be the religious origin of preferential marriage: if the ancestors have already formed a connection through an earlier marriage, they will probably be happy to bless the new marriage because they already know and trust each other.

band's village. As an example, we reproduce here an eye-witness report of this ritual among the Himba in Kaokoveld, Namibia, which reflects particularly well the multi-dimensional character of the procedure, although this is indicated only very indirectly by the narrator.

"The wedding rituals begin immediately after the arrival of the bridal pair. First of all a sheep is slaughtered. If possible, it should be a black one. It is called *ondu jondjova*, the guilt sheep. This 'scapegoat' is to cleanse the young couple from the sexual sins that both of them may have committed before their marriage. The real ritual begins with the preparation of this sheep. A hut is built out of branches for the couple. There is no rest for them inside. The young man must prepare the sheep during the night, and must not accept help from anybody, except from his bride. The shoulder and flanks are cooked in this house, and often the whole sheep. The two of them help each other in stirring the meat. For this they use a stick, which later on must be hidden so that nobody can find it. Otherwise it could be used for magic. This night is full of dangers, and they must be averted. The sheep's fleece is tanned during the night, so that it is completely soft and ready. This fleece plays an important role in the later life of the couple. When the meat is cooked, the people are called in, and the meat is taken out of the pot. The couple breath on it, but nobody must eat it. The bones must be kept in a safe place so that they cannot fall into anybody's hands, because by using these bones the marriage can easily be harmed by magic. Before daybreak, the bridegroom goes out into the fields, and buries them somewhere so that nobody can find them. Only the flanks and the shoulder are kept in the house. They hold the marriage together. The fleece that was tanned during this night is meant for the wedding couple. Nobody else must sleep on it. If they move into town, they only rarely take it with them, because the danger is too great that somebody else might chance to sleep on it. (In towns all these ceremonies are mostly omitted, because 'the fathers know that we are living in a foreign place, in captivity and that these rituals cannot be carried out'.) A branch of the makeshift hut is incorporated into the later home. In addition, the bridegroom slaughters an ox, or a sheep if he is poor, the so-called *otjoto*-ox. All his circumcision companions, who were present for the wedding celebrations at the bride's village, are also present now. However, only those who are already married and have slaughtered their own *otjoto*-ox may eat the meat of this one. The unmarried ones are made fun of and laughed at: they are still children, greenhorns, etc. The *otjoto*-ox raises the status of the young man. Through it he is accepted into the company of the married men, and from now on he may eat the meat of the 'sacred' cattle, the 'flesh of the forefathers'".

---

[102] H. Aschwanden, 1976, p. 225.

In the morning the bride and bridegroom go through the village, and receive good wishes and presents from everybody. During this procession they are accompanied by their contemporaries and friends. It is important that the bride now receives her *otizumba*, her 'powder' and her 'scent'.

The previous evening, or this morning, the bride was brought to the place of the ancestors' fire, where she was anointed. Until this point she had not been allowed to eat any food from her husband's house, she could not touch anything or enter the cattle kraal. The ceremonies are carried out by the bridegroom's father, or by the owner of the ancestors' fire.

In earlier times the father-in-law's 'walking-stick', which he had given his daughter on her journey, was brought back after a few years. Now this takes place earlier. The bridegroom must bring it back himself, and his young bride must accompany him. It is only when this stick is brought back that the wedding ceremonies are finally over, and the marriage is really completed.

However, for a long time the husband still does not speak of his wife as 'my wife', and he does not address her by her name. The woman must not leave her husband's house; at most, she may sit outside it. One day, however, she will get out and draw water. When she returns, the full pail of water on her head, and stands in front of the house, the newly-wed husband will take water from the pail or will drink directly from it, and say, "Ndiko (or whatever her name is), give me some water". From this moment onwards he will always address her by name, and speak of her as his wife. From now on, she will carry out her daily work in the village like every other woman".[103]

4. Mourning rituals

Many social anthropologists have described the precise sequence of the mourning rites among various peoples and explained their social functions. Death strikes deeply at the fabric of society. Rituals are understood as social and legal institutions which regulate the position of the survivors and restore the damaged equilibrium of the community. We will now examine an aspect which has so far been touched upon only in passing. In what way do rituals help individuals to solve their spiritual problems? Even in the small-scale societies of Africa, individuals are not entirely absorbed by their public roles; they are vulnerable, and have a longing for happiness and security like any-

---

[103] S. Kuware, in: T. Sundermeier, 1977c, pp.236ff.

one else. Of course, the way we pursue these goals is everywhere shaped by cultural factors.

Rituals are an elementary, non-verbal means of communicating spiritual tension. Not only is a personal problem 'expressed' and thereby given spiritual relief, but the people around are drawn into the problem. A community of mutual experience comes into being, giving support to individuals so that the pain can begin to heal. If the emotions necessary for healing are absent, then the ritual has an activating function. It calls them up, and at the same time subdues them. Ritual also conveys the religious beliefs of the community, which everyone knows about and finds plausible. The religion of the small-scale society is generally handed on by ritual, the cognitive and verbal aspects being less emphasised than the social and emotional. The meaning and content of ritual should be performed, not taught. Ritual is drama, not preaching.

The research of German psychotherapist Elisabeth Kübler-Ross and others has familiarised us with the sequence and process of mourning. We know that it is subject to certain laws, which reduce spiritual tension and help us to cope with grief. Comparing mourning rituals with the well-known stages of mourning, we find a surprising parallel, which cannot be accidental. The following will focus on the mourning rituals of the Pedi in the northern part of South Africa, and refer only occasionally to others.[104]

"Death calls his own", runs a Herero proverb. That can have several meanings: the dying want to be at home, in their own huts, among their own people. For this reason, the dead are not pushed to one side; their family come and remain with them. Even if nobody can save another person, in Africa death is not a very private affair, in which the utmost is demanded of the self ('my' death). As many people as possible will be present at a death, because it concerns them all. The behaviour of the dying person is determined

---

[104] I have developed the basic idea underlying the following explanations on the basis of the mourning rites of the Herero. Cf. T. Sundermeier, 1977a. The material on Zulu rituals was considered in the same author's Todesriten und Lebenssymbole in den afrikanischen Religionen, in: Leben und Tod in den Religionen: Symbol und Wirklichkeit,

by their culture: "You will die peacefully like cattle, and not disturbed and screaming like a goats". "Death calls his own" also means, however, that death is dangerous for those around the dying person. It is rare that a person dies alone; the dying person likes to take a second person along, it is said. Death is contagious. You have to hold it at bay, or even shake it off.

Among the northern Sotho, to whom the Pedi belong, a death must be reported immediately to the chief. His permission must be sought for the funeral. After that the relatives are informed. The 'death announcer' does not knock before entering a house, as is usual. Instead, he goes straight in. Without a word of greeting he heads for the fireplace, and places ashes on his lips. Then complete silence falls, for everybody knows that a misfortune has taken place. The housewife will begin to cry softly, finally asking who has died. The loud wailing begins only when the name of the dead person is known. The period of shock known to us from the stages of mourning is anticipated in this way and the danger of negating the death is averted from the outset.

The dead person is normally buried during the night following death, and that is why only the closest relatives can be present. In the case of a woman, one of her relatives must be there, if possible her mother's brother. If the death follows an illness, there will be enough women in the house to prepare the body for burial. In the case of an accident, the body is brought back to the home kraal. It is prepared for burial in this way: the arms and knees are folded close to the body and bound together, so that the body lies in a squatting position. Small stones are laid on the eye-lids. The tendons of the knees and arms are later severed, so that even in the grave the body remains in this foetal position. The head is shaved and the nostrils blocked up. After that the body is covered with a blanket. To prevent anybody stumbling across it, a black stick is laid in front of the hut in which the body is being kept. This is the sign that something here is no longer as it should be. Life has been cut off.

Darmstadt, 1980, pp.250–259; on the following topic, cf. H. O. Mönnig, 1967, pp.138ff.; H. Häselbarth, 1972, pp.66ff.

Death alters the usual customs. Among the Zulu, people greet each other differently, with just their finger-tips. "Death hangs over us", is what these differences say.

Meanwhile, one of the cattle is slaughtered in front of the house, and the hide is carefully removed. The corpse will be wrapped up in this hide. Just like the embryo in the amniotic sac, it will later be laid in the grave.

This position and the severing of the tendons has often been interpreted in an animistic sense. The dead person must be prevented from disturbing the family circle as a ghost. This interpretation is only partially satisfactory. The symbolic language should be understood in another way: the dead person is prepared for the new birth and therefore restored to the pre-natal position or, more exactly, prepared for the second birth.

When the body is wrapped in the cattle skin, the mother, wife or sister indicates the place where the grave is to be dug. Chiefs and heads of the kraal are buried in the cattle kraal, young men and women in the courtyard behind the house, small children under the eaves of the roof, babies in the hut itself. The grave is dug by those brothers who are present. The future heir turns the first sod. In this way, the new order is constituted.

The rituals are characterised by various inversions. Women wear their leather aprons inside-out. Among the Zulu, everything takes place on the other side of the house. The body is carried there, feet first, through the back entrance to the house which has to be broken through. People enter the house backwards.

Among the Pedi, the grave was originally round and reflected the ground plan of the round house. Many African peoples have a corner grave; this is dug on the right-hand side for women, on the left for men. The corpse is laid within this. The Zulu call this, 'iGumbe', or, 'navel'. Mother Earth...

A few of the dead person's utensils are put into the grave with the corpse, a calabash, a hammock, tobacco, pocket-money and eating utensils. Also wheat seeds. The dead person must be well provided for in the new life. However, the seeds are at the same time a request to the dead person to ensure a good harvest in the future. This is also expressed in prayer. The Xhosa pray: "Give us millet, give us maize, give us pumpkins".[105]

H. Häselbarth once noticed that when the corpse was being carried out of the house a child had to force its way in, so that it was in the doorway at the same time as the corpse. At that moment, an ox was slaughtered. "Exit and entry – the child entering with difficulty clearly represents the life continuing in birth", is Häselbarth's interpretation of this event. However else the event is to be interpreted, the identification of the dead person with a child is clear. Life and death go to meet each other.[106]

In Africa the day is the only time for action. Among the Pedi burial takes place at night. This is also an inverted procedure. For the dead, the night is like day. The ancestors like the darkness. At the same time, the dead must be symbolically deprived of what makes them human. H. O. Moenning's interpretation is: "The dead have no shadows. The spirit, 'sereti', has left the body, and no opportunity will be given to it to take possession of the body again".

The new birth can only be in the life of the world to come. Burial kills the dead definitively for the survivors. Death is not veiled, it is sealed.

The corpse is buried with the face towards the North, the direction from which the ancestors came. The path of the dead leads backwards into the past and is a sign of the indissoluble tie that exists with the forefathers.

The grave is filled in by the male relations. At the end everybody, in order of status and rank, throws a handful of earth or a stone into the grave. That is the final farewell. As soon as the grave is filled in the wife, who indicated where the grave was to be dug, approaches with an earthen pot, filled with water and medicines, and washes her hands. If the deceased was a polygynist, all the wives do the same. Then the water is poured over the grave, and the pot is dropped onto it so that it shatters. When a child is born, it is immediately washed with water and herbs from an earthen pot. "In this way,

---

[105] M. Hunter, 1969, p. 42.
[106] H. Häselbarth, 1972, pp. 37 & 139.

81

life also ends with a ritual washing and the breaking of the clay pot".[107] It is an end, but also a new beginning. At this moment, the women in the court kneel down in the same foetal position and begin to wail on a high shrill note. "Just as a child has to cry at birth, there must be the same cry at the time of death", say the Pedi. Mourning and joy go together. The dead person is mourned, and at the same time his new birth is praised. The group itself is led into new life. It is reconstituted. The women show by the position they have adopted that they have the power to create new life and to maintain the life of the group.

In the compound the real wailing now begins, and is continually renewed, day and night, every time a new mourner enters. Although this is an institutionalised form of wailing, genuine feelings are expressed. Ritual provides a channel for emotions, and brings them to the surface when they have previously been suppressed. People must mourn, because grief and tears heal the soul.

In this phase of mourning, the mourners can concentrate on nothing except the deceased. Ritual wailing makes this possible. Various peoples strike up songs of praise over the dead, although this is otherwise taboo. They also break into songs of mourning. The following texts show how forcefully personal grief is expressed in these songs.

From the mourning song for a boy of the Dama in Namibia:

"He, who bore my name!
see my grief!
Alas, you children!
And I am the young boy's mother!
There he is, my boy, dead and silent -
And I, my mother's firstborn -
Where shall I ever regain
such a child?
He, who bore my name,
the child with that small and fine mouth,

---

[107] H. O. Mönnig, 1967, p. 140.

youngest, prettiest thing,
who has died on me...
Alas, you bearer of my name,
come, take hold of me! Take me away with you!
My ancestors, it is said, shall
hear my prayer – today -
they shall tear me off this world,
for what is life to me,
now, that you, my son with this steep forehead,
my mother's joy, have died?
And I?! How could I possibly
live without you,
now that you have died away?
Alas, you bearer of my name,
brother of my sixth child,
who once were drinking
from my breast -
Could not death have
mercy on me? Leave you to me?
I must wander around like a refugee,
who is persecuted in the field.
Alas, you bearer of my name,
son of the busy collectress,
who is digging out there all day long -
it has become dark around me,
I am unable to find my path,
for my child has fallen asleep
and it lies in the dark.
Who is able to wake him up?
Full with pain I look at him! -
Come, that I may kiss you!"

From the mourning for a girl:

"Daughter, my dear daughter!
death is such a serious thing!
Every year one of my children dies!
Alas, that's what happens to me! Woe is me!

Mother, who dwells in //Gamab's hut,
take me, take me away as well,
that I shall die like the daughter,
whom you have torn from me.
Who can be given to me
to take the child's place?
...

What shall I do this year
now, that I miss my child?
Everybody else is alive,
yet alone my little daughter is dead!
Please get up, you, mother's girl!
She, who has the name from me,
who was lying on my breast,
she has perished and is dead!
And I – yet I am the mother!
Who will call my name
When you don't say "mother" anymore?
What are you looking for in //Gamab's shelter,
that you left me while dying?
Mother! Oh grief! My little child!
...

Your face was small, my little girl,
and mummy loved you just so!
Child, who always obeyed me,
please get up and come forward,
that I may see you once again:
How beautifully your eyes
were placed between full cheeks!
Little daughter, with rounded limbs,
please get up, your father appears!
He is watching out and in search for you!
Little daughter of the one who is like Kudu,
let me hear you once again!
Alas, the grieving women are mourning,

what that means, you all know well!
..."¹⁰⁸

From West African mourning songs:

"Woe! Afi! Woe! Afi!
We shall be longing for each other,
longing for a day that has passed.
Longing, longing not for today,
longing for the day that has passed
Forever we shall be longing for that very day!"

"Were death an animal -
the hunter could kill him and give me a loin,
he could destroy him and give me a loin.
The hunter could kill him and give me an arm.
The hunter could kill him, who came for my dear father.
The hunter could kill him, who came for my dear mother.
The hunter could kill him who came for my dear brother.
Were death an animal -
the hunter could destroy him and give me a loin".[109]

Concentration upon the dead person is so intense that the mourner identifies with him or her. The women's heads are shaved, like that of the deceased. And just as the latter can no longer take food, there are certain eating taboos for the mourners. For example, no salt is allowed, so meat is consumed unsalted. Among the Zulu, the widow may take only the liquid food of infants. Sexual activity is forbidden.

The following phase of mourning is characterised by depression and feelings of guilt. The Pedi express this as follows: the women must lay aside all adornment and blacken their hands, feet and face with a mixture of soot, burnt hair and blood or fat. The Nyakyusa of Tanzania feign madness.

---

[108] H. Vedder, 1923, vol. 2, pp.24ff.

[109] J. H. K. Nketia, in: H. Bürkle, 1968, pp.128f.

An important phase of mourning is hostility towards people round about. Very strong feelings of aggression develop towards others and the dead – they are even directed against the mourners. Among the Nyakyusa the war dance gives a meaningful expression to this phase. Participants in the mourning ceremonies are invited to transform their feelings of aggression into the movements of the dance. "The inner war must become outer war", is what they say. Many African peoples look for the culprit. The diviner is called and must establish who has caused the death. No death occurs blindly or is accidental. Evil comes from human beings. You have to know who the guilty parties are, so that in the future you can protect yourself from them and root out the evil. Among the Himba in Namibia a special ritual is carried out with the corpse. It must point to the guilty one – a frightening act of collective aggression. Ultimately, death can only be warded off by a death. At this point, mourning rituals, which are supposed to serve life, can do the opposite and increase death. The war dance of the Nyakyusa can turn into an actual fight against members of the 'outgroup'. Blood will flow. In other peoples an animal sacrifice draws the anger upon itself. The Nuer have a complex ritual for the sacrifice of reconciliation.[110] It seems to me that the ritual hunt also shares this psychological value. The Pedi go out to hunt a python, which is both an image of threatening danger and an archaic fertility symbol. Women wind strips of the snake-skin around their head as a sign of mourning. It is generally known that every form of sacrifice at the graveside, as well as laying gifts in the grave, can be interpreted as symbols of self-sacrifice or as sacrifices of atonement.[111]

The period of mourning lasts for several months, even a whole year, during which time the widows in particular are subject to certain rules of conduct. As a sign of mourning they carry a stick, like the one carried by girls during their initiation. Everybody must know that they are not a part of normal life, but are 'set apart'. They may not leave the homestead; others must

---

[110] Nuer rituals differ in a most interesting way but cannot be dealt with here. E. E. Evans-Pritchard, 1967, pp.144ff.

[111] Cf. Y. Spiegel: Der Prozess des Trauerns, 1973, p. 245.

even fetch water from the well for them. They observe sexual and eating taboos until the dead person is 'brought home', which formerly took place after a year. On this day all the relations gather at the grave once more, and take part in the ceremonial ritual which integrates the dead person in the community again. All the mourners are shaved, they wash with water and medicine, death is washed away. Small gifts are given to the survivors, and the widow offers the first-brewed beer to the man who will now care for her and to whom she will belong. Among the Pedi that is normally the younger brother of the deceased. Among other peoples children born to a subsequent marriage count as children of the deceased. Even where this right does not exist, it is important that life carries on and remains blessed by the ancestors, for whom the rituals were properly carried out. The ancestor is reincorporated into the family, despite the death which has been regarded and observed so seriously, and the survivors can turn back to life again. "Because we have the proper ritual behind us, our sorrow is now soothed", a Tallensi said, thereby expressing the experience of many Africans.[112] On the next morning, among the Nyakyusa, the children greet the man who has ritually gone through marriage with the widow with the words: "Father has arisen!"

The mourning rituals of various peoples have been moulded by their respective cultures and differ considerably, but they reflect in an impressive manner the individual phases of mourning. This can be shown by the following synopsis, drawn from two other Bantu peoples:

Phase of mourning	Herero rituals	Nyakyusa rituals[113]
1. Shock	Announcement ritual	Announcement ritual
2. Emotional release	Weeping and wailing	Weeping and wailing

---

[112] M. Fortes, 1966, p. 28.

[113] Space does not permit even a short treatment of the extremely rich rituals of the Nyakyusa. The following tabulation by catch-words, which of necessity must leave many difficulties unexplained, should at least make clear the phenomenological parallelism hidden under the variations in the details of the rituals. The reader should not fail to study the easily accessible, and exemplary presentations of the Nyakyusa rituals; M. Wilson, 1957, pp.13ff.; G. Wilson, loc. cit.

	Before the burial: sitting by the deceased; praise and mourning songs are sung for the deceased	Before the burial: The head of the deceased is held in the hand. Later: the deeds of the deceased are recounted
3. Inability to concentrate on anything other than the deceased		
4. Depression and guilt feelings	Food taboos. Turning to face the wall	Food taboos. People sit in the house of mourning on rubbish. Search for the guilty person. Feigned madness. War dance, destruction of banana groves
5. Hostility towards other people	(Himba before burial: search for the guilty)	
6. Refusal to return to normal life	Continuation of food taboos. Special sleeping customs. Slaughter of sacred animals	Continuation of food taboos. Animal sacrifice. Symbolic repetition of burial
7. Return to life	End of mourning rites. Distribution of the inheritance. Widow remarries. Selection of sacred cow. Relighting of ancestors' fire. Erection of grave stone	Widow remarries. The deceased is brought home[114]

Symbols give food for thought; rituals take the participant to the heart of what they seek to convey. Let us attempt to summarise what mourning rituals show.

1. Death is not the great leveller, as we often think. The difference that exists between people is preserved in dying and in death. A child is buried in a different way from a woman who was the mother of many children, or who was childless. The head of a kraal counts for more than a son of the house, and the death of a chief or king touches the whole society. The place of burial, the extent of the rituals and the length of the period of mourning indicate the status of the deceased. Social distinctions are maintained in death.

2. Death is the great enemy. It is feared, because it destroys the most valuable thing that exists, life itself. It makes a difference whether it is a good death,

---

[114] On the whole of this subject, cf. T. Sundermeier, 1977a. On the Nyakyusa rituals, cf. M. Wilson, 1957, pp.13ff.

i. e. the death of a person who has lived to a ripe old age, surrounded by grandchildren, and can now lay aside all cares; or whether an untimely death carries off a young person, who has accomplished little and left behind no descendants. In Africa death as a friend and brother is unknown. Only the death of old people is regarded as 'natural'.

3. Every death has a cause. There is death that comes directly from God, like being struck by lightning. This is to be accepted without rituals and mourning. If God intervenes, how can you complain, ask the Zulu? But in some cases even people can cause lightning to strike – if they are witches and sorcerers. Evil persons who cause death put society at risk. They must be opposed and punished, so that evil is rooted out of its midst. Mourning rituals are a means of defence.

4. Mourning rituals are rituals of separation. Because death is contagious, it must be held at bay. It is dangerous for mourners to succumb to melancholy. If the rituals have not fulfilled their healing function (among the Herero) the mourners are sent to the next funeral, so that they can ritually perform the separation once more, and weep away their sorrows.

Death must not be repressed, as often in Western society. The inversions speak an unambiguous language: life has come to an end. Everything is different now. We must come to terms with things in a different way.

5. The principal means of such separation is the coping strategy of identification. Everybody must die the 'little deaths' in many forms. Once more, death is right at the heart of things. Death is not 'the onset of a complete absence of relationships', as sometimes claimed in Protestant theology, but the establishment of a new relationship with the dead.

6. That is why these are rituals of re-birth. The dead are prepared for new birth and so are the survivors, who are born into a new status in society. That is why in many rituals the widow adopts the position of an embryo or of a woman giving birth. Among the Zulu, at the start of mourning, she may take only liquid (infant) food, and is slowly introduced back into life. Death is the great weakener of the lives of the bereaved. "We are weak", is a recurrent phrase. However, the ritual is ultimately directed towards new life.

7. The link between the living and the dead does not break. They are in close communication, each dependent on the other. It is the living who help the dead to begin their new life, by carrying out the appropriate ritual. The widow becomes the 'mother' of her dead husband, escorting him into his new life. On the other hand, the living are highly dependent on the dead. The latter's presence is felt everywhere; socially, when the living observe their commands and continue their roles; emotionally, when they think or dream of them, feeling the pain of loss; and religiously, when they fall ill or misfortune strikes, giving them a bad conscience for displeasing the ancestors. The presence of the dead is displayed at different levels in the mourning ritual: the ancestors are informed that someone has died, their blessing is sought and sacrifices are made to them. The main indication, however, is provided by the inverse procedures running through every custom in every culture.

These can be interpreted in various ways. In anthropological research the animistic interpretation predominates: dead people must be deceived. They are led out of the house through the back door, so that they will be unable to find the entrance again. This is a strengthening of the defence mechanism. The dynamic interpretation is also widespread: the corpse is contagious, it 'defiles', it destroys the power of good medicines and the healthy world. This is why the corpse must not come into contact with the medicines that are fastened over the main entrance. Both interpretations may be right, but they do not tell the whole story.

The psychological and religious dimensions seem to me to be fundamental. Inversion is a reinforced identification with the dead person who has somehow become the 'enemy' of the people. (Cf. Anna Freud's expression 'identification with the opponent'). The dead have departed from their families, leaving them with nobody to care for them. They have ruined their lives and reduced their vitality. In relations with the dead, normal life is turned 'inside out' – presented as its opposite. This is done to overcome death and its threats. Yet – and here is the religious dimension – people are thereby living in imitation of the dead, for whom the reverse is normal. An old Zulu woman once expressed it in the following terms: "We live like this", she said, and pointed to her open hand, palm upwards. Then she turned her palm down-

90

wards. "And this is how the ancestors live". The simple gesture said it all, and gave the key to the symbolism of inversion.

8. The rites contain no sign of a doctrine of reincarnation, as taught in Asian religions. Through ritual, the dead are born into a different life beyond the grave, not into this life again. Eternal life does not exist. Each life is directed towards death. But new life grows out of death, both here and in the other world. Only through death is there life. That is why participants die the ritual death. The son stands naked at the graveside (among the Zulu), the widow eats baby food, everybody shaves and washes – substitutions for dying. As the dead receive new life, the life of the survivors is renewed. In Africa mourning rituals often turn into sexual activities.

9. While the rituals speak of and interpret death, they are directed more towards life. Life is the highest good. Death is bad, evil itself. It must at all cost be averted. That is made clear in the ambivalent relations between the living and the dead. The dead are dispatched to the other world, and then brought back ritually into the compound. They must be close at hand, so as to support the lives of those who come after. They take their allotted place. But not everything concerns them. Too much of their presence disturbs everyday life.

The message of the rituals is that life cannot be relied on, and that the ancestors are not always well disposed towards the living.

10. God appears only marginally in rituals. The forest-dwellers of the Cameroons distinguish between 'God's death' and 'witches' death'. The first is the natural death of old age, the other is the evil death caused by human beings. In Africa the conviction is widespread that, directly or indirectly, evil people cause death. That is why the guilty are sought among humankind.

If God is not mentioned during the rituals we should not deduce that he is completely absent. The many taboos attached to his name can be understood as inverse presence, since even the name of the king, whose power is felt everywhere, is taboo among many peoples. Among some, God's presence is felt very intensively, e. g. among the peoples of the Sudan. The basic rule is that he is not directly involved. However, where he is believed to be the creator he is implicitly included in questions of life or loss of life. Mediation is still via the ancestors, who are closer to hand. Since they are known, their assistance can be invoked. It is difficult to imagine God in personal terms. How then can he comfort? He is not the judge (only very few peoples have this idea), and he does not draw the dead towards himself into his kingdom. The departed goes to join the ancestors, relating to the survivors through them. That is why the living appeal to the familiar circle of those who have gone before.

5. Daily life and survival – hunting

We have seen that rituals are mainly observed when life is most seriously threatened, that is, in times of crisis. Through rituals, the group supports individuals so that they all overcome the danger. They are not left alone. Ritual provides the space in which they feel safe. The group knows what people must do in such situations. It leads individuals through the tunnel of threat into the life beyond, giving them a new status in tune with the community. In this way, ritual becomes a healer for individuals and a regulator of public life. Ritual brings about change.

Up to now we have concentrated upon the rituals which have to do with the life cycle. The other cycle is regulated by the year, the cycle of seed-time and harvest, of dry and rainy seasons. Influenced by cultural, ecological and economic circumstances, there are rituals relating to work and the form of the community and state. Just as the biological course of life is strengthened by the crises of life, so is the daily life of the community through other rituals. It is not the case that ritual lays down every detail of life or that religion pervades everything. Ritual is religion in action. The sacred liberates life. It makes 'profane' life possible, without, however, allowing it to escape the ethical duties transmitted by ritual. Ritual initiates, but it does not replace the need for individual action or know-how. It would be ridiculous to maintain that Africans are unable to distinguish very precisely between everyday and religious matters, even if the separation is not so easy to recognise as in secularised Western societies. Of course they know that the success of the harvest depends on sowing seed at the right time, on the quality of the soil, and the correct care of the seed. Of course they know that accuracy, skill and perseverance mark the good hunter, and that, if a lion attacks or a snake looks dangerous, the outcome will depend on his own strength and courage.

If his own strength fails; if, in spite of all his efforts, he has no success in hunting, if the rains fail or a plague of locusts destroy the harvest and disease endangers the herd, the cause must be tracked down. In these circumstances, a superficial, as it were 'technological' answer is not satisfactory. The time for ritual has come, opening up a broader and deeper dimension. Misfortune causes the flow of life to flag; ritual contributes to overcoming the impediment.

Technical knowledge, ethical conduct and ritual acts are mutually dependent and enable each other. This can be demonstrated through the example of the hunting arrangements of the Lele in southern Congo, which Mary Douglas observed and recorded in diary form. I reproduce extracts here, because they give a good insight into traditional village life after the introduction of European technology and religion.

The Lele live on the border between primeval forest and grassland. While the grassland – dry, empty and infertile – is the women's area and has no religious significance whatsoever, the forest possesses a mythical religious quality. Women may not enter there, it is the men's domain. It is their hunting-ground, while the women remain at home. Both provide for life, the women by giving life to children, the men making a living by hunting. Both strengthen and increase life, yet the different tasks are assigned to different areas.

The significance of the forest and its religious implications should not be founded on its utility value: there is just as much game in the open country as in the forest, but no importance is attached to it. And then there are domestic animals and gardens. The Lele do not eat the domestic animals – goats, sheep, chickens, etc. They are regarded as unclean and sold on the market. Only what comes out of the forest is clean. The polarity of the sexes is here made a structural principle, dividing the world and its different activities. The division is not to be understood as absolute, because, through the interplay of roles, people come to terms with the totality of life. Hunting is a matter for the whole village, even for the women and children who remain at home.

Douglas does not report whether initiation into hunting exists among the Lele. Other peoples practise it though and a brief parenthesis here will add to the picture. Among the Bushmen in the Kalahari – highly skilled hunters – it consists of three acts. The future hunter is smeared with black paint. He smokes wild hemp, falling into a trance and coming nearer to God, so they believe. After that the dancing begins – imitative dances, which copy the gaits and behaviour of animals. It is not a question of hunting 'magic' as traditionally understood, however, because with the dances they seek to please God and show him which animals they want to kill. "Dance is the Bushman's worship and his prayer".[115] After the dancing comes the 'opening of the eyes'. A cut is made in the skin between the eyes, on the bridge of the nose. A powder is rubbed into the wound, made out of finely ground parts of various types of game. This medicine is supposed to sharpen their eyesight, so that they can spot the game and kill it.

Ritual makes hunting possible. It provides the space in which the hunt takes place. This is a thoroughly 'secular' activity, which depends solely on the skilfulness of the hunter. It is only after they have repeatedly returned empty-handed that they call for further ritual acts.

Among the Lele the preparation for hunting can take a long time. It goes along with preparing a group of medicines called *kinda*, which are supposed to ensure women's fertility and a good hunt.

Here are extracts from Mary Douglas's diary:[116]

Extracts from: Hunting Journal of Yenga-Yenga, (the name given by the Belgian Administration to the southernmost of three villages called Homba.), February-March 1950.
18 February: Fruitless hunt. The failure was generally attributed to the refusal on the eve of the hunt of one of the diviners, Ngondu, a fiery tempered man, to co-operate with his colleagues. In the middle of their consultation he had suddenly burst out complaining that his

---

[115] H. Vedder, 1934, p. 84.
[116] See M. Douglas, 1963, pp.17ff.

94

wife's groundnuts had been stolen, and that when the Administration came to inspect the crop he would be sent to prison, though it was no fault of his that an enemy had stolen them. He flung out of the meeting and someone whispered: 'See the diviner is spoiling the village.' The hunt was fruitless, in spite of the medicines prepared.

19 February: The whole day was taken up in discussing the cause of failure. ... Quarrelling went on in the centre of the village about this ... Ngondu brought up all his old grievances: one of his wives had died the year before, allegedly killed by the poison of the catechist ... He brought up complicated histories reaching back into the past. His friends tried to calm him, his enemies insisted that none of this was a reason for spoiling the hunting medicines; a diviner should feel more responsibility for his village. Finally, the matter was settled by a summing-up from a visitor, Bikwak, a famous diviner ... No one knew who had stolen the nuts. Perhaps it was some unthinking child.

20 February: Bikwak, the visiting diviner, together with two important local diviners, Ngondu and Nyama, prepared the medicine for the next day's hunt. In the night Bikwak sang in a trance, during which he was visited by spirits, who told him where game would be found the next day.

21 February: The medicines were finished at dawn. Bikwak, as superintending diviner, directed the hunters where to go, but he had to stay in the village all day. Women were forbidden to pound grain or to cut wood until he gave the all-clear.

[Everyone has to keep as still as possible, avoiding any noise. Naturally the taboo on sex applies now and at the appropriate time later. Sexual intercourse is debilitating; the hunt demands all a man's strength. This is not the time to create new life at home; it will come from the forest through the hunt.]

The kill was disappointing: one little blue duiker and one red duiker. In all, seven antelopes had been put up by the dogs, so the spirits had not deceived Bikwak. The village was undoubtedly spoilt, as they had only killed two instead of seven. The cause was diagnosed as follows: the village needed a new *kinda* medicine. So they began at once to make preparations for it.

24 February: Bikwak sang again in the night, after announcing that men and women should sleep apart, as next day there would be hunting.

25 February: In the morning he streaked each man's leg with charcoal and white clay. But it rained, and the hunt was postponed. As the medicine for the new *kinda* had been started, no visitors were allowed to eat in the village. A man and his wife from Mbombe were turned away, as, if they had taken food, they would have had to spend the night in the village.

26 February: The hunt was successful... Bikwak ordered that the backs, heads, feet, and intestines should be set aside to be eaten by the cult groups of the village.

[This hunt included an incident which sheds light on the tribal ethic and which will be related here for this reason.[117] A man had bought medicine for his new rifle. On this communal hunt, he shot a large yellow-backed duiker. The parts of the flesh that according to the rules of the medicine would have been allocated to him, were, however, awarded to a cult group, which had prepared the *kinda* medicine, and of which he was not a member. When he had no success during the later hunt on 3 March, he was asked the reason. He referred to the injustice that had been done to him in the distribution of the meat on the previous occasion. He had been refused the meat that was due to him, because of his rifle medicine. They admitted that he was in the right, and each of them gave him a franc as compensation.]

28 February: Bikwak still needed wild pig before he could proceed with the next step in the *kinda* medicines. He announced that today everyone must get on with their usual work, for tomorrow he would send the men off on a hunt.

Nearby a road was being built and in the afternoon a bloody fight broke out between two labourers and their wives. As the villagers gathered to watch the fight, the scratching and tearing of women's hair and head-wounds, nose-bleeding and insults, they were unanimous in their indignation: 'Fancy spoiling the village for other people! Disgusting! They are ruining tomorrow's hunt.' After the fight Bikwak, with the other diviners, ordered a fine of two raffia cloths and a chicken from the initiators of hostilities. They pleaded for time to pay. In order not to delay the hunt the village went bail for them, notching the ears of a goat in token of their payment. Bikwak did new medicine to cancel the effects of the fight, and announced in the evening: 'Tonight each woman her mat, each man his mat. Tomorrow we hunt.'

5 March: A hunt without medicines, undertaken because they wanted to taste meat. One red duiker only killed. This time failure to kill more was not ascribed to moral or religious conditions. The two best dog-owners were absent.

10 March: The leading dog-owner returned, so they went hunting. Nothing to do with medicine, just to chase up some little blue duikers for food. No game.

16 March: Wild pig spoor reported very near the village. The men went off quickly. A fruitless expedition, the pig had passed by in the night. A few young men were in favour of going on in the hope of rounding up some little blue duikers. Then one of the dogs fell suddenly sick, and the owner had to prepare medicines for it. As the dog looked like dying, the hunt was abandoned.

18 March: Another impromptu hunt. No kill, as the herd of pigs had escaped behind the place where the dogs were sent in. [People were dissatisfied with the local diviner. The matter was settled.]

---

[117] Cf. M. Douglas, p. 25.

23 March: Bikwak still absent. A local diviner, Nyama, prepared hunting medicines in the evening. He shouted his orders: No one was to sleep on *cokwe* woven mats, but only on traditional Lele mats; no one to sleep in European blankets; no one to smoke European cigarettes or to wear European clothes, only Lele raffia loin-cloths; each man to sleep on his mat alone, each woman alone. Next morning at dawn, before the hunt, they were all to meet and bring up their grievances, lest any secret grudge should spoil the hunt.

24 March: [The village assembly was held. Dirty linen was washed; the women's quarrel was settled. When the hunt was fruitless again this time, the oracle was consulted. He discovered that one woman still harboured a grudge. The medicine-man's wife left the meeting in anger. As a punishment she had to give two raffia skirts and a chicken. She had to destroy the skirt that she had worn, when she ran out of the meeting.]

25 March: They went hunting and killed two antelopes [with new medicine]. Nyama's wife paid the fine, protesting her innocence.

This text makes clear the deep interconnection between social relations, ethical standards and religious beliefs. All the inhabitants of the village have to observe the same moral principles. Nobody may disobey them. If anybody does so, society can bring them into line with appropriate sanctions. What modern civilisation offers of value is incorporated (rifle), but only in such a way that the traditional behaviour is not destroyed. At times of crisis the medicine-man takes over. The traditional triumphs over the modern, even if only for a short time. In this case, rituals become a defence mechanism against modernisation. The old ethical standards triumph.

The notes in the diary make it clear that hunting is a matter of skill and knowledge. Where it is unsuccessful, questions are asked about the equipment and skill. That applies particularly when the men have gone hunting, 'neutrally' or 'without medicines'. But if the hunt has been initiated with medicines, morality is seen to be at stake. In this case, religious causes must be sought. Ritual and moral behaviour are very close to each other. Hunting becomes a focal point of religion: divining, medicine, abstinence, harmonious conduct in tune with the community together make one great unity. Good fortune in hunting is a barometer of the wholeness or disharmony of the community, of the relations of the people with each other and in the sight of the spirits and of God. It is well known that when everybody has behaved correctly, as taught by the ancestors, the result is good fortune. If misfortune persists, it is a sign that human relations and the religious basis of the village have been disturbed. Hunting is more than a way of life; it is religious conduct put into action. It enforces moral convictions and strengthens group solidarity. The good, peaceful village is the highest goal. Where there is no peace, relations with our fellow creatures, the animals, suffer.

In this connection, we must also look at the sexual taboos which run through all hunting rituals. The Tonga in present-day Zimbabwe have a plausible explanation for this: "Married people are hot", they say. The sexual act releases passion. Passion would startle the animals and put them on heat. In hunting it is best to be calm and 'cool'. The law of analogous participation defines the behaviour of humans and animals and brings them into accord with each other. "Life is, so to speak, accelerated by the sexual act, and this acceleration is communicated to the whole of nature. Therefore: Keep quiet, be content!", advises H. A. Junod.[118] Anger and rage have an enormous power to spread; they influence relations with the animal world and the human environment in equal measure. Only when articulated and confessed can they can be overcome. Africa's profound knowledge of the meaning of relations between people comes in useful here. The communal, the normative and the religious form a unity. They are renewed and made effective in ritual. If one of these pillars is broken by contact with another culture and by modernity, the whole is not immediately at risk; the old order protects itself through regressive behaviour. However, adaptation or alternative action are now possible, as we shall see later.

6. The Smith

Hunting is not understood everywhere and in the same way as a ritual procedure[119]; as we have seen, it can be planned and carried out in a thoroughly 'secular' manner. But then it exposes the hunters to greater danger. That is why it is fenced in by ritual, to enhance their strength and activate

---

[118] H. A. Junod, vol. I, 1962, p. 189.
[119] E. Dammann, 1963, p. 199.

their relations with the environment. Two areas, completely separate in everyday life, have to be integrated. Hunting crosses boundaries. The transitions are secured by restoring harmony in home territory and by tuning in to the available network of analogous correlations.

This can be illustrated by the work of the smith, who enjoys a special position in all the peoples of Africa. Myths and rituals raise his work above that of others, even though rites involving potters and other occupations are also known. The reason for this can only be guessed, writes E. Dammann, adding, "Perhaps it is because of the use of fire. This was not granted to humankind by natural means. The phenomenon that it makes metal molten, which Africans cannot explain in physical terms, may also be a reason. Perhaps this is why iron is so esteemed and used as adornment".[120] We no longer have to rely upon this type of interpretation, with its roots in the nineteenth century (cf. Frazer). The symbolism of rituals and taboos speaks an unambiguous language, which only has to be translated. What makes the smith a special person and distinguishes him from others is his close relation to the objects with which he has to deal. These are packed with symbolism, therefore commanding respect. They are even dangerous. For example, the smith has to deal with red-hot iron, which will become rusty and dry as soon as it cools – just like spilt blood. And isn't the chimney itself a sexual symbol? A.-I. Berglund reproduces a conversation with a Zulu smith: "The smith took up some red soil in his hand and stretching out his open hand towards me said: 'Why is this earth red? Because it is blood, the blood of the earth... The earth is the mother of iron. Iron comes from its mother.' The red iron ore that trickled out was, in the eyes of the smith, a symbol and likeness to a woman's monthly periods. He insisted that he could work in the smithy only a few days each month, 'when the iron flows out nicely,' very clearly associating this time to that when women have their menstrual flows. He personally chose to work in his workshop just after the full moon, for about four or five days. 'After those days I am tired. The power has left my limbs. I cannot any longer smite the iron. It does not form nicely and the flowing (from the forge) is

---

[120] Op. cit, p. 209.

poor'. We discussed the black of cool iron. This colour, the smith claimed, was the colour of dried blood. 'When the blood is red, it is hot. When it is black, it is cool. So iron and blood are the same.' Dross from the forge is pounded into a powder and used as a medicine to cure painful menstruation. 'The sickness of women can only be treated with iron'".[121]

A herbalist in Zululand was convinced that the Europeans had such fertile estates because they fenced off their land with iron wire. Of course, he also knew about natural and chemical fertilisers, but iron stands for the fertility of women, animals and fields.[122]

The Dogon have built the calling of smith into their diversified cosmology. His status is singled out from all others. Like the hunter, the smith has connections with fertility. You do not have to be a Freudian to understand hunting in the primeval forest as a reference to sexuality. In every society, hunting has always been regarded as a 'male' calling, which is begun and concluded with ritual, even in modern society. It almost goes without saying that in many peoples both vocations require initiation, since the fertility of the village is at stake. When we include the ideas of bush, forest and animal spirits, which are widespread in West Africa, then it is perfectly clear why a ritual and religious dimension is particularly associated with the callings of hunter and smith. Both activities evoke feelings of awe and fascination.

7. Tools

Even in traditional Africa the hand tool is first and foremost a neutral instrument, which is used with skill and dexterity, which can be good or bad, and which is thrown away when it becomes unusable. If iron is used in its manufacture it is more valuable, which, in the light of the working hours of the smith described above, is not surprising. The tool, however, changes with use. It is altered by the sweat of the workman's hand; a relationship arises;

---

[121] A.-I. Berglund, 1975, p. 360. Making pots is women's work. There are symbolic reasons for dividing work according to sex. Men must avoid anything to do with pots (= uterus). It endangers their virility. Cf. F. Fischer, 1967, pp.396ff., 406ff.
[122] A.-I. Berglund, 1975, p. 356.

the connection can be expressed in personal terms. It becomes a part of its owner, above all when it is an object which is used to earn a living, and so has a place in important rituals. Then it takes on a religious significance and, in accordance with the laws of analogous participation, can become the representative of its owner, his *alter ego*. The difference between a 'dead' and a 'living' object becomes fluid. If we can understand such transitions, then the close links which exist between humans and animals also become clearer, as do certain aspects of the concepts of souls and spirits.[123]

The Nuer in southern Sudan recognise two types of spear – the fishing spear and the fighting spear. The first is necessary to maintain life, since fish provide an important supplement to the monotonous diet of nomads who live from raising cattle. The fighting spear is very expensive because it has to be bought from Arabs. The Nuer do not know how to work iron. The traditional significance of the fighting spear cannot be explained solely by its usefulness, however, as the lives of the Nuer have not been constantly threatened by warfare. Admittedly, the civil war subsisting in southern Sudan since 1956 has done much to change that.

After initiation the spear is handed over from father to son. It marks the transition to a new status in society. Up to this point, the youth has belonged to the company of girls, and milked the cows like them. Now, however, he is accepted into the society of men, and may no longer practise his earlier activities. The spear has a name, which also becomes the youth's name. Each clan also possesses a spear name, dating back to the time of the earliest known ancestors.

Sacrificial animals are killed with the spear. The Nuer call upon God before every sacrifice, and the sacrificer explains why he is offering the sacrifice. Without these words being spoken, the sacrifice is in vain. Words provide a name; the word makes the slaughter into a sacrifice. While calling upon God, the sacrificer holds the spear in his right hand and waves it over his head. He waves it as if he were about to strike, pulls it back, relaxes his grip, and grasps the spear anew. Through the movements of the spear he acts

---

[123] On what follows, see E. E. Evans-Pritchard, 1967, pp.231ff.

out what has been expressed verbally. The movements underline the words. Indeed, the eye sees more than the words are able to express, according to E. E. Evans-Pritchard.

The spear is always carried in the right hand. It forms such a unity with the spear that the left hand loses its power over it. For months the young man deliberately ceases to use his left hand so that it loses its strength and can no longer be used for hard work. The right hand, on the other hand, becomes a sign of power, strength and manliness. It is also the side of peace. They speak of a 'right-handed peace', never of a 'left-handed' one.

Nuer women cannot offer a sacrifice, neither can they speak the prayers on this occasion. Naturally, the reason is not any physical or intellectual deficiency on their part, but a symbolic one: they have no spear. When women speak to God, they 'pray' *(pal)*; men, with their spear, 'call on' *(lam)* God.

The spear bestows a special status on a youth so that he can take part in warfare, dancing and hunting, and it also alters his religious status. It creates a new relationship to the cattle, whose importance among the Nuer consists above all in being sacrificial animals. Accepting the spear also establishes a relationship with the ancestors and spirits of the clan. The spear is the visible expression of manliness, of bodily and spiritual strength.

The owner of a spear may name it during invocations. The prayer is not addressed to the ancestors, however, but to God, the 'God of our fathers', as the Nuer say. They address God in the clan through the ancestral spear, which one of the descendants is imagined to hold in his hand.[124] In reality, there is no ancestral spear. The symbolic meaning is decisive, because it makes the relation between the clan and 'the Lord of hosts' visible and real.

So the spear stands, on the one hand, for the bearer himself and, on the other, for the collective relationship to God, because it kills the sacrificial victim with which the clan identifies. The spear, a weapon in war, a plaything in the dance, a tool in the sacrifice, becomes a symbol of the life of the individual and of the clan, and stands for life itself. The instrumental becomes the sacramental; the material is given a spiritual dimension. People live in such a

---

[124] Op. cit, p. 247.

close relation to environmental powers that the external shapes and reflects the internal.

III. THE DEPENDENT HUMAN BEING

Human beings are the point of departure for African thought, and the focus of all religious practice. African religions can rightly be described as anthropocentric. Yet that must not be understood in a pejorative (Barthian) sense,[125] which would be to misunderstand the heart of Africa. Because thought is a human activity, the world can only be understood from a human point of view and as it relates profoundly to human beings. That also means that they suffer the finitude of the world, being finite themselves. This is expressed in myths in many variations. In religion, human beings do not wish to break through these limits in order to flee or overcome the world – they want to find their place in it. The Africans accept the limits, seeking strength and fullness of life, with good and peaceful days.

We have so far described the way in which human beings relate to the world around, approach it on the basis of its laws, and try to cope with it. The real content is still to be discussed. Whom does a human being encounter, when he or she encounters the world? How is the relationship between the visible and the invisible world to be understood? And what symbolic forms of expression have been found for it? A diagram will show the problem more clearly.

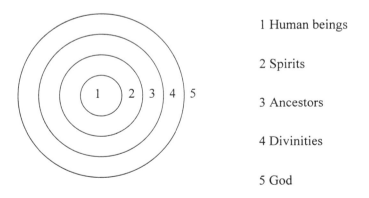

1 Human beings

2 Spirits

3 Ancestors

4 Divinities

5 God

---

[125] See above.

Human beings are in the centre. The world closest to them, that of the animals, is still part of the visible sphere. Yet in some respects animals are bridges to the invisible. As sacrificial offerings they serve as a meeting point with the ancestors; they are used as mediums by evil spirits. The world of spirits forms the next circle. They also belong, broadly speaking, to the human sphere. However, they are superior, and exert an external influence on humans. The ancestors are closer to people than the spirits, because they are more familiar. In this respect, the two circles could be interchanged. At the same time, however, the ancestors are further away from human beings in that they are bridges to the divinities, or more precisely to God. Therefore it is appropriate to put them more towards the periphery. God forms the furthest limit of all human experience. He enfolds all. Although far off, he can also be understood as being very near.

The diagram must, however, be amplified. The circles must not be seen as being on one level alone. They have a vertical gradation which indicates the pyramid of the powers. As we have already seen, no person occupies the same position in society as another. Seniority and relationships determine their place. At the pinnacle stands the chief or king, who, in turn, stands under the ancestors and functions as an intermediary.

A hierarchy of powers also exists in the invisible world. It is the opposite of the one in the visible world. We have already observed this in the case of death rituals, and this provides the key to further insights.

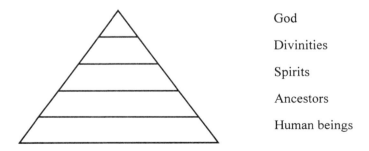

God

Divinities

Spirits

Ancestors

Human beings

Human beings are under an obligation. That is the most important characteristic of African anthropology. They are under an obligation to their parents who gave them life; to the ancestors from whom that life comes; and to the society with ist *rites de passage*, and which gives support in times of crisis. Finally, they are under an obligation to God, the ultimate origin of all life. However, in many religions this aspect is contemplated and expressed implicitly rather than explicitly.

This is reflected in creation myths. The overwhelming majority of them speak of the origins of the first men and women, not of an actual act of creation by God. They are about people. They are not interested in the origin of the world as such. They hardly mention the stars, or the cosmos, or the distant world. At heart they are mythical stories of 'anthropogenesis'.[126] The first people were already there, or came forth out of a stone, from reeds or a tree. Sometimes their place of origin is indicated. The Himba designate the place of the *omumborombonga* tree in the Kaoko Veld in Namibia as the place from which the first people came forth, accompanied by some domestic animals. Among the Zulu too, the reed *(uhlanga)* is described as the place. The royal kraal must have stood there, because the kings trace their origins back in a direct line to God through the first human beings. The Zulu people sees itself as the centre of the world.

Nowadays, the original story about how things began is often no longer known. Details remain hard to follow. This is partly due to the fact that we are dealing with stories of migration, which have been taken over from other tribes, or enriched with motifs from the stories of other peoples. The Kwanjama in northern Namibia tell the following story of the origin of humankind:

Human beings come from the palm tree (the finger palm): some children were sitting in it. An old woman, the servant of Kalunga (God), admonished them: "Don't be naughty. I'm creating you". She went to Kalunga and said, "I have created three children". But Kalunga asked, "What kind of children are they?" Kalunga said to two of them, "One is a boy and one a girl, they are to look after the West; the other is to remain in the East". The old woman came back to the palm tree, which had swallowed up the children. The

---

[126] H. Baumann, 1936, p. 163.

raven struck at the tree, but his beak broke. The woman sent the raven to Kalunga, to ask for help. He gave the raven a red ox. As this animal began to cry beside the palm, the tree fell apart and the children came out. The old woman went to Kalunga and said, "The ox has brought forth the humans". Kalunga answered, "They shall no longer go to the West, but come to me, so that I can teach them".[127]

Some of the students in the theological seminary in Namibia who came from Ovamboland knew this story, which I have told here in a shortened version. In reply to my question, they could even still give me the name of the palm tree, *omukua*, though no-one was able to say what it meant. However, one Herero student reacted as if he had had an electric shock. In Otjiherero that name means a part of the female body which he couldn't mention in class.[128] In this way, the symbolism of sexuality and fertility was recognised. For the Christian Ovambo, a door opened for the first time to traditional myths. A detailed analysis, with a structuralist approach, would reveal further dimensions.[129] For our present purpose, it is sufficient to establish the following points: God is involved only indirectly in creation. Human beings are "a part of nature", but this expression must not be pressed too hard, nor understood in ist modern sense.[130] They possesses fertility, and must hand on new life from age to age. They are destined to live and die (West – East). They cannot cope with life on their own – for that they need the ox. The ox's fertility serves to multiply human life (the Ovambo are cattle-raisers, matrilineal farmers). People are dependent on the ox. What gives life to an Ambo man in a matrilineal society, determines his origins and influences his life, can be summed up as: women – cattle – but also God.

---

[127] A fuller version of this can be found in 'Die Allgemeine Missionszeitschrift', 1910, p. 316.

[128] The word *omukua* does not appear in the 'Herero-Wörterbuch' of H. Brinker, 1886. However, I have in my possession the copy used by I. Irle, the editor of the Deutsch-Herero-Wörterbuch, Hamburg, 1917. This has the hand-written entry: Omukua: 1. Heute [today]; 2. Nabel [navel]; 3. Riss, Spalte [crack].

[129] A completely inadequate interpretation is given by E. Brauer, 1925, pp.18ff. This includes further myths relating to the origin of humankind.

1. Attachment to animals

People's dependence on animals and the profound bonds between them are among the most important characteristics of the African image of human-kind. This cannot be explained solely on utilitarian grounds. It extends into the religious sphere.

Close attachment

Cattle have a significance for the culture of the peoples of Central and Southern Africa similar to that of the camels for the North African and some Sudanese peoples. According to E. Brauer,[131] "in the eyes of the African cattle breeder, the ox is a part of himself". Among certain other societies we could even go further: people have so adapted to the life of cattle that they have become part of the ideal life that cattle represent. The general importance of cattle is felt in the social, political, cultural and religious sphere. For example, without cattle the Herero kraal loses ist status as *onganda* and is known merely as *onduo*, the village of the poor (*ondu* = sheep). A Herero without any cattle sinks to the status of a slave. It is cattle that makes a man, and in earlier times it was abundant cattle that made the head of a family a chief.

The cultural significance of cattle reflects people's economic dependence on them. Every part of the beast is useful; everything is needed. Houses are build of clay, mixed with cow-dung and cow-urine. Children wear wristlets cut from strips of cattle hide. Traditionally, women wear head-dress (*ekori*) made of cattle skin, and known as 'horns'. It is placed on their head during puberty rites. At a certain age, youths are given the 'tooth sign' (four lower teeth are knocked out, a V-sign is cut into the upper incisors), in partial imitation of cattle teeth, because cattle have no teeth in their upper jaw.

---

[130] Cf. H. A. Junod, who quotes a Tonga riddle: "What is it that created Heaven and Earth? – Nature"., Junod, 1962, vol. 2, p. 302. The word *ntumbuluka*, which is translated here as 'Nature', comes from the verb *kutumbuluka* = "to happen, to be formed".

[131] E. Brauer, 1925, p. 54.

Young men who do not have this sign are made fun of: "You smell like a horse!" (Horses have upper and lower teeth.) The ideal gait for woman is slow and swaying, in bovine fashion. Humans die peacefully and and with no sign of fear, like an ox that at most utters a gentle lowing, and not like a goat that struggles, bleats and screams when it is slaughtered. Boys are circumcised on a cattle-skin. After death, corpses are sewn into a cattle skin. Horns of cattle slaughtered during funeral rites adorn the grave.

Cattle are never the personal possessions of individuals. They are always the common property of the clan. The individual owner is only a trustee. He must put the cattle out to graze and attend to them. He may drink their milk, but he is not allowed to slaughter or sell them. In every Herero kraal there are at least three groups of cattle. There are the cattle inherited from the paternal line, which serve religious purposes. There are those inherited from the maternal line, which are for 'secular uses'. Finally, there are the 'sacred cows', which are assigned to the ancestral fire. There can be no ancestral fire without cattle, because, it is said, the ancestors enter the homestead with cattle.

We have seen above how, when an ox is slaughtered on special occasions, the flesh has to be distributed in a certain way. The dividing-up process is laid down 'as if on a map', a Herero once said to me. The network of all relationships within the family and neighbourhood is observed in the distribution. Killing the ox and eating the meat restores social relations. The ox brings families, friends and neighbours together and strengthens the hierarchical order. It has a stabilising function within the society.

The religious significance of cattle has been mentioned several times. Without them there is no veneration of the ancestors. Ritual at the ancestral fire, which is half-way between the cattle kraal and the chief house, promotes the well-being of the herd and of the village. It is supposed to guarantee their health and fertility. The forefathers are responsible for the life of succeeding generations and so must take care of the herd. If the herd suffered they would no longer be revered. So even the ancestors are (culticly) dependent on cattle, who become a place of encounter – a channel for communication with them.

The ox or cow is a protection and shield against the ancestors. Ist life stands for human life. That is especially marked among the Nuer, who ritually identify themselves with the beast before it is sacrificed. The following prayer for a sick person, recorded by Westermann, illustrates this: "God, what is this? Leave him with us; let him recover. Turn about, take thy cow. It has been decreed for the life. It is thou who has spoken thus. Take the cow that it may be in exchange for the life (*bi je luele yei*). It is thou who has created us; it is the cow who is exchanged for life (*e bi yang a luel ne yei*). Let him recover! In what we have erred! Give us the life. Thou art our father. Why must we always suffer? Give us the life, we pray thee, our father".[132]

In the earlier literature on this subject this close relationship with cattle was described as totemism.[133] That is just as incorrect as the judgements of missionaries that cattle had become an 'idol' to the Herero. What is correct in this comment is that keeping cattle and ancestor worship cannot be separated. The close connection of the ancestors to the presence of cattle serves only to express people's great dependence: their life is indebted to both, to the ancestors and to cattle: "*Omuinjo ueto uri mongombe*", "our life is in the cattle". The life of the African cattle breeder is an integrated whole. Political, social, cultural and religious connections form a unity. Nowhere is that made more clear than in cattle, in which all social, cultural and religious aspects come together in one living symbol. "*Ami mbi kambura m'ongombe*", a Herero once said to me, "I believe in cattle".[134]

Further forms of attachment

The attachment to domestic animals is a particular form of general closeness to the animal world. It is understandable that human dependence on oxen and cows has developed into a comprehensive relationship, shaping the

---

[132] Quoted by E. E. Evans-Pritchard, 1967, p. 224.

[133] E. Brauer, 1925, p. 98ff. For the opposing, but correct view, cf. E. Dammann, 1963, pp.36ff.

[134] For a detailed treatment of the above, cf. T. Sundermeier, 1977c, pp.160ff.; for the Nuer, cf. E. E. Evans-Pritchard, 1967, pp.248ff.

110

whole culture. Further forms of attachment to animals are more difficult to understand. An integral part of the African image of humankind, they have aroused a lively interest among researchers. Initially, however, this was the source of much misunderstanding, because the line between humans and animals was blurred, suggesting the existence of an early, 'primitive' stage of the human spirit. While such theories have been rightly criticised there is still no interpretation of this aspect of African understanding of the world that is satisfactory in every respect.[135] Structuralism has given us fresh insights and we must tackle the topic again, even if there is no question of ever obtaining a full picture.

Roughly, two types of attachment to animals can be distinguished: those that are transitory, and those that are timeless. The first display a broad range of social and cultural participation in the world, which we shall examine in detail.

1. As we have seen, hunters and villagers are subject to certain taboos during the hunt, because people's conduct is transferred to the prey. That was shown by the example of the Lele. A few other examples will fill out the picture. Among the Bakwiri in Cameroon, the hunters themselves are not allowed to tie rattles around the necks of the hounds, leaving this to a girl who has not yet reached the age of puberty. Sexually potent people are regarded as 'hot'; they drive the hunted leopards wild, jeopardising hunter and hounds. If the Bobeal go hunting whales, peace must reign in the village, otherwise the whales will get excited. Conversely, animals also have an influence on people. If a fisherman is bitten, then it is known that his wife has been unfaithful to him. The man becomes a laughing stock.[136]

The reciprocal influence of human beings and animals can be interpreted dynamically. There exists a play of forces between them that must be controlled through ritual. The animistic interpretation reveals another aspect: the human spirit enters into contact with the spirit of the animals. For this reason, the latter has to be asked forgiveness after the hunt. The hunters want to be

---

[135] Cf. E. Dammann, 1963, p. 181.

[136] For the whole of this topic, cf. J. Ittmann, 1939, pp.151ff.

reconciled with the spirit of the animal, so that it does not turn against them and the village in the future. This is why the forest- dwellers of Cameroon bring the dead animal a 'sacrifice of excuses'. The heart of the dead animal is cut out. It is cut open and spat into. Breath and spittle count as expiatory gifts.[137] Among the Waito in Ethiopia, prayer is offered before hunting the hippopotamus: "Dear father hippo, dear little father, let yourself be eaten by your children".[138]

The Lele are convinced that the spirits reward the hunter with prey; at the same time, however, the spirits punish the animal because it has offended against their laws.[139] Among the Bavenda, when a bull has to be killed it is addressed in these words: "Oh *makhulu* (old man) you are now too old and we must kill you, because of your age, but we replace you by a younger animal. Do not take offence at our action but continue to be good to your people".[140]

The detail speaks a clear message: an interdependent, participatory relationship exists between the world of animals and the world of humans. It includes every part of human and animal life; animals are not merely soulless physical beings. They have lives in the same way as people do. They participate in the 'spirit world'.

2. Only against this background can we understand the role of animals in the preparation of medicine and divining. Animal bones play a special role among the instruments of the diviner. Among the Tongo in Zimbabwe, the bone of a goat's foreleg is a vital element. The justification is telling: goats live with us in the village; they 'know' us; therefore their bones will also tell us what is wrong in the village. The link existing between humans and animals in life does not cease with death, but can be renewed through ritual. The animal speaks through a part of itself. It functions as an intermediary, so that a structural analogy usually exists between the animal being questioned and the case to be investigated.

---

[137] Op. cit., p. 156.

[138] According to T. I. van Baaren, 1964, p. 86.

[139] M. Douglas, 1963, p. 10.

112

3. The same idea underlies the transitory attachment to animals and the attachment between the ancestors and animals. The ancestors disclose their presence to people through animals, but not through all of them. Snakes are favourite mediums of revelation, but only those which display certain characteristics. The Zulu explain their selection as follows. The snakes of the ancestors must not have forked tongues, and they must shed their skin. Shedding their skin is a sign of dying and renewal. The analogy to the birth of a child is obvious: the child is born out of a skin. As a child glides out of the after-birth, so a snake glides out of ist skin. Snakes only shed their skin where there is a heavy dew. In the same way, the child is born out of water. For the snake, the discarded skin is 'litter'; it is valueless and is discarded. The after-birth is valueless and 'dirty', the Zulu say. Ultimately, a dying person leaves the body. The corpse is counted as 'dirt', has no value, and is buried. There is a further analogy: the snake changes ist appearance only in the dark. The ancestors also work in darkness, in the mother's womb. They unite with the mother's blood, and the child is formed.[141]

It is the analogous relations to human beings which make an ancestral animal. In the last resort it is the 'symbol' which speaks, even if the symbolism is not familiar to all the members of the community, or has been forgotten. It is not a matter of 'incarnation' of the ancestors, but of human beings ultimately encountering their own world in animals.

4. Finally, a transitory attachment to animals can be seen in the widely held belief that people can turn themselves into animals. More is meant by this than imitating animals in dancing and ritual. Naturally the traditional African recognises the distinction between animal and human. Humans can speak, they have intelligence and a will. This distinguishes them from animals, the Rwanda say.[142] What then does belief in transmogrification into animals mean? In Namibia, I had to give a course for a group of student teachers from different ethnic backgrounds. This topic came up in the discussion. All as-

---

[140] H. A. Stayt, 1968, p. 243.
[141] A.-I. Berglund, 1975, p. 84.
[142] J. J. Maquet, in: D. Forde (ed.), 1963, p. 174.

sured me that they had heard of such cases, and believed they were true. Some told of their own experiences. They had seen a man's tracks in the sand which had suddenly changed into animal spore. They could also name people in whom the change had been observed. It happened to people who did not conform to accepted norms and were 'evil', they thought. An analysis of comparable reports in the literature shows the same result. These 'outsiders' always change into wild animals.

Belief in the possibility of transmogrification serves to enforce standards and implies social sanctions for assumed or actual deviant conduct. When examining this phenomenon, we should keep in mind the importance of day-dreaming and delight in fanciful narratives. For Westerners, statements about someone being changed into an animal can only be fictitious. In Africa, however, verbal reality is socially conditioned reality. Verbal symbolism possesses an existential dynamic. It has event character. If you believe somebody can change into an animal, you believe he or she has evil powers. Giving them a name is a defence mechanism and assists in self-protection. It divides people up, into 'good' and 'bad'. Significantly, most of the cases reported to me involved people from another ethnic group to that of the story-teller.

Totemism

The non-transitory attachment to animals is generally called totemism. Specifically, there is the totemism of individuals, and more commonly that of families, clans, and tribal moieties. Let us focus on the bond between an animal and a clan. A people is not only sub-divided into clans, but also according to the animals after which the clans are named. Among the Sotho we know of jackals, leopards, monkeys, etc., sometimes connected with the origins of the clan. The father of the clan, as he is called, was seeking a new dwelling place. He chose as his totem the animal he first encountered at the new place, or which had 'shown him the place. From then on, the animal was 'respected', i. e. not hunted or killed. Wherever they encounter this animal it is protected, because they feel attached to it in some way. The 'link' to the animal keeps alive the memory of the founder and the history of the clan.

Different families, which need not be related to each other, may share the same clan animal. The totem unites them in an all-embracing community. People who possess the same totem have a responsibility to look after each other as if they were related. If they meet somebody who shares the same totem they will help them with food and accommodation.[143] To find out whether someone is a member of the same clan, one question is, "What do you dance?" The answer is, "I dance such and such an animal". The answer refers to a – now obsolete – custom which (according to Mönning) "represents solidarity" with both the clan and the totem animal.

Identification with the totem animal has transforming power. It is a catalyst for feelings. A Sotho student, whose clan totem was the monkey, reported: "It makes me feel ill when I see other people eating monkey flesh. I feel as if somebody were eating one of my relatives. To my ears, being called a monkey is not an insult, but a compliment. Monkeys are clever. Our clan is cleverer than the others, especially the crocodile clan..".., and then there followed a string of stories of how their tribal ancestor (a monkey) had led the crocodile by the nose. The conclusion is significant and shows the functions of totems: "We are better than other clans!"

Emotions are channelled through the totem animal. This has great significance for social coherence. It holds the group together, distinguishing it from other groups. The inner tie means separation from things outside. The totem animal is relevant to classification. The laws of exogamy, which are coupled with totemism, become understandable in terms of social psychology. Siblings cannot marry. Or, as a Herero proverb says: you don't break a stick in order to join it again (instead, you link two different groups together, which increases their strength). So marriage has to be between two clans with different totems.

E. E. Evans-Pritchard conducted investigations among the Nuer to see whether there was a principle by which animals were chosen as totems. The list of animals shows such enormous variety that this is not immediately recognisable: lions, water buffaloes, lizards, crocodiles, various snakes, tor-

---

[143] H. O. Mönnig, 1967, pp.235f.

toises, ostriches, silver herons. Then there are plants, e. g. pumpkins and papyrus; even the river and stream can be totems. Utility plays no role in this. Plants and animals useful to the Nuer are completely absent from this list. The totem animals do not appear to possess any special characteristics and are not particularly prominent in stories and myths. They have only one thing in common, nearness to the spirit, to God. Birds fly in the air and have a particular spatial nearness to him. Trees which cast shadows, especially sycamores and tamarisks, are considered to be gifts of the spirit in the sun-scorched land of the Nuer and are in close relationship to him. The same applies to creeks and rivers.

So all animals which make the Nuer think of God can be chosen as totems. They only have to point to God to qualify. As symbols of the spirit, they can be considered totems, as can all those objects with which they come into contact. In order to be able to understand the meaning, order and choice of the totem, we must understand the chain of associations and the value assigned to them. The symbolic value of the totem applies only within a particular culture and can only be understood there. Even when ist meaning cannot be put into words by individuals, it makes sense to those who have grown up in the local milieu, and is binding upon them. Anybody coming in from outside must look for the key in order to understand the coherence and logic of the system.

The consequence of the totem symbols for the wholeness of the culture are far-reaching, but can also remain peripheral. They can be limited to a few food taboos. They affect the marriage system, and sometimes permeate the ordering of the household. When, for example, the Vai in Liberia regard the crocodile as a pet, it is obvious that they treat each other 'carefully'.[144]

There is a special form of non-transitory attachment to animals which does not fall within totemism, in the strict sense of the word. Yet it does possess an important hermeneutic function in decoding the symbolism of to-

---

[144] E. Dammann, 1963, pp.39f. A similar personal experience is related by G. Lienhardt, 1961, p. 132.

temism. I refer to the 'identification' of twins with birds among the Nuer. It is closely connected to the classification of totem animals, mentioned above.

Twins are birds, according to the Nuer, they are not 'persons'. But the Nuer can also say that twins are *one* person. For example, if a twin dies no funeral rites are performed as long as the other twin is still alive. "Isn't my soul still alive? I am alive, and we are really children of God", said a bereaved twin.[145] If both twins die, they are not buried in the ground in the traditional way, but in a tree, in the fork of a branch – like birds. What is the basis for this link between twins and birds? Birds, not people, hatch out more than one offspring at a time. So twins are birds due to duplication. Since crocodiles and tortoises also lay more than one egg, twin have a special relationship to these animals and will never eat their flesh. They show their respect by never killing them.

The analogy of multiple birth alone is not a sufficient basis for the whole classification. A further argument runs as follows: birds are from a higher sphere. They build nests in the trees, they fly around the heavens. They are nearer to God and therefore are assigned to him. Twins are called 'natures from above'. They are regarded as a special revelation of God. It is not said they are *like* birds; they *are* birds.

It is this identification formula which time and again confuses Westerners and which led earlier scholars to the conclusion that no clear distinction existed in 'primitive cultures' between animals and people; that things which for us are quite separate could be regarded as identical there. A could equal B. The symbol and what is symbolised are the same thing. Van der Leeuw expressed this pithily: "The picture *is* what it depicts; what you see is what is meant".[146] However, this claim is not always true. When a Pedi points to a fellow-tribesmen walking by, and says, "There goes a monkey", or when a Herero says to the staffs of the ancestors, "This stick is my father", or when the Nuer say, "Twins are birds", "Lightning is God", or "Rain is God", then we must observe the asymmetry of the expressions. The sentence cannot be

---

[145] E. E. Evans-Pritchard, 1967, p. 129.

[146] G. van der Leeuw, 1956, p. 511.

117

reversed. Birds are not twins, the Herero's father is not a stick. God is neither rain nor lightning, and the description of a Pedi as a 'monkey' is no more than a clan designation. However, the expression of identity is more than a poetic and symbolic form of expression. It expresses a particular means of coping with the world. It may strike us as 'materialistic', in that the spiritual world is always expressed through earthly, material things. In Africa, the spiritual cannot, in the last resort, be separated from the natural and material. There is no symbol without ist 'material', or 'natural' side. There is no life without the here-and-now. It is only in death that the body is separated from the spirit – but life in the hereafter is still related to the present life and is dependent on it, as we shall see in the account of ancestor veneration. For Africans, writes J. V. Taylor, "the supernatural is natural, it is strange and unaccountable, but there is no element of otherness about it, for it belongs with everything else to the here and now. So they accept it and take account of it in the most matter-of-fact way".[147] Since encountering the natural environment and coming to terms with it are never a matter for the individual alone, society's desire for order is also reflected in non-transitory attachment to animals. Nature must be 'incorporated' into society if people want to share in ist powers. In the same way society is 'incorporated' into nature, because people live against the backdrop of nature, and alongside it. If the environment is understood in terms of personal relationships, the same must apply to the social order. The attachment to animals is a means of making society transparent. It is an important structuring principle.[148]

One more aspect remains. The dynamic interpretation saw in totem animals a 'reservoir of power' which people felt to be superior to themselves and demanding of submission. According to G. van der Leeuw, "this makes a

---

[147] J. V. Taylor, 1961, p. 280. "Nevertheless a great deal of African 'materialism' is accompanied by the most lively sense of the spiritual world". p. 275.

[148] As long ago as 1922, A. R. Radcliffe-Brown wrote that "for primitive man the universe as a whole is a moral or social order governed not by what we call natural law but rather by what we must call moral or ritual law"; A. R. Radcliffe-Brown, 1952, p. 230. This conclusion of his fundamentally altered research into totemism. Lévy-Strauss, 1965, later adopted the same view.

118

religion of totemism".[149] He does not claim that the totem is deified. But where is the distinction to be drawn between 'deification' and 'religion'?. In any case, can such assertions be justified in the African context? The ideas of the Dinka in the southern Sudan come closest to it.

The giraffe clan honours the giraffe, because a giraffe helped their primal ancestor. They institutionalise the original event of assistance, as it were. They are convinced that the 'giraffe' (note the singular) will continue to help them. That is still the case, even though there are no longer any giraffes in the whole of the area and various members of the clan have never seen a giraffe in their lives. The animal has become a symbol of help, used to address the clan deity. It is the spirit of the animal that counts. The animal makes this deity immanent, as it were, and gives it tangible form. The members of this clan can describe themselves as 'children' of 'the giraffe'. This has social consequences. All members of the clan are distinguished from one another in age and status, but in the eyes of the clan deity they are equal and are seen as 'half-brothers'. The clan deity determines their ideas of morality and standards of conduct. Even if the various groups within the clan do not have connections with each other, they 'meet' in the clan animal.[150] The clan deity enters into the thoughts, ideas and experiences of the people, and becomes a part of them.[151]

Is this then the deification of an animal? Certainly not. Again the animal is merely an emblem, the material, 'tangible' side of a spiritual reality, which can only be grasped with the help of 'natural', 'personalised' horizons of experience. In Africa nature is neither deified nor prayed to, neither as a whole

---

[149] G. van der Leeuw, 1956, p. 73.

[150] M. Lienhardt, 1961, p. 131.; for the whole subject, pp. 104ff.

[151] It "is incarnate in them and it is intrinsically part of them", idem, p. 146. C. Lévy-Strauss, 1963, draws our attention to the same phenomena. During the First World War units of American soldiers identified themselves with natural phenomena to such an extent that they were comparable in every respect with the totem animals of traditional religions. Such identification, e. g. with the rainbow, led to separation and differentiation from other units. The inner cohesion of the unit, the creation of a new sense of meaning, special moral ideas, separating from others, are all parts of this. The emblem takes on a significance which gives structure to the group or society.

nor partially in one of ist manifestations.[152] However, people do indeed participate in nature, and with the help of animals enter into a close relationship with it that defines their ethics and emotions. It also profoundly affects religion, which always includes the whole of human experience.[153]

2. Veneration of the ancestors

"The chiefs, the chiefs, to whom do they pray?
The ancestors, the ancestors!
The Europeans, the Europeans, to whom do they pray?
Money, money!
Muslims, Muslims, to whom do they pray?
Mohammed, Mohammed!
The Baptised, the Baptised, to whom do they pray?
Jesus Christ, Jesus Christ!"

Years ago Monica Wilson heard this song among the Christian Nyakyusa in Tanzania. It demonstrates something of the keen powers of observation of Africans, who infer values and meaning from deeds. Just as money governs the life and thought of Europeans, so belief in the ancestors permeates the traditional religions in Africa. With few exceptions, it forms the core of religious practices. It was so central that missionaries utterly opposed it, because they saw in it the most fundamental threat to belief in God and a flagrant denial of the first commandment. Africans have never been able to completely grasp why one thing should exclude the other, which is why – in spite of European opposition – veneration of the ancestors continues to be practised, with a greater or lesser degree of openness and intensity.

---

[152] This also applies to the religion of the Khoisan-speaking peoples of southern Africa, the Nama and Bushmen. The oft-cited *mantis religiosa*, the supposed 'Hottentot God', was never worshipped as a god. European settlers deliberately distorted the content of the Bushmen's religion, albeit a particularly 'pure' religion, in order to ridicule and belittle it; so they could oppress, and even exterminate them with a good conscience; cf. M. Gusinde, 1966, pp.72f.

[153] I will not go into the other aspects of links with nature, because they do not throw further light on the African view of humankind. They merely substantiate the principles already set forth; cf. Sundermeier, 1987.

The relationship between belief in God and belief in the ancestors can be described as two concentric circles, which do not exclude each other because the smaller is a way into the wider, more distant circle of God; alternatively it can be understood as two ways of life, which do not clash with or contradict each other because they serve different ends. They are like two parallel lines which meet at infinity.[154] In 1955 the well-known Ghanaian theologian C. Baeta stated categorically: "Our people *live* with their dead".[155] With this statement, he initiated a debate about the theological and ecclesiastical relevance of the veneration of the ancestors which continues to this day.

1. For a long time social anthropology was sceptical about a one-sided religious interpretation of veneration of the ancestors, emphasising ist social aspect. In the 1950s E. W. Smith started a discussion on J. H. Driberg`s interpretation. A final consensus on the matter has still not been reached, even if there is little support now for the radically social interpretation originating with Durkheim. Driberg says: "What we have mistaken for a religious attitude is nothing more than a projection of (the African`s) social behaviour". Africans do not pray to their ancestors, they request, or beseech, or expostulate. "The term `worship` is strictly reserved for religious dealings with the absolute power and the divinities. The Latin word *pietas* (profound respect) probably best describes the attitude of Africans to their dead ancestors, as well as to their living elders".[156]

Driberg rightly draws attention to two points. In various languages a distinction is made between 'pray' and 'call upon', in which the latter concept is applied to dealings with the ancestors. However, we must ask whether this linguistic differentiation is really observed consistently in everyday religious practice. I myself in conversation with Hereros found that they knew of the difference, but they gave it a different weight than the original meaning of the words allowed. This may be a later development, but we should beware

---

[154] On this latter point, cf. Sundermeier, 1973a, pp.142ff.
[155] Cf. in: Christianity and African Culture, Accra, 1955, p. 59.
[156] J. H. Driberg, quoted by E. W. Smith, 1950, pp.25f.

of an overhasty definition. (The same distinction exists in the Catholic church with regard to venerating the saints and praying to God, yet this important dogmatic distinction between invocation and prayer is often confused in practice.)

The elders are addressed like the ancestors, giving the impression that there is no distinction between living and dead ancestors. In the practice of *pietas*, the levels in fact overlap. The elders are held in honour and their advice accepted as being from wise older men. Likewise the ancestors are invoked because they were known in life, and were familiar with life in the village. They know what is good for their successors. Forms of address are extended beyond the frontier of death. It would be to misinterpret the symbolic language of funeral rites, however, to assume that in traditional religions death was not perceived as a grave danger and threat, and was not respected as such. Our discussion of rites has shown that belief in the ancestors cannot be understood as a denial of death, a lack of perception of ist solemn nature. Rather, it seeks to overcome the danger which death represents. Precisely for this reason, it takes death and the fear of death very seriously.

Is belief in the ancestors a religious or a social phenomenon? Apart from the fact that in African religions this distinction does not exist, and Africans reject the division between secular and religious action as artificial and Western, we would ultimately have to opt for religion, without overlooking the truth contained in the sociological interpretation. Every year the Bakossi in Cameroon[157] celebrate the feast of the ancestors, the *ndie*. It is a village festival, in which (originally) all the inhabitants of the village took part, something no longer possible today, because of the intrusion of Christianity. A village elder summed up the significance of the *ndie*: "The *ndie* was formerly our church". This statement is illuminating. Belief in the ancestors enhances the well-being of the whole village. It affects everybody, even if not everybody takes part in the festival. The festival is not an everyday event, but seeks to unite everybody at a special moment in time. Just as in Christianity, there are active and less active 'believers'. Not everybody observes the cult

---

[157] For what follows, cf. H. Balz, 1984.

122

of the ancestors to the same degree in everyday life. The festival of the ancestors, however, inspires people to ask for peace and well-being, and to become conscious of their origins and social interdependence. The following prayer was pronounced at the festival of the ancestors in 1981:

"E e! Quiet, e e, don't make noise!
Peace! We who are gathered here today,
We are following the footsteps of Ngoe,
And that is why we gather here.
Ngoe, whose name we call,
came from a place, and when
He reached Mwebah, he ended.
Peace! After the death of Ngoe,
He left children who were to follow his footsteps.
He showed some points, and those
are the points we are following today.
    ...
If we are working in your name today,
if other children of yours should forget you,
we can still not forget you. ...
O wine, peace, wine, peace,
we are really suffering too much:
suffering production of children,
food; we are suffering many things,
mostly money.
We suffer, but we remember,
as you people are there, you
remember us your children who are poor.
    ...
O wine, peace! We who are here
we are suffering
food, human beings, money and other riches,
the following: Sango Akwokume, Ngwese-Meko
Enodiabe awe Sobe, Metukmenome
Ebonome who was down there, his name came.
Mekokame also came because of your name.
Ajembule who was also here, came to live because of you.

You yourself should remember
for us all those whose names we have called today,
and everybody should tell his brother what we need.
Is it not so?
Yes!
Peace! Women – since even great
men come from the woman,
Etane was Ngoe's wife with whom he moved about.
You should also remember us on the side of the women,
since Ngoe is for the interest of all men.
Not so?
Yes!
...
Peace! Even if we call somebody's name or not,
anybody who is powerful, you should tell him yourselves
so that he should be able to
defend us from all things which are evil.
Not so?
(Yes!)
If a man should have a hen,
then the hen should give seven chicken
among the chicken, there should be four hens and three cocks
which will be killed when there are strangers.
If evil is spoken of you,
you should be blessed. Not so?"[158]

The text is a prayer. To classify it as anything else is to misinterpret it. The prayer is directed to Ngoe, the primaeval ancestor. Other ancestors are named as intermediaries. The chain is unbroken with Ngoe as the ultimate point. He is not understood in this text as providing contact with God. There is no thought of God in this festival. Whether his presence is implicit might be stated only on the basis of a careful analysis of the symbols used, but he has no function. The prayers are not addressed to him. The controversial question of whether the ancestors are only being addressed in their mediatory function,

---

[158] H. Balz, 1995, pp.260–262.

124

or whether they themselves are addressed in prayer, must be answered in the second sense at this festival. The ancestors dispense blessings. They are responsible for the well-being of their successors. They are invoked as figures known from the past, without whom the present generation would not be here. Among other peoples, God is addressed via the ancestors. Nowadays African scholars, in particular, widely regard this as the genuine and original form of African religions.[159] Yet the practice is very likely a secondary phenomenon, one of adaptation to Islam and Christianity. An internal shift of emphasis towards one or another side must also be regarded as possible. In Africa, belief in God is generally not associated with cultic acts, and God's name is occasionally taboo. Belief in the ancestors may have repressed belief in God. In terms of the psychology of religion this would be understandable, given the strong tendency of African religiosity to highlight what is near and familiar. The strong impulse to personify all the environmental forces would support this. However, it is quite possible that a primal pattern of belief may re-emerge. The idea of a chain of intermediaries is essential to belief in the ancestors, as is shown by the invocation of the ancestral line. The continuation of this line as far as God is not necessarily an essentially foreign element which has been subsequently linked to the ancestor cult. Instead it would appear that the adaptation exposes the original intention and, under pressure from contact and intermingling with other cultures, strengthens it.

The sociological and social significance of the cultic side of belief in the ancestors is considerable. It explains how this belief has survived in African society right up to the present day.

Not every person automatically becomes an ancestor through death. With few exceptions, having children is one of the most important prerequisites. In a patrilineal society there must be sons. During his lifetime, the son guarantees the status of his father, just as the deceased father establishes the social status of his sons and heirs within the society. The oldest son stands in a special place at his father's graveside. Everybody can recognise that he will

---

[159] J. S. Mbiti's presentation, 1974, shows the widespread impact of this. For a discussion of this view, cf. J. F. Thiel, 1977, pp.128ff.

be the head of the family and will now enter into his inheritance. His father and grandfather are approached through him, which cements his position, regardless of what moral qualities the father possessed during his lifetime.

"Never speak ill of the dead" – this maxim applies here as well. The ancestor is an idealised version of the present life. They set the standards to which people aspire, even if they have not observed them themselves. The ancestors are guarantors of the received moral order. If anybody in the village transgresses community rules, the ancestors intervene and make their presence felt by punishing him. Belief in the ancestors restores the old order.

The ancestor must be known by name. Ancestors whose names are no longer known cease to exist, in the legal sense, and have no significance for the present structure of the locality. The name stands for the lineage.[160] The dead who during their life have not occupied any prominent position, and who have earned no more than due respect, are already forgotten by the second generation. Once their inheritance is distributed, the succeeding generation only turns to the line of ancestors higher in the hierarchy, who encompass the clan and distinguish it from others. However, so long as there are questions of inheritance to be settled, the ancestor remains in people's memory.

Unquestionably, the relationship with paternal and maternal ancestors is moulded by warm bonds established during the person's life-time. Belief in the ancestors cannot, however, be explained in this way. What follows makes this clear. Among the matrilineal Ashanti there exists a specially close relationship between a father and his children which is not supported by any legal relationship of authority. The person wielding legal authority is the mother's eldest brother. After the death of the father, the relationship of *pietas* does not survive. It is to the deceased brother of his mother, not to his father, that the son will dedicate a stool, which forms the symbol and centre of ancestor veneration among the Ashanti. The legal position of the recognised head of the family is guaranteed and continued by reverence for the ancestors. However, M. Fortes is right in saying that ancestor veneration does not

---

[160] M. Fortes, 1965, p. 124.

belong to the realm of father-son relationships, which is controlled by spiritual laws, but to the public and political order.[161]

Belief in the ancestors represents an awareness of history at the clan as well as the family level. If the father, on some special occasion or on his dead-bed, lays down that special food taboos shall be observed in the future, the family will keep to this. Avoiding these foods is an ever-present reminder of the ancestors and of the events that they have institutionalised. Where the presence of the ancestors is given material form through a fetish, a stool, or any other object, these help to keep alive the memory, and make the past present. The history of the ancestors contributes to fixing the identity of the clan.

If the village authorities have the impression that the ties holding together the village community are loosening and that the moral order is weakening, or if people are afflicted by sickness or storms or drought, they seek refuge in the ancestors. The social cohesion of the village is renewed by a festival of the ancestors. The Herero say that the ancestral fire has become 'tired'. They extinguish it and rekindle it ritually in a festival held either at the grave of the ancestors or at some other place at which a great ancestor has committed mighty acts. The history of the people and of that particular place are recited in songs of praise. Belief in the ancestors serves to integrate the members of the group and provides social stability, particularly among those societies which have no dominant form of chieftaincy.

2. We have seen above that posing ontological questions makes understanding African religiosity more difficult, if not impossible. 'Being' does not constitute the situation in Africa, the situation and the context determine being. The same applies to the ancestors. We have looked into this question by attempting to understand the levels at which belief in the ancestors is defined. Among the Zulu, the dead can be named in eleven different ways, and by using the right form of address they can be invoked in different situations, from different angles. However, we must go a step further with the various religions, and ask what it is that ultimately distinguishes an ancestor from mere

---

[161] Op. cit., p. 130.

mortals. How does 'spirit' relate to 'soul' in an ancestor, to use concepts taken from Western anthropology?

In order to explain the problem clearly, let us turn to the Lugbara in northern Uganda.[162] A person consists of a body, breath which gives it life, and the *orindi*. Breath is the sign of life, but not (as with other peoples) life itself. At death, both pass away. The body is of no use; the Lugbara forget the site of the grave. The place of breath is the lung; that of the *orindi*, the heart. Middleton translates this concept by 'soul', but that does not correspond to what is meant; it is the core of what expresses the ability of the spirit to leave the body and to appear to others, especially after death. This does not preclude the belief that the *orindi* also goes to God after death. "What you keep apart we hold together", an old Bergdama once said to H. Vedder.[163] That applies here too. The idea of 'shadows' is of absolute importance for belief in the ancestors. The dead have no shadows. That is a persistent idea of the Bantu. At midday, when there is often no shadow to be seen, people grow afraid. The shadow belongs to the self, because it is the proof of life. A person's shadow must be protected from witches, who can cast a spell on it and bring harm. It is regarded as quite normal if a dead person appears in a dream, and this can be a good sign. If he or she appears at certain times during the day, e. g. during a whirlwind, this will be regarded as an evil omen.

The Lugbara have more terms to describe people: i. e. *talj, dro* and *ori*. *Talj* describes people and their special abilities; *dro* means those who are protected by God. Middleton, however, translated *dro* as 'protective spirit'. It comes from God and will return to God after death, remaining with him in a bush or stream. It enters into the collective of the 'children of God'. It represents the dark side of God, which is not predictable. *Talj* also goes back to God, but abides with him in heaven; it represents God's good side.

According to the ideas of the Lugbara, the forefathers are not 'physical entities',[164] and yet they are a reality. They are there in the same way as the

---

[162] For what follows, cf. J. Middleton, 1969, pp.28ff.

[163] Reports of the Rhenish Mission Society, 1920, p. 121.

[164] J. Middleton, 1969, p. 32; cf. G. Dieterlein, 1965, p. 16ff.

elders of the lineage, and must be respected in the same way. The same term is used to name them both – *ori*. Yet the distinction between them must not be blurred; sacrifices are to the dead, not to the living. If they have earned a significance extending beyond the bounds of the family, they are honoured with a special shrine.

We must break off here. Once more it is clear that the terms do not allow for hard-and-fast definitions, but denote people in their many relationships in community. They are an attempt to find words for the multi-facetted mystery of humankind. They are not analytical terms, but could rather be described as ascriptions, in which space and time and experience are summed up in one term.

The dead are not dead. This is why Mbiti describes them as 'living dead'. In this way he combines two aspects which do not really belong together, and which are ultimately mutually exclusive. Africans love life and fear death, like all people. It remains to be asked whether the classical expression 'shades' is not the appropriate one, as it is also used in African languages. It expresses the other mode of existence after death, which is both stronger and weaker. Fullness of life exists only on earth. As all the rituals show, the life of the ancestors is lived conversely to that of the living. Life 'there' is not a simple continuation of this life. It 'copies' life in the here-and-now, and can be nothing but a copy, a watered-down version of it. It is a 'shadow existence'. The ancestors depend on the living. Only if the living duly perform the rituals do they become ancestors. The ancestors need to be fed by the living and demand their sacrifices. "They are always hungry", it is said. That is why they demand sacrifices from people. If they are forgotten they can make the living remember them. However, except for the greatest ancestors, they do not escape oblivion. They lose their importance for the living. What are they then? Africans no longer answer this question. They are interested in life, not in shadow existence.

At the same time, the ancestors are more powerful. Since they are invisible, they are superior to mortals. They can send sickness and they can punish; they can grant good fortune or deny it. People are afraid of them, but still want them to be near them, not too close. The living have mixed feelings about them.

Whether the ancestors are obliged to confer blessings or whether their function lies more in the realm of punishment is still a matter of controversy in research.[165] Balz has shown that for the Bakossi the religion of the ancestors is a pure 'religion of grace'. They know of no ancestors who punish. This corresponds to the heart of belief in the ancestors. Fathers can indeed punish their own children, but they will never destroy them, for that would endanger their own existence. Consequently, the Lugbara attribute the ultimate punishment, a never-ending chain of misfortune which finally leads to the downfall of a family, to God himself. The ancestors can only hand out minor punishments to bring people back into line with traditional morality. However, this does not apply to all peoples. I have heard impressive lamentations from the Mbanderu at the graves of ancestors, in which they complained that the ancestors had withdrawn and the family was dying out.

3. Max Gluckman once rightly stated that the wealth of customs connected with ancestor veneration was coupled with only a small number of beliefs.[166] The stronger the *praxis pietas*, the less the dogmatic content. This is a general characteristic of African religions. They are not about doctrine, but are a way of life. This is stimulated by symbols rather than by values and concepts, since "symbols speak louder than words", as the Karanga say.[167] They invite participation, as we have seen. That is of crucial importance. Yet we must not overlook the content of faith. It is influential in ist own way, in explaining the existence of human beings in their world. This account of a Nyakyusa is representative of many:[168]

"People think that in the land of the shades they build homes like we do, they marry wives, they have children, they plant food and build houses. I heard this always from old

---

[165] Cf. African Systems of Thought, loc. cit, pp.16ff.
[166] In M. Fortes, 1965, p. 126.
[167] H. Aschwanden, 1976, p. 184.
[168] M. Wilson, 1957, pp.210f.

men, but they only guess. They say: 'Perhaps it is nice, perhaps horrible.' They do not know very much. They fear to die. I have never met any old pagan man who wanted to die, they always fear. Property is important. People are much taken up with the idea that riches are there in the land of shades. They say: 'If a man dies, his fathers come to receive him, but if they find he has no cows with him they are angry, they do not receive him with re-joicing. If they do not kill some cattle at the burial of a dead man, without doubt illness will come to the home. If they consult an oracle, then the oracle says: Your fathers beneath are angry, because you did not kill cattle for the burial of So-and-so.' So then they go and kill a beast. When they kill cattle at a death, they do not kill for the mourners to eat, no, but they say it is that the fathers may receive him well, that they may not be angry".

The basic chord which is struck here reappears in different variations. The dead need a proper funeral, otherwise the spirit wanders around, possibly as an evil spirit. A judgement which consigns a good person to a particular place and damns an evil person is foreign to this belief. Admittedly, the Koko and Basa in Cameroon believe that the wicked go to a kingdom of coldness and that the rest will live in a kingdom of light, while those who are doing penance are in a kind of limbo, and will be accepted into the kingdom of the 'free' only after a trial period.[169] But these beliefs may have been influenced from outside Africa, e. g. by Islam or Christianity. In any case, they are atypi-cal of the rest of Bantu Africa.

Little is known about life after death. It can generally be described as 'up there' or 'down there', or both at the same time – which is not impossible, as we have seen. What is more important is that people know where, and how to encounter the ancestors. The place is determined by the cultural context of the religion. The main means of sustenance of the Nyakyusa is bananas, which is why the place of sacrifice is a banana grove. The banana tree is an eloquent symbol of the fertility of the ancestors. Cattle-raising Bantu prefer to seek a meeting place in the cattle kraal, where the ancestors are often bur-ied. "Cattle and ancestors are one", the Herero say. A Zulu medicine man ex-pressed the 'identity' in symbolic terms. A woman conceives and gives birth in the tenth month (i. e. after nine months). A cow also calves in the tenth

---

[169] M. Ntetem, 1983, pp.35f.

month. Both sleep in the kraal at night, and go outside the kraal during the day. "So a cow is like a human".[170]

The large and complex societies of West Africa have a house of the ancestors containing their images, a 'materialisation' of their presence in fetishes. There are also special places in the houses and villages. Fire is often associated with the ancestors. A familiar location is preferred for a private talk with them. The Lugbara also recognise silence, a wordless communing with the ancestors.[171] They are addressed in the same way as old people, confidentially and intimately. However, the 'scolding prayer' is also occasionally permitted, as in the case of stubborn old people. Don't you sometimes have to tell them off too, when you can't stand it any more?

An example from Zululand shows the intimate approach and the atmosphere of secrecy surrounding a conversation with the ancestors.

"I had been much troubled by dreams. They even led to sickness. But I had nothing, so I could not enquire. If I had had some money, I would have gone to the diviner at X who divines well. But there was nothing (in the purse). Simply poverty. So I remained, doing nothing. Then I went to the cattle-enclosure and sat down. I sat down, just sitting there and waiting. Then I stood up and went to the cow of the shades. I walked to the place where it was standing. It was standing next to the red cow, there on the left side. I came to it. I rubbed it with ash. I rubbed just nicely with ash. It licked the ash in my hand. I was very happy. When I was rubbing up-and-down I put my hands on the back of it. It stood still, doing nothing. Then I spoke some words. It was the words that I had planned when I was sitting there in the cattle-enclosure before going to the cow. I said, speaking in a pleasant voice, speaking to the shades, I said: 'Oh, ye fathers of my father! What is this thing troubling me? First dreams every night without an interpretation. Then sickness. Yes, even yesterday I was vomiting the whole day without ceasing! Everything came out. Everything, even the gall! That was yesterday. Then today, it is the head. The pains fill the head everywhere. Besides these things there is poverty in this home of yours. I am saying poverty, poverty in this home of Ns. There is not even something for divination that I may know the reason for these things in our midst. That is the reason for my standing at this place, fathers of my father! So I am saying, do not become angry, saying, 'What has the child brought,

---

[170] A.-I. Berglund, 1975, p. 110.

132

when approaching us in this manner? We do not see anything (that he has brought).' I have brought nothing but this animal which I have brought before, some time ago, and bringing it, knowing that there would be a gateway to you, Ye of N! That is the reason for my standing here. So do not become angry, asking for something. I am here, speaking nicely, so that I may know (the reason for the illness)'. Then I spoke about the poor fields because there had been no tilling due to the sickness (my informant had been ill during the planting season). I begged pardon again for coming empty-handed and bade farewell. All the time I stood there beside the cow, speaking nicely all the time. It also just stood quietly, doing nothing. When I completed the speaking, it stood still in the same place. I knew that they had heard my words, in that the cow had stood still all the time, doing nothing, just remaining quiet".

The Zulu was convinced that he had really encountered the ancestors. He was able to sleep well that night and soon recovered his health again.[172] The tone of the following prayers from Swaziland is quite the opposite:

"You, son of So-and-so, why do you kill us your children? Why do you turn your back on us? Here is your beast. Take it. Look after us for we are looking after you. Why did you send illness on this child? You are greedy, you are always ready to find fault".

A prayer of the Tonga:

"You are useless you gods! You only give us trouble! For although we give you offerings you do not listen to us! We are deprived of everything... So come to the altar. Eat and distribute among yourselves our ox (it is only a hen) according to your wisdom".[173]

The ancestors work by night. If they show themselves by day, they create fear. They work at night, or to be more precise, in the dark, because the dark is their day. They 'work' within the womb, and ensure that the seed bears fruit. They work in the seed on the land. They like the darkness of huts (that is why they do not feel at home in European houses with their windows). They appear in dreams. They may be invisible to the European, but not to the African. "How can you say they are invisible?" a Zulu asked one of

---

[171] Cf. the striking example in J. Middleton, 1969, p. 36.

[172] Quoted in A.-I. Berglund, 1975, pp.204f.

[173] Quoted in G. Parrinder, 1962, pp.64f.

my friends. "No, we see them; sometimes more, sometimes less. No, they are not invisible".

They do not 'appear', they are not ghosts. They are seen in dreams, as they were in life. 'Seeing' is more than physical perception. Seeing means involvement with something and exposure to it. You see the ancestors, because you know their activities, for good or ill. "I beseech you So-and-so, my grandfather, hear me", prays a Hutu from Burundi, when he enters a house of the ancestors beside the grave. "Cease your anger, receive your gifts, bless us. Come out of the cows, out of the seed, out of the children... Bless us, give us peace and happiness in the home, in the cows, in the fields". After laying down the gifts, all the participants bow, clap their hands and say: "Accept, accept and bless us".[174]

"Peace and happiness" – these terms are the themesong of the invocations. This is what people yearn for in their belief in ancestors. This is reflected in ethical and religious acts. *Pietas* in this context means striving for peace.

Where this peace does not exist, people first look for the fault in themselves. The diviner finds the cause in strife in the village, or in the neglect of the ancestors and their traditions. Only if he or she has thoroughly investigated the life of the community, and can find no cause for criticism, is the fault looked for among the ancestors. If they turn out to be tormenting spirits, the Zaramo in Tanzania exhume the dead and scatter their bones.[175]

In the light of what has been said, it is hardly possible to maintain that the ancestors become gods or that the primeval ancestor himself is condensed into the image of God. This is a Western rather than an African interpretation.

However, there are points of interest. While the ancestor belongs to the family, and to the family alone, there is an occasional tendency to glorify the dead chief more and more. Specific powers are assigned to the various ancestors. They are 'responsible' only for special tasks and are invoked in this

---

[174] R. Guillebaud, in: E. W. Smith, 1961, pp.182f.
[175] According to E. Dammann, 1963, p. 17. Cf. on this subject J. F. Thiel, 1977, pp.132ff.; for further information cf. H. Sawyer, 1970.

regard. The original ancestor increases his power, so that he comes even closer to God. Where the cult of fetishes is bound up with belief in ancestors, a dispute over precedence can arise between fetishes. But these are felt to be secondary developments that substantially alter the original cult. Raids to get control of fetishes, and destroy them, are part of traditional belief.[176] The belief in ancestors is subject to a kind of self-purification. The diviners, the traditional guardians of this belief, then assume the role of prophets. It is no accident that in the religious revival movements and African Independent Churches the images of the 'diviner' and the 'prophet' have matching symbols.[177]

E. B. Idowu says:[178] "Certainly, the cults of the ancestors do not constitute African traditional religion; and it is a gross error to equate them with religion. The proper meaning of the ancestral cults derives from the belief of Africans that death does not write `finish` to life, that the family or community life of this earth has only become extended into the life beyond in consequence of the `death` of the ancestors. Thus the cults are a means of communion and communication between those who are living on earth and those who have gone to live in the spirit world of the ancestors". Transplanting the Western dichotomy between the spiritual and the secular into African religiosity does it no favour. Belief in ancestors is deeply rooted in African village life, and is thus at the heart of African religions. It serves the community and ist life, which is always thought of primarily in physical terms. The spiritual is the expression of the corporeal, not the other way round. It is directed towards the corporeal, because it arises out of it. Belief in the ancestors cements the distinctions between people within a society. It imposes obedience to ethical standards, and sanctions judicial decisions. It makes it possible to identify the family and the clan, and records their history. In a word, it sustains the conservatism of the traditional African way of life.

---

[176] Cf. on this subject J. F. Thiel, 1977, pp.132ff.; for further information cf. H. Sawyer, 1970.

[177] Cf. on this subject, among others, B. Sundkler, 1964, pp.384ff.

[178] E. B. Idowu, 1973, p. 186.

By believing in ancestors, Africans symbolise and personalise what they strive for most of all – life. Those who are chronically ill cannot become ancestors.[179] "*Yepe nkwa*" (Akan), "We want life" – now. This is the secret of ancestor veneration.

3. Spirit Possession

In the ancestors Africans encounter only a small part of the world of the invisible that surrounds them, the part relating to the family. It is relevant to life within the family circle. Beyond that, the other world is ineffective, even non-existent. The invisible world is, however, larger than this. The dead who are not counted among the ancestors – cripples, lepers, those who have not been buried properly, those who in their lifetime cut themselves off (ethically) from the tribe – drop out of reach, and cannot be appeased with the usual means of ancestor cults. They are frightening and unpredictable. In the ancestors, the individual encounters the collective conscience, as formed by the tradition of the people. In the various spirits, the spirits of the dead and the spirits of nature, something different enters the scene. Here humans encounter a further sphere of life, which we could ascribe to the natural and physical realm, bounded by the horizon which blends heaven and earth together into a unity.

But even this broader physical world is mediated personally. It cannot be otherwise in the African understanding of reality. Africans encounter their natural environment, as we have seen, not as something available for objective usage, but the other way round – they are ist victims. It takes possession of them, filling and 'inspiring' them. Being filled with amazement is the mildest form of encounter. More often, they are filled with shock and fear. The encounter shatters them, and makes them ill. Possession is the most elementary form of such experience of spirits. For Westerners, illness is an objective fact, brought about by objective causes. They say that the mentally sick 'lack' something. According to the African understanding of the world,

---

[179] H. Aschwanden, 1976, p.272

sick people have contributed something to their illness. They do not 'lack' anything; rather they have 'too much' of something, they are filled with something from outside. A spirit 'possesses' them, so that they become ill. It must be removed, driven out. People who are possessed attract everyone's attention. They become the focus of a whole gamut of rituals, intended to bring healing.

In contrast to Western idealism, the spirit is not separate from nature, nor is it a quantity existing for itself; it is inherent in existence, essentially part of nature. In Africa, spirit is not defined in contrast to matter or as the opposite of the body. The spirits are present in and with nature, they are manifest in the physical as symbolic interpreters of reality, and are understood anthropomorphically. Because they are given personal characteristics, they make it possible to deal with the world. Spirit is manifest in nature, in the animal world, in so-called inanimate objects; you encounter spirit through your own spirit. When a Mende walks through the bush and sees a striking object, e. g. a special stone, he will want to pick it up and take it home. It could be that the spirit of the stone has something special to say to him. Why else did the stone 'catch his eye'?[180]

The languages of Africa have an abundance of names for the various spirits. They are defined in terms of the circumstances in which they manifest themselves. Yet it is not their name that is so important, but the way in which they impose themselves upon people. They are 'wind' (*luwo*), it is said, "because we don't see them. We recognise them by what they do. Just as we don't see the wind, but we recognise that it is there by what it does".[181]

Among the Tonga in Zambia, the *basangu* are spirits which speak through mediums and say things of general interest and importance. *Masebe* are spirits which enter into people, make them ill, and force them to dance the Masebe dance. On the other hand, *zilube* or *zelo* are spirits which have no

---

[180] Cf. K. Little, 1963, p. 126.
[181] On what follows, cf. E. Colson, in J. Middleton, 1969, pp.69ff. & 72.

other purpose than to kill. They stand for evil and are controlled by sorcerers.[182]

The general name for them is *umuuya*, 'spirit'. In Tonga it describes not only air, wind and breath, but also that 'being' which possesses everything that manifests itself to people. People have spirit, but so do animals and things. The concept of *umuuya* expresses that which forces people to behave in special ways in keeping with the spirit.[183] *Umuuya* is the 'impressive' part of all things and phenomena, their way of imposing on human beings. The *basangu* (spirits) choose their own medium. There certainly are people who are predisposed towards this, but the decision lies with the particular spirit. Constantly recurrent dreams and other signs indicate possession. Convulsions, shivering, cries, and loss of consciousness are the hallmarks of ist presence. However, there is no ultimate certainty. Even a diviner cannot provide this. The apparition seem genuine if it sounds convincing. More precisely, you are only absolutely certain when the spirit's announcements have proven true. Until then you play along with it, and go through with the ceremonial.

When the spirit announces ist presence in a medium, all the members of the household assemble, and clap out the rhythm appropriate to the particular possession. Songs are sung to the spirit referring to natural events, such as the coming rains. In greeting you ask for the name and history of the spirit, which has revealed itself previously and possesses a shrine. The name is known, but an unknown spirit can also reveal itself, since it is not tied to a particular circle of adherents. The Tonga have no traditional authorities or chiefs.

What the spirit has to say through the medium is not revealed the first time. The medium only tells what he or she has seen and heard in dreams or trances. If the medium has proved to be a true representative of the *basangu*,

---

[182] *Mizimu*, on the other hand, are spirits of the ancestors. They, too, are *umuuya*, spirit. They are not responsible for possession. They send sickness upon members of their own families only when they feel neglected or when their families have mistreated them.

[183] E. Colson, 1969, p. 72.

questions may be asked. Then the medium has to fall into a trance. A small circle is formed inside the hut. Most of the people sit outside and beat out the appropriate *basangu* rhythm. When the medium has fallen into a trance, the participants put the questions in a shrieking, imploring, threatening voice. The medium lies on the ground, groans, rolls around in convulsions, and cries out answers in a high falsetto, differently stressed from normal speech. A few Tonga words are recognised in the disjointed utterances.

The seance ends informally. The spirit leaves the medium, whose face slowly loses ist fixed expression, and voice becomes normal. A light hand-clapping is the sign of thanks for the message, of which the medium has usu-ally not been conscious. The content and meaning of the message are then discussed. People do not hold back with their opinions if they question the genuineness of the words. Blind belief is not demanded. Small gifts are pre-sented to the medium, who otherwise enjoys no special place in the society. If people are not satisfied with the spirit's answers or do not believe the me-dium, they turn to another one and seek out another spirit. Just as the spirit is not tied to one place and one medium, so people do not feel themselves obliged to seek help and information from one single spirit. Generally people turn to the *basangu* spirits only in desperate cases. The Tonga do not like to be watched over much, either by elders or by spirits.

Masabe possession is quite different in character. While the *basangu* seances take place only in small circles, *masabe* possession has an exclu-sively public character. People want to know the spirit's wishes, because they want to control ist manifestations in the future. Possession can take place spontaneously. It is always linked with a dance. First of all, the medium 'dances' his or her spirit in the circle of members of the family, then outside in a larger circle. The dance must take place three times within the family. On the day after the first dance, the medium is well cared for; a chicken is slaughtered specially. During the second dance, the names must be mentioned which have 'transmitted' the spirit. It is only after the third dance that the medium receives the clothes appropriate to the colours and appearance of the spirit. In 1954 the 'aeroplane spirit' manifested itself for the first time when an aeroplane flew over the village. It took possession of a girl, who fled into the bush as if stunned and had to be dragged back by the inhabitants of the village. She learnt the spirit's demands in dreams and visions, the drum rhythm, the dance steps, the drama, which had to be presented during the intervals of the dance, and also the items which the spirit wanted for itself, and finally plants for medical treatment. At the first aeroplane dance, the medium was both patient and instructor. She taught the drummers, dancers and choir. After ist first performance, the aeroplane dance spread very quickly. More often than not, when an aeroplane flew over the village it unleashed further possession dances. At first the girl was fetched to teach the dance, but soon so many could do it that her presence was no longer necessary. The phase of possession was then at ist height; after that it died down, to be replaced by other phenomena and dances.

The spirit, *umuuya*, can transfer from one medium to another who is then contagious and can cause a further possession. That is regarded as simple, but acceptable, magic, because the spirit causes no permanent harm to anyone. Women are said to be more vulnerable, because in their hearts they harbour more resentment and evil intentions than men. The reason for the possession is communicated in a state of trance. Often there are only trivial motives: the other woman has not been helpful and has neglected her guests. Relatives are understandably often the victims of such contagion. Since healing can only take place through dancing, medicine and gifts, it is an expensive affair. During this time, the medium occupies the centre of attention.

The person has to show great ability to dance, because the dramatic imitation of various animals, objects and people requires a high degree of empathy and talent, even when the dancing takes place in a trance. The spectators are able to judge the ability and enjoy the performance as entertainment, even if the danger of contagion is always under the surface. Most women are possessed by a spirit at least once in their lives, and many of them make a career out of it, becoming possessed with the appearance of every new spirit.

The phenomenon of possession is understandable in terms of social psychology. In small societies mass psychotic movements are outlets for the release of tension in times of social change. The Tonga are thoroughly aware

140

of these connections. They point out that women are particularly open to possession after marital strife or a quarrel with neighbours. They begin to brood, which makes people 'hot', the first symptom. Yet social tensions are not the only cause of possession. Research has shown that spirit possession likewise affects people who are mentally healthy and respected within their society. The heart of spirit possession will be made clear by compiling a list of the types of spirits who have called forth possession dances. The following possession dances were collected.

There are *masabe* which are named after *animals.*

Sokwe	Baboon
Ceta	Monkey
Inzovu	Elephant
Mwaba	Jackal
Bashumbwa	Lion
Ingulube	Pig – all known before 1940

Named after a *tribe.*

Manyai	Banyai
Manyoni	Ndebele
Mazungu	Europeans – before 1940 except for the Ndebele

Status or *occupation.*

Mapolis	Policemen
Maregimenti	Soldiers
Madyabantu	Cannibals – before 1940, except the last two

Means of transport

Citima	Train
Incinga	Bicycle – known before 1940
Indeki	Aeroplane
Kanamenda	Motor boat
Kandimu	Ship's motor

Symbolic acts

Impande	Mussel ornament
Pumpi	Pump – known before 1940
Guitar	Guitar

Madance	European dance
Cilimba	Accordion

Spirits

Bamooba	Spirit of the bush
Mangelo	Angel
Cannibal spirit	Visitors from Kenya with fat stomachs

Through spirit possession the new and unusual breaks into a society. At first every new thing threatens the balance of power in a small-scale society. Possession is mastered through the dance and so robbed of its danger. Whatever breaks in from outside is modified through possession and incorporated into the society and its life-style. Spirit possession and the public dance which follows it are the means of overcoming what is new. The ritual encounter internalises what is external. People do not remain passive, invaded and attacked; they lead the dance. Possession activates people to accept something new. They enter into dialogue with it. The phenomenon is personalised, becomes negotiable and assumes a social form.

The Mende in Sierra Leone have another form of spirit veneration.[184] Here it is not the exceptional that leads to awareness of spirits. Instead it is return of events and the familiar environment. For the Mende, God is far off but the ancestors and spirits are near. The concept of God is vague. The spirits are as real as natural phenomena. In Upper Mendeland the local river regularly breaks its banks in September. The diviners interpret this as a warning. The bad morals of the villagers have angered the spirit of the river. It will flood the whole country unless placated. And so a day is announced for the festival of reconciliation. Usually this is fixed for the time when there is enough rice, at the end of September. Everybody contributes to the organisation, bringing sheep, chickens, fish, palm oil and salt. Cooking utensils are carried under cover of night to the place where the spirit lives, usually under trees and beside large rocks in the upper course of the river. Certain taboos must be observed. You must not cross the river, otherwise the sacrifice will

---

[184] For what follows, cf. K. Little, 1963, pp.111–137, especially pp.126ff.

not be accepted. The men take over the cooking. Double portions are cooked, one of everything for the spirit. Its presence is confirmed by questioning. If the omens are favourable, the people return home happy after completing the sacrifice, in the knowledge that the river will retreat and once more occupy its normal bed. The spirit is placated. If there is an unfavourable answer to the questions, the sacrifice has to be repeated after a while.

While appeasing the river god is a completely communal affair, the sacrifices that are brought to the *dyinying* (cf. Arabic djin), or *genii*, are private in character. The genii appear in human shape, and are regarded as white-skinned. They are naturally good-natured, but it is better not to get too involved with them. They need a firm hand. Anyone losing control of the situation will have to serve them or sacrifice something very dear – even a child.

Among the Mende, and this is typical, encountering such spirits can actually have its comical side, so that people enjoy telling stories about the spirits' pranks.[185] There are precise rules on how to act if they surprise you on a lonely path. This type of belief in spirits is marked by unexpected events, and the kind of personal contact that does not affect society.

K. Little points out that these rules imply their own ethical ideal. Their bargain with the spirits reflects the Mende's own values: open-handed generosity, discretion in private matters, and calmness in difficult situations. Being smart is a good thing, and women are expected to be tough and cunning both in trade and love.

The example of the Mende expands the picture of belief in spirits given by the Tonga in two important aspects. It can develop the imagination, rooted in that narrow borderline between the comical and deadly danger. Both can be accommodated in the belief in spirits. This belief activates people and helps them to resist threats. Where they can conquer or outwit the spirits they feel more alive, and where they can make use of spirit powers village life becomes easier.

---

[185] Cf. the stories of the Pondo in M. Hunter, 1969, pp.276ff.

The daily threat from nature which faces every African is personalised in their encounter with spirits. Nature is not understood in the physical and biological sense, i. e. as morally neutral, but as a force to be reckoned with. Natural phenomena are experienced as a spiritual power which impinges on people, leaving them fascinated and spell-bound, and – at the same time – appalled and terrified. It is therefore no coincidence that both J. S. Mbiti and E. B. Idowu, in their presentation of African religions, begin their description of belief in spirits by recounting their own experiences, to demonstrate the feeling of being at the mercy of natural phenomena.[186]

Belief in spirits is not only concerned with fleeting phenomena, but with the environment and material things. A place communicates with people through itself, not only through events that take place there, e. g. a river which overflows its bed, or the unusual stones and trees which give a place a unique atmosphere. 'Atmosphere' is a poetic concept for Westerners. In Africa, however, natural phenomena are forces to be reckoned with. They profoundly affect relations with the world *around* us (our 'environment' = German *Umwelt*), for which English lacks a word to describe, in the African sense, as the world *with* us (German *Mitwelt*), i. e. the world with which people live in a symbiotic relationship.[187]

When the Chagga on Kilimanjaro in Tanzania build beehives, a lengthy ritual involves forging iron for axes, to fell trees, and knives, to strip off hides. The whole family is involved, the women being specially careful to settle every argument. Every woman declares: "If I had any anger for any cause whatever, it is over and there is peace once more... Iron, grant us children and animals; axe, grant us beehives to feed our children".

One of the trees to be felled, of a type which is found only in the Chagga area, is called the 'sister' of the man who owns the land on which it stands. The felling of this enormous tree is prepared like a wedding. On the day before, the land-owner goes to the foot of the tree with milk, beer, honey

---

[186] Cf. J. S. Mbiti, 1974, pp.81, 86f.; E. B. Idowu, 1973, p. 133.
[187] Cf. K. M. Meyer-Abich: Wege zum Frieden mit der Natur, 1984; especially pp.245ff.; for the following topic, cf. B. Gutmann, Die Imkerei bei den Dschagga, Archiv für Anthropologie, 1922, pp.8f.

and other gifts: "'*Mana mfu*', (daughter of my sister), I give you a husband to marry you, my daughter!... do not believe that I drive you to it, but you are now grown up... May all go well with you, my child". When the tree is felled the next day, the owner is not present; it would be too painful for him and would insult the tree. After a detailed ritual, involving libations, the leader of the work-party himself strikes the first blow with these words: "You, child of a man, we are not cutting you down, but are marrying you! And we are not marrying you with despotic force, but with gentleness and goodness". Later the land-owner comes back, sees the fallen tree, and breaks out in weeping and lamentation: "You have robbed me of my sister". Finally he allows himself to be consoled, and peace is restored.

People talk to the tools and the trees, especially to the tree in which the bee-drums are hung. They relate what they are doing, often cloaked in metaphorical language, and ask the trees for protection and blessing. These are not magical incantations, as has often been alleged in the literature. Words accompany the actions, because a relationship of communication exists. People live in close association for protection. This must not be destroyed 'in cold blood'. Through rituals people adapt to the totality of events, in which there is no division between the human protagonist and the material object. Instead, everyone has their place in the closely woven fabric of life, and must take care that this is not torn through their own action. That would bring misfortune for the environment and for humans. Why? Because they would have destroyed their own past with cold, heartless action, and drawn upon themselves the anger not only of the trees, but also of the ancestors, who felled trees and collected honey in the same way. In these rituals the past is restored, and with it the fertility of the land. The growth of the new trees is made possible. Life is a unity. Even if there is a hierarchy of life forces, the whole biological world is bound together osmotically in a special way. Destroying these links unilaterally would have fatal consequences.

These rituals, and others dedicated to belief in spirits, express reverence for all life. It would, however, be false to link this reverence with romantic feeling. The ritual does not protect the tree as an individual. It is felled. However, this fundamental attitude does not permit the domination of nature. A senseless clearing of the forests for the sake of gain, a senseless extermination of animal species just to satisfy a passion for hunting, is unthinkable. This is only possible through 'demythologising' the environment and dethroning the spirits of nature by the god Mammon and his accomplice, greed.

Belief in spirits represents one aspect of how Africans relate to nature. So far as I can tell, this contains no sign of understanding the world as creation. It is just that people see themselves as being at the mercy of environmental forces, and have some how to cope with them.

In Tanzania I bought a Makonde relief. Two men are sitting on the ground, one smoking peacefully, the other cowering in fear. Above, beside and between them, float spirits, big and small, horrible in their distortions; although lightly sketched they are still recognisable as human beings. The picture is a graphic representation of belief in spirits: this is how people see themselves, abandoned to the powers of the world, threatened and protected, questioned and affirmed. The ambivalence of their feelings is the subject of the relief. Belief in spirits shows up the dangers, and at the same time makes the world inhabitable. People know that the supernatural reveals itself in smaller powers. These are subject to a greater power. This is why people can put up with them.

Theories about the belief in spirits

In descriptions of 'primitive' religions, belief in spirits was said to have been replaced by science. Even though we have today become more cautious in our judgements, this aspect of traditional religion is still the one which is least understood. At best it is regarded as a kind of transition between a religion linked to nature and the religion introduced by the prophets. Nathan Söderblom was typical of this attitude.[188] "In the impersonal power of the *mana* type the idea dawns that the divine penetrates the whole world, and that it is supernatural in character. Belief in the soul and in spirits begins to recognise the existence of the mind, more accurately characterised as the realm of the will, firstly of ill-tempered and capricious individuals, but later, through the prophets or other religious and ethical achievements, of more reasonable beings or organisations acting on the basis of internal laws". This proposition, dubbed 'brilliant' by G. v. d. Leeuw, is to be examined as a representative of this type of judgement.[189] Söderblom maintained: 1. There exists an idea of an impersonal power, exercised over everything (= *mana*). 2. It points to the divine, which penetrates everything. 3. The transition from the first to the second stage is determined historically; over time belief in *mana* becomes belief in spirits, and ultimately belief in God. 4. This takes place under the influence of the prophets. 5. Belief in *mana* is the first stage; belief in spirits the second stage; belief in God the third stage. 6. Belief in spirits is characterised as the realm of the capricious, inhabited at best by 'individuals'. The term 'person' is not appropriate, since it only belongs to the third stage.

This set of propositions is wrong in nearly every respect.

1. *Mana* does not describe an impersonal power. Codrington, with whom the term originated, understood it in a different sense.

2. The history of African religions does not show that belief in God emerged from belief in spirits. The contrary is true: because people know God and understand him as spirit, they can integrate belief in spirits. This can be seen most clearly in the religious history of the Nuer. It is not the prophets who overcome belief in spirits through moral preaching, and replace it through belief in one God possessing a moral will. Belief in spirits has always and everywhere had to do with the moral ideas of the particular people in question. This applies equally to veneration of the ancestors and spirits: they punish and reward, they oversee relations between the society and the individual.

3. Söderblom has rightly seen that there is a certain element of caprice in the spirits' actions, but it must be immediately added that their victims by no means regard this in the same way. E. E. Evans-Pritchard says very clearly: "To the European observer, they seem to be greedy, capricious, and hostile, but this is not how they appear to the Nuer... They are jealous spirits who demand tribute from their votaries. The Nuer fear them but they do not feel resentful so much as guilty when they bring sickness upon them. They recognise that an angry spirit generally has right on its side, and they seek to make amends so that it will cease to trouble them; and in making amends through sacrifice a bargain is struck in a much cruder and more human way than when a sacrifice is made to God".[190]

4. E. E. Evans-Pritchard rightly raised the concept of guilt feelings. This is an important motive for the strength of belief in ancestors and spirits. It often seems that the spirit (or the ancestor) functions like the long arm of conscience. Whenever misfortune occurs, the

---

[188] N. Söderblom, Gudstrons Uppkomst, 2nd ed. Stockholm, 1914. [Quoted here from German trans.: Das Werden des Gottesglaubens, 2nd ed. 1926, p. 283.]

[189] G. van der Leeuw, 1956, p. 84.

[190] E. E. Evans-Pritchard, 1967, p. 51.

question of guilt arises: Where have I gone wrong? How have I neglected the ancestors, etc.? Belief in spirits does not so much incorporate the irrational as make sense of irrational happenings. It is the sense within the capricious. A way of explaining life, this belief is based upon the moral conscience of humankind.

5. Finally, the concept of spirit in the quotation from Söderblom must be questioned, and also the relationship between 'supernatural' and 'natural'. Spirit is not an ontological dimension, existing for itself, before and over above matter, but something inherent in existence and essentially linked to it. As we have seen, spirit must not be understood as something invisible. It is not defined in contrast to the body, like the supernatural in contrast to the natural; it is not idea in contrast to matter. The spirits are in and with nature, in and with the corporeal. They are manifested in this, and are understood anthropomorphically. The special and individual quality of African religions lies in this: that the spirits are understood in terms of personal morals, and so make the world negotiable. Ultimately, people experience themselves in the spirit which is manifest in nature, animals, and so-called inanimate objects, if they have a bad conscience and are striving for good fortune and security. J. V. Taylor speaks in a nice turn of phrase of the 'centrifugal self', and quotes a Twi proverb: "The human spirit is without limits".[191] This should not be taken to mean that belief in the soul and spirits is merely a projection of the inner world of human experience. We would not seek to trivialise African belief through such interpretations. The concept of the existential can help here, since it makes two things clear at the same time: it has to do with comprehensive structures and phenomena which go far beyond the self, and at the same time with real areas of human experience. People are at the mercy of everything they experience as being the world of spirits, but it exists for them only at that particular moment. If people forget the spirits, they are irrelevant, and ultimately non-existent. Belief in spirits is concerned with the reality of experience, not with ontology.

4. Uncontained and Unconditional

The divinities

The boundaries between spirit beings and divinities are not fixed. It is not easy to draw a clear distinction. Many authors change from one expres-

---

[191] J. V. Taylor, 1965, chap. 5.

sion to the other within a single chapter.[192] E. E. Evans-Pritchard speaks of spirits among the Nuer, while G. Lienhardt describes the same subject among the neighbouring Dinka as 'free divinities'. I would see the distinction in the following terms: divinities are nearer to God and have a wider sphere of effectiveness than spirits. They have qualities which major religions attribute to the one God. At the same time, they dwell further away from the earth than spirits do. The spirits' home is always the earth; that of the divinities, even if in varying degrees, is predominantly heaven. However, there are also earth divinities.

Let us turn to the Nuer in Southern Sudan. They say that originally they knew only God and people. They learnt of the existence of 'divinities/spirits' from the Dinka. (This justifies our dealing with their idea of spirits in this chapter.) God is spirit. That is the most important thing that the Nuer have to say about him.[193] He is the omnipresent creator and father of all his children. There are no ancestors between him and humankind, as in most African religions. The Nuer have no belief in ancestors. The space between God and humankind is filled by the divinities/spirits, which people have gradually come to know. The most important divinity is *Deng*. He 'fell' from heaven and was called *Deng kwoth*, son of God. He causes sickness and stands for what is alien. His mother, *Buk*, is a female divinity and, like her two daughters, is associated with rivers and water. The first fruits are brought to them on the bank of a river. They are honoured by the pouring of libations. God is said to have taken the two daughters and placed them in the water, where they turned into spirits. How do *Deng*, who belongs to air, and *Buk*, who is associated with the river and water, i. e. to the material side, fit together? The Nuer say the divinity is in the air as spirit, but in rivers and streams as matter. Heaven and earth cannot be separated.

The Nuer have a series of divinities; many names come from the Dinka and were forgotten; they have had no wide-reaching significance or efficacy.

---

[192] Cf. Parrinder, 1961, chap. 4.
[193] For what follows, cf. E. E. Evans-Pritchard, 1967, chaps. 2 & 3.

A relationship with the divinities comes about through possession and through heredity. The divinity takes possession of individuals like a sudden illness. After being healed, they know that they are bound to this divinity. Their children inherit this bond. If they struggle against it, the same sickness can suddenly strike one of their descendants. The divinity appears and influences people in this way. This applies particularly to those called to be prophets. The divinity is everywhere. Wherever there are people, there is the divinity. People cannot get away. They are surrounded on all sides.

"A man who wants to escape the Deng,
Will find Deng in front of him.
He will find Deng on his left,
He will find Deng behind him".

Cattle are another medium of communication with the divinity. A cow is dedicated to it, and ashes are rubbed into the back of the chosen beast. A similar procedure takes place in reconciliation sacrifices, identifying the animal with the divinity. A consecrated cow is fitted with a metal ring, so that everybody can recognise its special status. It must not be sold, or slaughtered. If it dies, it must be replaced. If the cow calves, a male calf is sacrificed to the divinity, whereas a female calf serves as a bride price. However, the divinity must be informed in advance of this change of purpose.

A festival is held after harvest-time to honour the divinity, bringing together the whole family. A large quantity of beer is brewed. Normally an ox is slaughtered. However, the divinity can inform the family through a medium that something smaller will do, e. g. 'just' beer. Some beer is poured over the stake to which the consecrated cow is tied. Various members of the family perform this libation. Everybody takes some beer in their hand and flings it in the air. Then they sit down and drink the rest of the beer. Family matters are discussed. It is expected that anybody who has a grudge of any sort against another member of the family will speak out on this occasion. They can, in fact must, mention any injustice committed against somebody else. They should express their feelings and say when they feel insulted or overlooked. In this way, all problems and tensions come out into the open and can be dealt with. Anything which is not mentioned now must not be brought up in the future. The Nuer say that on this occasion evil is driven out of the heart. Throwing the beer into the air is the symbolical representation of this process. "All evil is laden on the cow", they say. All those taking part take ashes and rub them into the cow's back, which is afterwards cleansed with beer.

The divinity has a firm hold on the life of people, giving them life, which is why there exists a close link between them. This is seen most clearly in sacrifice: the life of animals for human life. People are dependent on the divinity and on a harmonious relationship because this is the only way in which harmony, and that means peace, can be maintained within the family.

The following song expresses the dependence and gratitude of the people. It is sung during mourning rituals, but also when setting out to fish and on other occasions.

"Mother of *deng*, the ants (i. e. the Nuer) ransom their lives from thee,
Mother of *dengkur*, the ants ransom their lives from thee,
The mother of *dengkur* brings life,
The mother of *dengkur* brings me life,
Life is revived.
She brings life and our children play,
They cry aloud with joy,
With the life of the mother of *deng*, with the life of the mother of *deng*.
The pied crows (= *buk*) are given life and are filled.
Our speech is good, we and *buk*,
Our speech is excellent;
The country of the people is good,
We journey on the path of the *pake*.
(Derived from the Arabic word *faki*, a fakir or holy man, but used in Nuer for a merchant.)
We are here, we and *buk deng*,
Buk, mother of *deng*, the ants ransom their lives from thee,
Mother of *deng*, the ants ransom their lives from thee.
We give thee red blood.

The ants of *deng* are simple people, they do not understand how their lives are supported ..".[194]

The Nuer give a great deal of thought to the relation between the divinity and God. We are told that the divinities are called the children of God. This is a metaphorical way of speaking and indicates that they belong to God's world. They come from him and 'fall' upon mankind. They are spirit, but are thought of in more anthropomorphic terms than God. Their nature is different from God's. God is purely good, but the spirits are touchy. They can get angry and they demand more attention from humankind than God does. When the divinities punish, they are always in the right, according to Nuer ideas. They have good reasons for being angry. You can bargain with them, but not with God. You can put them off, in the knowledge that they can wait and (for the time being) take the intention for the deed. It is possible to speak with them in a personal way, which no-one would dare to do with God.

Even though the divinities are not like God, God is involved in appeals to them. As spirit, they are close to him and have access to him. They are 'images' of God, as E. E. Evans-Pritchard puts it, hypostases of God's various qualities. Divinities differ among themselves, but they have one thing in common: they are spirit, they are God. God appears in them in various modalities. God hypostasises himself in them.[195]

Let us now turn to West Africa. It is natural for peoples who have a long and varied political history that the different forms of contact between peoples, whether warlike or friendly, (e. g. trade, migration) should lead to the superimposition of religious ideas and selective integration. This makes it difficult to reduce their ideas to a system, all the more so since African religions are concerned with experiences, not with articles of faith.

---

[194] Ibid., p. 46.

[195] The Nuer have two further categories of spirits: the 'spirits from below', and hobgoblins, who are associated with medicine and fetishes. The Nuer show little respect for either group. They are so strongly connected with matter and with certain objects that they should rather be regarded as belonging to the kinds of spirits that were discussed in the previous chapter.

The range of divinities and their relation to the one God are well expressed in the following Yoruba myth from Nigeria:

"The one thousand seven hundred divinities conspired against Olódùmarè [the highest God of the Yoruba], and decided that he must abdicate power and authority. They went before him and demanded that he should hand over power to them, at least for an experimental period of sixteen years. Olódùmarè suggested to them that it might be wise for them to experiment for sixteen days in the first instance. This suggestion they joyfully accepted. Olódùmarè then told them the world was theirs to run the way they chose for that period of sixteen days. They immediately set about their task. But after only eight days they discovered that things had gone wrong – that the machinery of the universe was, in fact, at a standstill.

They devised every means they could think of to keep things going – but made no headway; they adopted all the tactics they knew but failed; the heaven withheld its rains; rivers ceased to flow; rivulets became glutted with fallen leaves; yams sprouted but did not develop; the ears of corn filled but did not ripen; the juice of trees was licked to quench thirst; Orúlìmà was consulted but his oracle was dumb and the appliances of divination refused to work; the daily feasting in the houses of the divinities stopped; the whole world was certainly going to perish! The divinities thus found themselves at their wits' end. There was nothing else they could do but to go back to Olódùmarè. And so, in shame, and with drooping heads, they went back to Him and confessed their folly, acknowledging His absolute sovereignty and supremacy over all, and pleading for mercy. The Benevolent Father laughed at their foolishness and forgave them. Then He switched on again the machinery of the universe and it immediately resumed normal running. The divinities went away singing:

Be there one thousand four hundred divinities of the home;
Be there one thousand two hundred divinities of the market-place,
Yet there is not one divinity to compare with Olódùmarè:
Olódùmarè is the King Unique.
In our recent dispute,
Édùmàrè it is who won.
Yes, Édùmàrè".[196]

---

[196] Quoted by E. B. Idowu, 1973, p. 159.

This myth is not only concerned with the relationship of the divinities to God, but also with the world and the risk of getting lost in it or of no longer being able to cope. The myth is a mirror of Yoruba society, which is becoming ever more complex as it grows. How can a society continue to function, when an individual can only get to deal with a small part of the administration? How can the totality of the world continue to function, if an individual turns to only one of the many divinities, or knows very few of them? The new, large societies offer people a range of choices for changing their space, i. e. their place of residence or work, so that they continually enter into new dimensions of the world and feel homeless. How can they find certainty there? The myth has burst the barriers of the small community and considers the problems of a large society. While this is not its full meaning, this aspect must not be overlooked.

The correspondence between myth and society can also be established among the Fon people in Benin (Dahomey). "Dahomean culture is based on control by an officialdom, which, under the monarch, was of an essentially hierarchical character similar to that ascribed to the gods... and just as each principal chief who governed a region had minor chiefs under his direction who were responsible to him, so each pantheon-head has minor deities under his control who are responsible to him".[197]

Mawu-Lisa, the twofold divinity (Mawu = feminine, is subject to the moon; Lisa = masculine, is subject to the sun), created the world through a power which is called *da*. This power could be called the first created thing, but sometimes it functions as an impersonal power, which has been eternally coexistent with God from earlier creations, and which is needed as an instrument by Mawu-Lisa. Creation really means 'ordering' the world; earth and water must be gathered together so that they can grow together in an orderly fashion. The power which makes this possible is *da*, which manifests itself in the rainbow. The rainbow (in Fon the word also means 'snake') encircled the earth and squeezed it together. This is how the earth originated. "The rainbow

---

[197] M. J. Herskovits, quoted by P. Mercier, 1963, p. 233. For what follows, cf. op. cit., pp.210ff.

gave us life", they say. It still encircles the earth, holds it firm, and gives it permanence. Mawu-Lisa led *da* over the whole earth. Wherever it came, life arose. Like Mawu-Lisa, *da* itself is understood as a two-fold divinity, or as a divinity in two modalities. In the rainbow, the colour red stands for masculinity and its power, blue for femininity. With its 3,500 coils, *da* holds the earth below, and with its 3,500 coils in the other direction, the heaven above. The coils are not fixed, but they change and move. *Da* circles around the earth and moves the heavenly bodies. Life is movement. Even the sea receives its movement and life from this source. *Da* is the greatest power that humankind can imagine, ceaseless movement. But it is subordinate to Mawu-Lisa, because movement is subordinate to life: "*Mawu-Lisa* is thought, *da* is life".

Among the Fon's pantheon there are the Vodu, Mawu-Lisa's children. Their function is not to participate in creation, but to maintain it. They help, they rule. Their power is great, their punishments are feared, which is why respect towards them often takes first place. The most popular divinities in the pantheon are *Heyvoso* (Sogbo) and *Sapata*. Sogbo rules over phenomena within the atmosphere; his weapon is thunder. Sapata rules over the earth; his weapon is smallpox.

Sapata has the greatest number of devotees among the Yoruba, and is called 'King of the earth'. A day of the week is named after him. On this day work in the fields is not allowed. This day has become market day. This divinity has his own priesthood to serve him.

The continually growing knowledge of the world is reflected in corresponding special functions of the Vodu. This leads to a hierarchy of the divinities. Vodu genealogies arose with each different language, so that individual groups can no longer understand each other.

Fon cosmogony acknowledges the task of maintaining the world, as well as the act of creation. In the first act, *da* was the right hand of the creator; in the second, it is *gu*. Living in the world is part of the process of maintaining it. *Da* is the power which all the Vodu use. It guarantees continuity, and is the servant of all. It does nothing by itself, but without it nothing can be achieved.

The world of fate is also represented in the pantheon by a divinity, by *Fa*, the hypostasis of the word, *Mawu*. The fate of humankind is fixed. It can be experienced in symbols.

There is one divinity, however, who can cut through fate, namely *LEgba*. He is full of tricks, is moody, and teasing – the opposite of the strict divinity *Fa*. It is not a matter of chance that Christian missionaries used him to describe the Devil. This, however, is a one-sided interpretation and a false portrayal of his character. He is both good and evil, he can both protect life and make it difficult, particularly for those who are not reconciled to him.

A picture of LEgba, a wild dog, is found outside many villages and houses. It is hoped that he will not bite the hand that feeds him. However, he will attack the stranger and enemy. His gaze is always directed outwards, never towards the house. Since he is supposed to provide assistance, people also like to call him 'Father'. Among the Yoruba he is venerated under the name of Eshu. He is said to have 200 names altogether.[198] He plays the role of a demon, without being demonic. He represents the unpredictable, malicious, unreasonable evil in the world.

This divinity does not possess his own priesthood, unlike other divinities. Similarly he has no 'school for priests', in which his adherents are trained. LEgba is a messenger between the divinities, and between humans and divinities, which is why the priests of all the divinities serve him.

Attention should be drawn to one peculiarity of the structure of the pantheon: its complementarity or duality. The powers of heaven and earth, of good and evil, of the masculine and feminine, are each expanded and complemented in their respective opposite number. The King is one, complementarity becomes unity in him, but in holding court and in administering justice, etc. the principle of duality reigns. Indeed it stands for completeness, totality. So the one God Mawu-Lisa contains the two poles of life. She/he is one, but the lower divinities have different, polarised tasks. "Two guard the property of their father, Lisa, whose domain is the sun; two play the same role for their mother, Mawu, who lives in the moon; one is the protector of

---

[198] Cf. G. Parrinder, 1961, pp.56ff.

156

trees, one the goddess of the hearth. In the pantheon of the earth one divinity cares for drinking water, one is the messenger of her father and inflicts illness upon people, one watches over the fields, one spreads sunlight over the growing corn..".[199]

"Polytheism is a qualitative and not a quantitative concept. It is not the belief in a plurality of gods, but rather the lack of a uniting and transcending ultimate which determines its character", says Paul Tillich.[200] African religions confirm the truth of the first of these propositions. Whether Africans, however, lack the ability to conceive of 'the One' will be discussed below. At this point we must establish that it is the multiplicity of experiences of the world which leads to belief in the multiplicity of spirits and divinities. People see themselves as exposed to the thousand faces of the world. Because they do not encounter the world in a rational and objective way, but create personal relationships, the reality of the world has to be reflected in the belief in gods and spirits. The experience of society cannot be separated from the experience of nature. This applies to belief in the ancestors within the family circle, and also to the belief in spirits and divinities in the larger society and in the cosmos.

In order to grasp the idea of spirits within primal societies, the term the 'soul outside' has been used.[201] I have not used this term so far, because it seems too vague and possibly misleading. However, it does express one aspect accurately, the 'ex-centricity' of humankind. People are essentially directed towards the other thing or being which exists outside themselves, yet they remain with themselves when they are with the other.[202] Humans experience this essentially in the polarity of sexuality and their own bodies. They discover this to be the structual principle of the cosmos, which then becomes a home. They can identify with the cosmos, and can cope with it.

---

[199] M. J. Herskovits, quoted by P. Mercier, 1963, p. 233.

[200] P. Tillich, Systematic theology, 1968, vol. 1, p. 246.

[201] G. van der Leeuw, 1956, para. 42.

[202] This should not be understood as meaning humans, animals or natural phenomena are all 'kindred spirits'. Analogous participation means something different.

African religions are not 'nature religions' in the strict sense of the word. Nowhere in Africa is there worship of natural phenomena. People do not offer themselves up to them in prayer and adoration; they feel they are at the mercy of nature. People are so small and insignificant that they can describe themselves as 'ants' in comparison. Yet they are something more, because they can address the external world as a personal 'opposite number', as a spirit, or a divinity. People can influence them, because they influence people. They fall upon, and into people. They take on shape, form and being, through being named. Blind fate is not in control. The dense web of life can be given shape. Libation and sacrifice have no other purpose than to express participation in visible form. Admittedly, the divinities are not dependent upon people in the same sense as are the ancestors. Their greater sphere of activity makes such an idea impossible. However, they are also directed towards humankind, in so far as they are not in themselves the ultimate. They represent parts of life, never the whole. The divinities are a means to an end, never the end itself.[203] They have many names, but there is one common one: they are spirit.[204]

A final aspect, not yet mentioned, underlines the 'ex-centricity' of humankind, as expressed in belief in spirits and in the idea of the divinities: death is not seen as a personal opponent. There is no spirit dedicated to death, and no divinity of death. If people could address death, they would no longer be with themselves, they would not transcend themselves, but would lose themselves. In the same way there is no spirit or divinity representing evil. There is no devil in African religions.[205] Any form of dualism is alien to them. Admittedly, LEgba among the Fon and Marcadit among the Dinka have certain aspects of evil, but they are closely interwoven with positive functions. In African religions no absolute power is ascribed to evil. Evil does not come from outside, but from people themselves. It is they who pervert things and that is why evil can be overcome. Life (which is good) is

---

[203] Cf. E. B. Idowu, 1973, pp.168ff.
[204] G. Lienhardt, 1967, p. 56.

stronger. In spite of their profound knowledge of the dangers and risks in life, African religions are fundamentally optimistic.

The all-embracing God

There was a time when researchers thought that there were ethnic groups in Africa with no concept of God. Today, African historians and theologians, in particular, vigorously claim the opposite. Africa has not just had a vague knowledge of God: the foundation of African religions is monotheism, albeit in a diffuse form. E. B. Idowu and, above all, J. S. Mbiti have attempted to present the African belief in God, making it compatible with Christianity. Mbiti uses a scholastic approach for his presentation of the history of religion. He tells us something of the nature of God, of his eternal, intrinsic and moral properties. We learn that God is 'omniscient', 'omnipresent', 'omnipotent', 'transcendent', and 'immanent'. He 'is of himself', he 'antedates' all things, he is 'fathomless', he is 'spirit', 'invisible', 'pre-eminent', and 'everlasting'. Material from more than 360 peoples was collected for each of these terms. Mbiti has produced indispensable reference works with a great deal of information about the many-facetted way Africans imagine the greatness of God.

In the following, however, we are concerned with something different, and it is the subject of this book. What has religion, or belief in God, to say about Africans? How do they experience that reality which we call 'God', and for which they have many names? The many difficulties in answering this question start with terminology. African religions have no 'name' for 'God', in the strict sense of the word. An expression of foreign origin whose meaning is no longer known is often used, e. g. Njambi, Nzambi, etc. Just as a Roman never knew the real meaning of '*deus*', or the average American or Australian cannot explain the meaning of the word 'God', Africans do not know what the various names for God mean. This does not rule out enlisting the aid of lexical associations and popular explanations, which may make

---

[205] The idea of a 'black God' (Wele Gumali) is the exception to prove the rule; cf.

sense; but in the final analysis they say little or nothing about the original meaning.[206] Thus a traditional name can become an epithet, which expresses experience. For the most part, however, little interest is shown in such interpretations, because it is improper to name God. Naming somebody is an act of domination. For this reason, many African peoples use an archaic term of unknown origin, which has often been taken from other languages. In Africa too, archaic and remote language give extra dignity to the concept of God. It is no accident that God's name was made taboo. Circumlocutions and idiomatic expressions were used, as in ancient Israel. Thus attributes became names. One result of making the names taboo was that sometimes the first missionaries, after spending years with a people, studying and writing down its language, never heard the term for God, and so introduced a non-African, biblical name, or picked a wrong one.[207] Making the name taboo does not mean suppressing the idea of God, nor that God is replaced by divinities or ancestors; it intensifies the awareness of God. Anything that is taboo makes a specially strong impression on people. It cannot be forgotten. However, there is a danger that in the course of time it may become peripheral in people's awareness.

I will illustrate this with a small personal experience. On a car journey a Herero student and I were talking about traditional religion, and I asked him about the meaning of the term for God, 'Njambi'. He became considerably embarrassed so I changed the subject, after a while asking him what was wrong with my question. "I grew up with my very pious grandmother, and was brought up in the Christian faith. However, this (pagan) name for God was so holy to us, that we could never use it. If we did, we were heavily punished. And now I find myself here sitting next to a white man and he uses this old Herero name for God as if it were of no significance!" After three or four generations the name is still significant and able to instil fear, thanks to the taboo. The first missionaries did not hear this name, and placed a peripheral,

---

G. Wagner, 1939, p. 218.

[206] On the Nzambi and the Nyambe, cf. E. W. Smith, 1961, pp.156f.; on the Mulungu, ibid., pp.58ff.; on the Leza, cf. ibid., pp.75ff.

[207] Cf. T. Sundermeier, 1973a, pp.149ff.

or even an incorrect, name at the centre of the new faith, a mistake which could not be corrected later. If God's name is not used, this should not be taken as a sign that the idea of God has lost its significance.

Dietrich Westermann once said that in Africa God is understood as un-defined and remote.[208] This assertion may refer to a wide-spread myth, to be found in varying forms in many peoples in Africa.[209] Whether this interpreta-tion is correct, remains to be seen. Here is the Giziga version from North Cameroon.

"Once upon a time heaven was close to the earth. God lived among men. Heaven was so close that men could only move about bent over. They did not have to worry about food. They only had to stretch out their hand, and break off pieces of Heaven to eat.

One day, however, a young girl, the daughter of a chief, a *mukuwan*, (a naughty child, who does everything wrong, and does the opposite of what others do), looked at the earth, and, instead of breaking off pieces of Heaven to feed herself, took the grains which she found. She made a pestle and mortar for herself in order to pound the grains which she had picked up from the ground. While pounding, she knelt on the ground, but when she lifted up the pestle it struck against Heaven and against God. As she felt annoyed while working, the girl said to Heaven: 'God, can you not move a little further away?'

Heaven moved further away, and the girl could stand more upright. She carried on with her work, but the longer she pounded the grains, the higher she raised the pestle. She complained against Heaven for a second time. Once more Heaven moved further away. Finally, she began to raise her pestle high in the air. The third time she complained, Heaven, feeling hurt, moved far away, to where it now is.

Since this time men can stand and move about upright. They no longer feed them-selves with pieces of Heaven, but millet has become their food. God no longer comes among men as he once did, when he led their palaver every evening. Now men are alone in their palaver; there is war".[210]

This story about the origin of death exists in different versions:

[208] D. Westermann, Africa and Christianity, 1937, pp.65f., quoted by E. B. Idowu, 1973, p. 171.
[209] H. Baumann, 1936, pp.327f. gives further examples.
[210] Quoted by L. V. Thomas & R. Luneau, 1975, p. 136; for the Dinka version, cf. P. W. Schmidt: Ursprung der Gottesidee, vol. 8, p. 131.

"When the first men arose out of the reeds, the Lord of the earth sent the chameleon to men to convey this message: 'Men will die, but they will rise again.' The chameleon set out, but, as was his custom, he went very slowly. Then the great lizard with the blue head was sent to say to men: 'You will die and decay.' The lizard went quickly on his way and soon overtook the chameleon. They delivered their messages to humankind. As the chameleon arrived with his, people said to him: 'You are too late. We have already accepted the other message.' That is why men are destined to die".[211]

The myths speak of a time when God was lived among human beings. But this time has gone, once and for all. It was not a 'golden age' in the sense of a lost paradise. However, people had enough to eat, as other versions of the story make clear. There was enough for every day. More was not needed. Anybody who wants more than their 'daily bread' is regarded as 'greedy', and is behaving badly. Myths contain ethical teaching. Bad behaviour on the part of people destroys their relationship with God. He withdraws, therefore there is no chance for people to span the intervening gap. God has the power to come to them but they cannot go to him.

In the version handed down here, the special feature is the fact that the separation between God and human beings leads to the latter 'becoming human'. Their 'autonomy' is walking upright. The girl turns to the earth. God's nearness is felt to be 'crushing'. People walked about bent over, but were provided for. Now they walk upright, but have to provide for themselves. They have to work. This form of 'self-fulfilment', to use a modern expression, does not lead to world peace. On the contrary, so long as God directs our discussions, peace reigns. Left alone, even the words lead to death. Palaver without God is warfare!

Turning to the second myth: the word can bring life and death. Human beings decide which it is to be, depending on whether they accept the message. Once the decision is taken, it is irrevocable. This is why Africans who

---

[211] Quoted by H. A. Junod, 1962, vol. 2, p. 350. Among the Bavenda, it is the chameleon which is the messenger of death. A centipede which is relaxing on a tree by the wayside is the messenger of life; H. A. Stayt, 1968, p. 362. Among the Vasu in Tanzania lambs and lizards are the messengers, and they ask the question: Do you want to die like a pot that is smashed to pieces, or like the moon, which returns? cf. C. K. Omari, 1991, pp.97f.

162

are familiar with this myth have a hostile attitude towards the lizard even to-day. It is teased, it has tobacco smoke blown into its eyes, it is covered with branches or killed (among the Zulu, Tonga, etc.). The 'scapegoat' is punished, but the message remains.

The myth proclaims the distance between the worlds of heaven and of earth. This spatial distance is at the same time factual and moral. The distance is something like a *camera obscura*, in which everything appears in a mirror image.[212] Heaven and earth, God and people, behave in opposite ways to each other. Quick things, like the hasty message, represent death. This still applies today: lightning from God causes death, as nobody can resist it. The slow animal has to convey the message of life. Slowness and the chameleon's peculiar way of moving are not signs of earthly life, but of the ancestors. Among them, 'rest' is life. "God walks, he does not run", is a proverb among the Kwanyama in Namibia.

God's message arrives among people the wrong way round, but it does establish contact with God. Heaven and earth are separate, but are not essentially different from each other. They belong together. People see Heaven, they hear God's messages, they either accept or reject them. In spite of the separation, the earth continues to be the realm of God's action. God overcomes the distance through messengers coming from the realm of nature.

Why God sends two messengers is not explained. Questions relating to theodicy are alien to African religions. However, the fact that he does send two messengers is important. Their messages together describe the total reality, which always includes both features, becoming and decaying, life and being-no-more. The existence of life and death is the only issue. The text of the myth invites people to accept death as something immutable. God himself represents this immutable quality, which can no longer be analysed.

---

[212] D. Zahan has rightly drawn attention to this, even if he interprets the myths, in my opinion, in an excessively structuralist manner, 1979, pp.38f.

I will illustrate the above by selecting one people from South Africa and describing its concept of God, in order to deduce what belief in God in Africa says about humankind.[213]

1. The Sotho-speaking Tswana call God *Modimo*. This term belongs to the second basic category in Bantu languages, and not to the first, that of people. It contains terms such as smoke, fire, wind, mist, in other words, things which cannot be grasped, "things which are not personal".[214] The spiritual nature of God is indicated by this category, but also his non-personal superiority, which does not allow of anthropomorphic symbolisation. G. Setiloane logically does not speak of a 'HE', referring to God as 'IT'. While unusual in the African context, this accords with the phenomenon of using foreign or archaic terms for God; it makes his name more numinous and is a barrier to using gender-specific forms.

God is named in the way that he is experienced. He is intangible and alien. People know about him, but cannot feel him. Even though God and Heaven are closely linked together in various myths, this does not mean (see above) that they are identified with each other, any more than God and the sun are, despite the identical terms for them.[215] Heaven 'explains', 'clarifies' God, belongs to God. God is as broad as the heavens, and encompasses everything. Experiential reality is not God, although he underlies and overarches it.

It does not follow from this that he cannot be addressed, or is not addressed. This would be unthinkable in Africa. However, forms of address are taken from the human sphere and people's daily lives. "The word, God, has

---

[213] On what follows, cf. G. N. Setiloane, 1976, especially pp.79ff. Cf. also E. W. Smith, 1961, pp.116ff.; H. Häselbarth, 1972, pp.132ff.; D. Bosch, 1973. I refer particularly to the interpretations of K. Nürnberger, 1975, with whose objectives I largely agree, even if I would sometimes emphasise other points.

[214] E. W. Smith, 1961, p. 118. Originally it was thought to mean the place where the ancestors were, or, where they ceased to be revered as ancestors. cf. H. Häselbarth, 1969, p. 88.

[215] For the relationship between God and the sun among the Meru, cf. R. Harjula, 1969, pp.50ff.

no meaning for us, if God is not understood anthropomorphically".[216] If reality is coped with through experience, then God, the basis of reality, cannot be expressed other than in symbolical terms. In Africa this means being named in symbols that are more anthropological than cosmological. This is why the Tswana used to call God, 'Montshi, Modihi, Mothei, Motlodi... Giver, Maker, Founder, Creator'.[217] 'God our Father' is another form of address. Or even more movingly, 'Madam', 'My Mother'. E. W. Smith gives the following prayer: "O God, my Mother, grant that I may see my children grow old like me but not crawling on their stomach, objects of scorn".[218] When God is called 'Father', 'My Mother', it means that he is understood to be above gender, but not non-sexual. The double form of address means that God includes both aspects in himself, the nature of man and woman. God stands for wholeness, the whole. The androgynous character of God which is sometimes found in Africa (see Mawu-Lisa above) is a symbol of this.

The same idea is expressed in the following praise-song: "He is the scorching light of the sun; he is the soothing light of the moon; he is the flash of the lightning; he is the glittering of the stars!"[219] The whole of Heaven is described in complementary terms – sun and moon, lightning and stars. The praise-name 'Thobega of the black and white clouds, love of the first mother!' says the same thing. painting a lovely picture of thunder clouds. It combines the colours of Heaven (white) and of earth (black). The clouds appear white and peaceful above, yet they hide the dark danger underneath. The first mother's love encompasses and gives life to everything. God stands for the horizon of experience which, like heaven and earth, encompasses and gives being to everything. He is called 'the Source'. *Umvelingqangi* is one of the most important Zulu names for God. It says exactly what God means (*vela* = come forth, *nqangi* = first, or rather first of twins). "Heaven and earth always belong together. They are one, but one is above the other. Heaven is

---

[216] E. B. Idowu, 1973, p. 21.

[217] E. W. Smith, 1961, p. 122.

[218] Ibid. He also gives here another prayer of a woman who was miraculously rescued in the desert: True God, my Mother, grant that this food is also water.

[219] H. Dehnke, in an unpublished manuscript, quoted by K. Nürnberger, 1975, p. 163.

the first-born, but they are of the same nature. That is why he who lives in Heaven is called the first-born of twins. He came first. Then came the earth. They belong together. They have their children, humankind". Without earth, there would be no heaven; it would collapse, because it rests upon the earth at its uttermost ends.[220]

To us one of the strangest-sounding Tswana names for God is the 'one-legged one'.[221] Does this take anthropomorphism to its limit, and does it limit the idea of God's all-encompassing nature? Some years ago, in St. Ansgar, a Christian centre outside Johannesburg, I saw an artist – I don't remember whether he was Zulu or Tswana – who had made a linocut of a picture of God. God had *one* ear, *one* arm, and *one* leg. My astonished enquiry was answered spontaneously: "God is so great that he needs only one leg, one arm and one ear to do and hear far more than we do with two legs, arms and ears". Paradoxically this was a strong statement. Where death, the ancestors and God are concerned, inversions must be understood as strengthers in the area of ritual and symbols.[222]

2. The Tswana have no creation myths. However, God is described as the originator of all life and people. He is addressed as 'Montshi'; this means 'midwife', 'enabler', i. e. the one who enables us to come out.[223] God does not intervene directly in the course of earthly events, yet he is the source (Motlhodi), the power, without which nothing happens. His action does not exclude human deeds, but makes them possible. "When you sow seed in the earth, the earth does nothing, but the seed germinates", an old Tswana diviner said in reply to the question as to how God works. "He does nothing, it hap-

---

[220] A.-I. Berglund, 1975, pp.34f.

[221] Cf. H. O. Mönnig, 1967, p. 45.

[222] According to D. Livingstone, the term 'one-leggedness' is an image for the unity of God and means that he is 'exceptional', 'just and benevolent' (op. cit., p. 34). Since symbols allow of different interpretations, in fact require them, this interpretation cannot be ruled out. However, whether it conveys the whole idea seems doubtful to me.

[223] G. M. Setiloane, 1976, p. 81.

pens".[224] His working is indirect. He grants life to people and animals, but he is not their life. He is always beyond.

Being beyond, he is at the same time present and near. The myth that speaks of the God who distances himself is not intended to describe the ontological distance of God; it means that human beings have lost the way to God and cannot cross the gap between them; they cannot sway God, or influence him, or control him. God is close, like the light – that is one of his many names. You can no more grasp God than you can hold on to the light.

To experience God's nearness is terrifying. Among the Zulus, they say: "When the clouds come low, then the sky comes down over us. Sometimes it is fearsome, sometimes it is good. It (the sky) moves up and down as he wishes it to move". Another Zulu said: "When the clouds are high up, then the sky is far away. When the clouds come low, then the sky is low. This time is awesome, because he (the Lord-of-the-sky) is close. Then people should be indoors and keep quiet. The great one is near".[225]

3. The dialectic between lightness and darkness, the polarity between transcendance and immanence, distance and closeness, is consistently maintained in African concepts of God. It also affects the way God is understood as the giver and guarantor of order and morality. He himself is beyond good and evil, because ultimately everything is controlled by him and comes from him. That does not mean that evil derives directly from him. People are always the agents of evil, but where do they get their power to do evil from, if not from God?! IT controls everything, even, in the last resort, natural catastrophes and the wickedness of *baloi* (sorcerers).[226]

Great natural catastrophes, inexplicable calamities, sudden death, death by thunderbolt, great droughts and terrible floods are attributed to him in a special way. When people can no longer lay the blame for misfortune on the wrath of the ancestors, the power of sorcerers, or their own misconduct, then

---

[224] Quoted by K. Nürnberger, 1975, p. 162.
[225] A.-I. Berglund, 1975, p. 32.
[226] G. Setiloane, 1976, p. 82.

167

God himself has certainly intervened. He stands for the boundaries to human understanding. He is the ultimate Beyond of those things which are to be borne and to be experienced, and which can no longer be questioned. The Tswana say: "Modimo has killed", when somebody has been struck by lightning. His terrible greatness is felt in a hailstorm, and his deadly assault in a thunderbolt. A Zulu from the neighbourhood of Rorke's Drift, Natal, describes one such experience, as follows.

"We were all in the house, when suddenly the door was flung open and lightning came in, taking this one and that one. All fell to the ground, but I stood up because of the medicines I had taken, and because I wanted to defend the home with the medicines. I was holding them in my hand. So I stood up. Looking, I saw the thing. It was fearful to see and moved very quickly. But I saw it clearly. It was a bird. The feathers were white, burning, the beak and legs were red with fire, and the tail was something else, like burning green or the colour of the sky. It ran quickly, saying nothing, simply snatching those whom it took. Then it touched the grass with its fire. It vanished through the door again. When it had left there was one who shouted. So we all ran out of the hut, except those whom it had taken".[227]

This is not an encounter with God that is described here. The ball lightning is only the messenger of the Lord-of-the Sky, 'the bird of heaven' as he is called. But everybody knows that it is sent from IT, in order to carry off a human being.

The person who is killed by lightning is not buried in the traditional way of the ancestors, but in a manner which is pleasing to the Lord-of-the-Sky. When possible, he or she must be buried by a lightning magician in a damp place, so that the heat abates and is not passed on to others. The person will be buried only a yard deep, stretched out and not in a foetal position. One finger pokes out of the earth and points towards Heaven as a sign that God has taken him or her. Everybody should know this. No funeral rites will be conducted at home, nor will a period of mourning be observed. If the victim is a man, his widow will not re-marry. She should not remain within her hus-

---

[227] A woman and two children had been killed by a lightning strike; A.-I. Berglund, 1975, p. 39.

band's family in order to bear him further issue. "It is clear that if the sky has taken a man, that is the end of him. Even if there remains nobody to carry on his life, it does not matter. It is the decision of the sky, so what can we do?"[228] The inexplicable will be accepted as fate. It would, however, be wrong to conclude from this that, for human beings, God is merely 'fate'.[229]

4. Apart from a few exceptions (the Ashanti, Nuer, etc.), God is not the object of cultic acts in Africa. Ultimately, it cannot be otherwise, when he stands for the indescribable and the great, unique experience. Cultic rite aims at repetition, yet the indescribable cannot be accommodated within ritual. Ritual deals with minor threats and daily needs. God, however, is too great for people to bring him their 'everyday' cares and the petty, tiresome conflicts of life. The fragmentary is the province of the ancestors and the spirits; God stands for the whole. "God is too great to be reached with our sacrifices, he has no need of them", the Akan say.[230] It is only when they are completely at a loss that they turn to him. A brief cry of thanks, of pain or of supplication suffices in such a case. "Ka Modimo" ("my God!"), "Oh, Modimo, please help!", "If Modimo is with me..".., "May God give us luck", etc., are examples of these calls upon God.[231] Some peoples call upon God only in times of great good fortune. Occasionally, longer prayers are acceptable. The following Tswana prayer has been handed down from days of old:

"God of our fathers,
I lie down without food,
I lie down hungry,
Although others have eaten

---

[228] Ibid., p. 41. Further details are given here.

[229] K. Nürnberger, 1975, p. 168. Nürnberger seems to dismiss or completely ignore other aspects of the relationship to God in Tswana tradition.

[230] W. Ringwald, 1952, p. 29.

[231] H. O. Mönnig, 1967, p. 47. Among the Kikuyu a short invocation to God is customary at morning and evening, ('God, you have supported me during this night,' and 'God, support me in this night'), and also before making a sacrifice to the ancestors; L. S. B. Leakey, 1952.

169

And lie down full.
Even if it be but a polecat
Or a little rock-rabbit
(Give me and) and I shall be grateful.
I cry to God,
Father of my ancestors".[232]

5. That God is One and can only be One is evident from what has been said. The widely used Bantu term for God, *Njambi*, (for example), exists only in the singular. There is no plural of the word. It follows from this that talk of an African 'high God', often found in older research, is inappropriate. It is meant to emphasise the difference from the Western concept of God, but says nothing about the nature of God as perceived in Africa. A distinction between the God of heaven and the God of earth is occasionally to be found (especially in West Africa), the differences lying more in function and attributes than in there being fundamentally different gods. Austrian anthropologist Father W. Schmidt maintained that monotheism did exist originally. We could agree with this if it did not imply the Western theistic idea of a self-sufficient God existing for himself. But this does not apply to the African concept of God. God does not exist without the world, and is not conceived of in Africa apart from the world. Therefore, access to him can only be via the world. God's name and his symbols must invoke the world, otherwise they may name something, but it will not be God.

God is experienced in, with and through the world. Although African religions are not 'religions of revelation' in the strict sense of the word, God speaks – not loudly, and not directly. He speaks through the world. "We catch a faint whisper of God, but we cannot see him", runs an Ovambo proverb.[233] He can be perceived through his works. Though omnipresent, he is visible only there.[234] That is why everybody knows him. It is not necessary to tell a child that there is a God. When children lie on their backs, they see the sky,

---

[232] E. W. Smith, 1961, p. 121.
[233] Ibid., p. 146.
[234] T. Evans, in E. W. Smith, 1961, p. 245. This refers to the Akan.

the bright place, 'Onjame'. "Even a hen points to Nyame when it drinks water".[235] You only have to teach children not to point, nor to poke their fingers at the sky, lest that brings its wrath down on you. After all, you don't point your finger at other people, do you?

No, we cannot get away from God, and it is impossible not to be aware of him. The world, even human order, speaks of him.

"Odomankoma;
He created the Thing (= world).
Infinite Creator;
He created the Thing.
What did He create?
He created Order,
He created Knowledge,
He created Death,
As its quintessence".[236]

6. This sets God within the moral order. Does this not contradict the maxim that God does not intervene in good and evil happenings because he is beyond this order of things? Even if we have to distinguish between the statements of different ethnic groups and peoples, one thing is common to all of them: there is no one doctrine of God, any more than there is a code of conduct in one way or another derived directly from him. There was no African 'Moses'; the laws are those of the ancestors. And yet ethical knowledge is communicated in such a way that God is brought in through proverbs. They point towards God.[237] Proverbs contain the wisdom of a people, they speak of human beings, of their experiences and patterns of behaviour which have stood the test of time. They give warnings and speak the language which is appropriate for encounter with the world. They teach knowledge of God.. If God sends you an illness, he sends you a remedy also. If God does not kill

---

[235] J. B. Danquah, 1968, pp.38 & 41.

[236] Ibid., p. 132.

[237] Cf. on the Akan J. D. Danquah, 1968; on the Ovambo, cf. E. W. Smith, 1961, pp.144ff. & 149f.

you, you do not die. (Akan) – Sodomy is not done by free will; cowardice comes from God. (Ovambo).[238] The cause of orphans is put in order by ants, say the Tswana, i. e. God works invisibly through little things, without our noticing.[239]

"It is my task to distribute medicine and to give it to the woman, but the work of creating a child rests with God", said a Vasu herbalist in Tanzania.

How closely human wisdom, ethical teaching and belief in God are connected becomes clear in the apparently neutral-sounding saying which women employ when they see a new-born, obviously ugly child. In itself, every child born of woman is beautiful, say the Vasu. In the rare exceptional cases, however, they whisper: "How was this child made? It was created at the crack of dawn". This statement contains a reprimand for the father, a reference to God's continuous presence, and a statement about the right relationship in marriage. Humans beget the child, but God 'creates' it. He needs time to make it beautiful, just as the potter needs a longer spell of time to give a pot the final polish. Now, apparently, he did not have enough time. The child was begotten at the crack of dawn. Something is not right in the marriage. The sexual relationship is wrong. "The wife was there only to bear children and this is why the husband came at any time he wanted and never bothered to be there for the whole night... Sexual relationship should take place early enough so as to allow God to finish his work on the new baby before dawn".[240]

Very few peoples in Africa see God as a judge in the next world.[241] The rare occasions when he is described as a judge refer to his judicial action in this world. He sees what people do. God sees and hears everything. He is present. Misdeed and punishment are seen in Africa, rather as in ancient Israel, as being very closely connected with the person's subsequent life, and this falls within the domain of the ancestors.

---

[238] Ibid., p. 150.
[239] G. Setiloane, 1976, p. 83.
[240] C. K. Omari, 1991, pp. 103ff. & 106.

172

To sum up: God is near as the One who is far off. He is there as the origin from which everything comes, without which what exists would break down. He is there as the omnipotent one, as the mighty one, as '*Usomandla*', who possesses all power.[242] Yet how and when he applies it cannot be foreseen by anyone. Compared with him, people feel like 'ants'. They are at his mercy. God's being is good and trustworthy, which inspires trust and thankfulness in human beings. Yet, because his action cannot be calculated, awe is the appropriate stance. Finally, it is good to know that there is something above the ancestors and the spirits, which sets a limit to everything and that the limitless and the incomprehensible is in God's care.

"Great Deng is near,
But some say 'far'.
O Divinity,
The creator is near and some say, 'He has not reached us'.
Do you not hear, O Divinity?"[243]

For Africa, God is what ultimately concerns everyone, at all times and in the same way. However, he can be thought and spoken of only in symbols taken from the whole created world.[244]

---

[241] The Akan are an exception to this. Cf. W. Ringwald, 1952, p. 24, and below pp.204f.

[242] This is a Zulu praise-name. 'We call him *uSomandla*, because he has all the power. If a man wants power and cannot get it from the shades or from medicines, then he can obtain it from the one above only, if he is willing (to give it to him). He is very powerful, far more powerful than even the shades or medicines. Indeed, we say that the shades have power. (Quoted by Berglund, 1975, p. 36)

[243] G. Lienhardt, 1967, p. 38; for the whole of this, cf. T. Sundermeier, 1983.

[244] For the theological interpretation of the African concept of God, cf. H. Rücker, 1985, chap. 3.2. He gives a succinct summary: African "religiosity is anthropomorphic, because it is concerned with human beings; it is monolatristic, because it is based on the ultimate unity; it is not polytheistic, because, as an earthly phenomenon, only plural experiences are possible for it; it is not deistic, because the world of God is speech; it is not modalistic, because it transcends the ontological system". (ibid., p. 137).

IV. ETHICS

1. Reverence for your neighbour

One of the greatest mistakes of travellers, scholars and missionaries of the last century was to deny that Africans had a moral sense. Their own ethics had made them blind to other values and standards prevailing in different social circumstances; they believed in the moral education of the human race under the leadership of Westerners. When they did come to adopt a more sympathetic stance, influenced by Romanticism, African morality was indeed recognised as autonomous. Yet their experience of traditional religion was too fragmentary for them to appreciate the inner logic and coherence of the whole world-view, and so the connection between tribal ethics and religion.[245] In fact, the question of how ethics relates to belief in God is one to which few African peoples give an explicit answer. An Akan text from West Africa is one of the exceptions:

"The sun shines, and burns down brightly.
The moon rises in its splendour.
The rain falls, and the sun shines again,
Yet God's eye is above all these things,
Nothing is hidden from him.
Whether you are in the house, whether you are on the water
Or in the thick shadow of the trees,
He is above you in every place.
You think you are more than an orphan child,
You strive after his goodness, and you betray it.
Your thought is: nobody sees me.
Think, however, you are in God's sight,
He will give you your reward one day,
Not today, not today, not today,
One day he will give you your reward

174

For what you are thinking in your heart:
You are a slave, an orphan child,
God will give you your reward one day
Not today, not today, not today".[246]

Research into symbolism has shown how few key concepts are needed to indicate the close mesh of different levels in a religion, and indeed how the interdependence of the whole can be explored from a single concept. This key, i. e. the deep-structural symbol underlying everything, unlocks the whole moral system, which does not require codification. The details follow from the general philosophy of life, each detail shedding light on the next.

This also applies to individuals and their relations within the village. Since all inhabitants share the same general context, symbols do not need to be deciphered and set down in a statute book. They know what to do because they are familiar with the environment and live in a community where situations rarely arise which cannot be dealt with from past experience. Proverbs can interpret the circumstances and point to solutions. They transmit the accepted moral code. Discussions, reactions from the neighbours, the open disapproval of an elder, show what is to be done. Taboos are signs of looming dangers. People live within the complex fabric of the community and have so internalised its standards that they spontaneously submit to them, even when this is not directly required.

An anecdote will show what I mean. Students of the Lutheran Theological College in Umpumulo, in South Africa, were playing a board game in our house. The point of this game is that each of the four players tries to erect 'barriers' against the opponents' four pieces or to get them out of the game, in order to bring their own pieces 'home'. The player who first gets a piece home has won and the game is over. I explained the rules to the students, played with them for a few minutes, and then turned my attention to other guests who had just arrived. Returning to the players after a while, I saw how

---

[245] On this problem, cf. J. N. Kudadji, 1976; cf. further, E. A. Adegbola, 1968.
[246] Quoted by W. Ringwald, 1952, p. 24; cf. also E. A. Adegbola, 1968, pp.236f.; J. V. Taylor, 1965, pp.146f.

they had fundamentally altered the rules. At first I thought they had misunderstood the easy rules, but on closer inspection the new game fascinated me more and more. The alterations were not haphazard, there was method in them. The pieces were now called 'oxen'. Then the rule of having to get another player's piece off the board had been abolished as being 'too cruel'. Even the purpose of the barriers had been changed. Instead of putting them in the way of the others, they had to get them out of the way altogether and put them where they would probably do least harm. The winner was the one who got all four pieces home first. The game only ended when the last player led their four 'oxen' into the 'kraal'.

African community mindedness and the matching moral code had asserted itself. The alterations to the game became a mirror in which I could recognise myself as a European, and also the different outlook of Africans. Europeans emphasise opposites: 'in play' we learn to beat and exclude our opponents, and to be the only winner. In contrast, what is striking about the African version is the complete elimination of competition. The point is to help others, and to remove hindrances from their path so as to reach the goal *with* them, if possible. In the last resort there is no winner or loser. In the European view this would be a boring game – and life would be boring without challenge and struggle. The African view, on the other hand, is of a peaceful interplay of forces, dependent on the luck of the game.

The defining elements of African ethics were shown in this way of playing games, as was the inner link with religion, even though nothing was said on the subject. It is all about life in community. When the life of the community is at risk, so is its whole tradition, i. e. the past, which is determined by the ancestors, and which must be carried over into the future. A person 'serves' the cattle in which the ancestors are present and make life possible. Is not the neighbour, with whom life in the village is shared, an enabler of the whole, so that any risk to his or her well-being affects others? Wherever community and life are at stake, wherever there are taboos involving sanctions, religion 'comes into play'. Anybody who does not discover this, or wishes to break away, damages the whole network of social relations.

The basic principles of African ethics can be set down in a few expressions:

1. *"Good company"*

This is the title of a book by Monica Wilson which aptly describes the subject under discussion.[247] Since 'we' is constitutive for the existence of the individual, the over-riding ethical principle is to behave in accordance with the community, i. e. to promote good community and to strive to maintain it. You become a human being through (your fellow-)human beings, in the words of a Zulu and Sotho proverb. Community creates humanity. It follows from this, firstly, that the community evokes *loyalty*. The lone wolf is regarded as antisocial. Little importance is attached to meditation. A Sotho student whom I regarded particularly highly on account of his perceptive comments told me that his father had often hit him across his shoulders with a stick when he 'was sitting thinking'. He had never understood why his father had done this, seeing in it only the demand that he join in and be sociable. And that is what he did.

To be a loner and to 'meditate' is regarded in African society as the first sign that the ancestors are 'brooding' over somebody and want to single him or her out. This is to be prevented if at all possible since, even today, diviners always live somewhat outside the community in spite of their standing. Someone can only learn what it means to be a human being in fellowship with others. Young people must hear what the elders say, and compare impressions with their peers. How else can they learn how to present a case convincingly, or practise the art of public speaking, regarded so highly in cultures without a written tradition? If they were to get into a dispute, they could not defend themselves. Since words help to create a feeling of community, *well-spokenness* makes for 'good company'.

Helpfulness is a further feature. It is not unlimited, however, but 'relative'. Just as a stone, when thrown into water, forms circles – the closest are the strongest and those further out weaken and finally disappear completely –

---

[247] M. Wilson, 1963. For what follows, ibid., pp.66ff.

the obligation to help others and offer hospitality is greatest towards members of the family. Relatives, whether biological or classificatory, are received like brothers and sisters. Helping your neighbours, who for the most part are kin, is a natural duty. If a meal is about to take place, every chance visitor is served too. Among the Tswana a mother never gives food to her child alone, but invites all children present to share in the meal she has prepared.

A missionary I knew had only one sweet in his pocket when he met a group of (Bushman) children in Botswana. He gave it to the oldest girl, but was worried lest it should lead to a fight. The girl put the sweet into her mouth, sucked it, and gave it to the next child. Thus the sweet went all the way round, until it had all gone. Sharing is a part of good company.

Sharing with your neighbour means taking part in all communal family and neighbourhood rituals, birth and marriage festivals, mourning ceremonies, and at harvest time; it means being present when reconciliation rituals are performed; it means bringing your share of cattle, when expected or called for by family relationship.

Anybody absent from a ritual endangers the cohesion of the group, and runs the risk of being suspected of wanting to destroy it. This applies in particular to funeral rites. Anyone who is absent can easily be accused of causing the death of the deceased. Since people participate in each other inwardly, the fact of belonging together must be visible. The person who refuses outward participation, disturbs the life that holds all people together, and is guilty in regard to the others. Rituals seek to bind people together. Only when all take part is it certain that nobody is seeking to disavow the ritual and that nobody has hostility, anger or envy in their heart. The reconciliation ritual is a fixed event preceding many rituals and festivals.

If we were to sum up the subject under discussion here in one phrase, it could be '*seeking peace*'. However, this should not be confused with the Western understanding of peace. This latter first focusses on the individual ('Leave me in peace'), and only then only on others. In the context of Africa, peace is essentially linked with community. Peace is not possible on your own. Neither is peace simply the opposite of war, or the absence of strife, but means 'to live in harmony'. It includes the family, the neighbours, the cattle and nature. Strife separates, peace joins – peace and alliance are sometimes used interchangeably. Peace is thus not a gift, but an assignment, a social duty, a religious exercise. In many Bantu languages, the term for 'peace' shares a common root with 'to lie'. The person who lives in peace can lie down, and need not keep watch. When peace is achieved, a condition of quiet, calm and inactivity reigns. A man can stand in front of his hut and take pleasure in the fertility of the fields, the lowing of the cattle, the children at play, and the contentedness of the women. He can enjoy time, and does not need to 'create' it – as when at work. Peace means time is standing still. Fear and strife, on the other hand, drive thoughts into the future, while activating memories of the past. When Zulus slaughter cattle at certain times they ask, 'Will we have peace now?'

As we have seen, Africans are able to sum up in a single expression, in a single symbol, what for Europeans needs a broad analytical exposition. The colour white and the emotional equivalent, 'cool', indicate the ideal. White is the colour of peace, and says that people have no anger in their hearts, and that relations with the family and the neighbours are clear and transparent. In various languages, 'I have peace in my heart', and 'I live in peace', are expressed by the symbol 'white'.

Water is white in colour. It is pure and it purifies people by 'cooling' them. In all purification rites, which in various respects are also rites of reconciliation, water is used, if possible running water, because it is 'living' and pure. Human anger and fury, which disturb good relations between people, are cooled by water. After somebody has spoken of everything which they have stored up in their heart against another, all the participants sip water and then spit it out. Even simply spitting out (white) saliva counts among certain peoples as an act of purification, which serves to restore friendly relations. It is not heat but coolness which appropriately expresses the ideal of right ethics.

This description of the basic pattern of African ethics is ideal, and it is obvious that village life is not free from conflict; strife and tension need to be continually overcome. Because they are felt with particular intensity and pain

179

in a small society, there is a need for exhortation and the commitment to be-have in a community-minded way. In this 'intensely corporate society', as J. S. Mbiti writes, 'all is neither grim nor bright. It is hard to describe these things: one needs to participate or grow up in village life, to get an idea of the depth of evil and its consequences upon individuals and society.'[248]

2. Reverence for humanity

This virtue embodies the virtues of 'good company', and at the same time limits them. Reverence, or *respect*, for other people are among the fundamental forms of conduct which render village life pleasant and harmonious. 'He respects people' is the highest praise for an Ewe.[249] Respecting people means according them the regard due to their status and position. The African village is not socially amorphous. It is not ordered democratically, with all enjoying the same rights and duties, yet it is democratic in that everyone shares in its life and events, depending on their position. Respecting people means respecting the order in which they live. People in lower positions must accord due honour to those of higher rank; elders and the high-ranking must be aware of their duty to provide welfare for the less privileged.[250]

Respecting your neighbour determines the decorum of living together, something which is more than mere etiquette. A man greets a man of higher

---

[248] J. S. Mbiti, 1969, pp.209–10; further: "there are endless manifestations of evil. These include murders, robberies, rape, adultery, lies, stealing, cruelty especially towards women, quarrels, bad words, disrespect to persons of a higher status, accusations of sorcery, magic and witchcraft, etc. A visitor... will immediately be struck by African readiness to externalise the spontaneous feelings of joy, love, friendship and generosity". This ambivalence is well expressed in the following Akan proverbs: "The image of man is like the sun; look on it, and it is peace". And: "Because of man the sword is made". (I. G. Danquah, 1968, p. 193, Nos. 2404 & 2413).

[249] D. Westermann, 1937, p. 169.

[250] "For a boy it was considered very important to know his exact position in the clan, his relationship to other members, and his whole genealogy, so that he might be able to make such claims as he had to seniority, to prove his membership in case of dispute, and above all, to prove that he was a true Muganda". (L. Mair, quoted by J. W. Sempebwa, p. 136). On the whole of this subject, cf. idem, pp.106ff. & 154ff.

rank differently from a woman, and a child differently from an adult. Whereas in many cultures a woman greets somebody by kneeling down, often a man merely bows his head. While a man usually sits in an elevated position in his house (on a stool or chair), a woman sits on the ground. In the presence of a chief, a man naturally also sits on the ground, if he is allowed to sit at all. A man expects a woman to be shy, modest and respectful, and to speak with a man or an older woman with lowered looks and with her head on one side (particularly among the southern Bantu tribes). This applies in both matrilineal and patrilineal societies.

Expressing respect takes on different forms in different societies. The separation of the sexes has many facets. Respect for others can mean that men and women do not eat together, or that a daughter-in-law may not look upon her father-in-law, nor remain in the same room with him, as is the custom among the Nyakyusa in Tanzania.

While children do not have to oberve the conventions, adults have no choice. Bad form is a sign of the deepest lack of respect, and is regarded as a moral offence, leading to sanctions by the ancestors. In this connection, the Pedi use the concept *sebe*, sin, which dates from pre-Christian times.[251] Anyone who does not respect older people does not respect the ancestors either. '*Go nytsa badimo*' (= not respecting the ancestors) is the worst possible offence, and will have terrible consequences. Sickness will certainly afflict the family.

Why then must respect for others be expressed so strictly in proper form? We have seen in many instances that in Africa externals are not just of superficial value. They are the thing itself. Emotions which possess a moral value, as shown by the concepts 'coolness' and 'heat', must be expressed in one way and not otherwise. Ignoring your emotions, however, means ignoring yourself.

This has serious consequences for a person's sense of justice. Theft, murder and adultery do not only cause 'damage' in the normal sense, but also emotional damage, which also requires compensation. Placide Tempels made

---

[251] Cf. H. O. Mönnig, 1967, pp.64ff.

this clear with an oft-quoted example. A man had entrusted a lamb to an elder from the neighbouring village. On day he discovered his dog gnawing at the lamb's bones. To assuage his emotional pain, the elder gave the man not only one lamb, but a second and a third one, and finally 100 francs as well, because 'the loss of my sheep pains me, it causes me sorrow.' It was only after the payment of the money that he could forget his pain and feel happy again.[252] The biblical principal, 'An eye for an eye, a tooth for a tooth', was seen as setting a limit on punishment, not only in the Old Testament, but also in Africa.

Furthermore, respect for the humanity of others means being helpful and respecting their position in society. Everybody behaves in a spirit of decorum, and does not try to outdo others in a competitive spirit. If individuals perform too well, that is grounds for suspicion. If they boast, they are suspected of witchcraft, or else driven into isolation. This code of ethics with its emphasis on conformity penetrates the smallest details of everyday life. If a woman carries more wood on her head than others, if she works longer in the fields, beginning earlier or stopping later, she will soon be talked about. On the other hand, if she works less than the others, she will be isolated. Adam Smith's principle of the struggle for economic progress through individual effort has no counterpart in Africa. There you adjust to others and behave in the same way as your peers and gender models, in order to act like them again in the next phase of your life. You do not work your way up into the next stage, or earn it; you grow into it, or are born into it through the appropriate ritual.[253] Each stage of life places particular obligations upon people. It is part of being younger to obey and submit. On the other hand, old age imposes other obligations towards the community. Older people may give orders, provide advice, and settle problems. They not only expect the honour which comes with age, but also demand it.

Developing a Western understanding of democracy is undoubtedly difficult to achieve under such circumstances. There is a danger of the abuse of

---

[252] Cf. P. Tempels, 1959; J. Jahn, 1958, p. 121; J. V. Taylor, 1965, pp.149f.

[253] J. W. Sempebwa, 1983, pp.178f.

seniority. The possibility of absolute power is inherent in various state systems. However, awareness of participatory interdependence sets a certain limit on such an abuse of power in traditional Africa. The elders still rely on the opinion and agreement of the younger men. Part of the wisdom of the elders is to respect the latter's feelings. Sickness (as a sanction for alleged witchcraft or sorcery) is no respecter of age.

Within such a framework there is little scope for individual development. *Knowing your place* is what counts. This is the real form of respect for others, for your neighbour. 'The person who does not let himself be ruled suffers much,' says a Ganda proverb.[254] The ideal pattern of African education, followed at home, in the village and in initiation rites, aims at adaptation to the overall context, and not at independent thinking, or getting people to reflect critically about the acceptance of tradition. What P. Fuchs said of the Hadjerai in Chad is generally applicable, even if the 'theological' basis varies. 'Personal qualities and gifts are inborn just like belonging to a particular family or tribe. This all determines an individual's fate. What he or she can learn in the course of life is techniques and social behaviour. Everything else is in them while still in the womb. This understanding of human nature shapes the upbringing of Hadjerai children. It does not aspire to development, but to conformity.'[255] The history of migration within Africa and of colonialism has often shown that this conformity can easily turn into an attitude of subservience, or be confused with it.

Respect for another person, as an aspect of 'good company', ends, as does the latter, at the boundaries of the people's territory. Beyond lives the enemy; a number of peoples limit the application of the concept 'human being' exclusively to their own people. 'Reverence for people', as a basic value of African ethics must therefore be formulated more precisely as 'reverence for your neighbour'. As in the Old Testament sense, the 'neighbour' is a member of the same community, not a fellow human being living at a distance.

---

[254] Ibid., p. 119.

[255] P. Fuchs, in: W. Raunig, 1980, p. 90.

The attitude to the strangers who live in your territory is described in different ways. On the one hand, the 'sanctity' of hospitality (Tallensi) surrounds them, because they are under the special protection of the divinities; on the other hand, experience shows what a burden strangers can be. "There is always some trouble after the stranger departs", says an Akan proverb.[256]

Under the influence of Islam and Christianity, the scope of this ethic has been definitely broadened, so that nowadays even strangers become neighbours. Monica Wilson relates that, at a Nyakyusa wedding, she once heard the bride's mother say to her daughter in her traditional exhortation: "Give the stranger something to eat as well. Remember that you are a Christian".[257]

3. Power

Life is expressed as liveliness. Where the expressions of life are weakened, danger lies ahead. Every effort must be aimed at strengthening life, at gathering strength, so that the threat can be overcome and the course of life may continue. Life is meant to expand. That is the law under which humans come into being; it corresponds to the natural law of growth. That is why human beings strive to overcome everything which weakens life, and to strengthen everything life-enhancing. They strive for strength and power. 'Strength' in this respect is a comprehensive term, covering various mutually contradictory aspects, which profoundly influence ethical behaviour. (Among the Zulu, *amandla* means strength, power, wisdom, fertility and, occasionally, even modesty.)

Self-control is one of the basic qualities of African ideas of morality.[258] From an early age the African boy is taught self-control. Circumcision rites,

---

[256] J. B. Danquah, 1968, p. 191, No. 1403. Cf. also ibid. No. 1404: "The stranger on your threshold brings you some money – and some debt". For the whole question, cf. M. Fortes, 1975.

[257] Cf. also M. Wilson, 1963, pp.70f.

[258] D. Zahan, 1979, pp.110ff., rightly points out that up to now this idea has hardly been dealt with in the ethnological literature. However, if we were to regard what is only one

184

with their tough demands, are a training in this art. They foster the "integration of the Muntu in oneself",[259] i. e. they teach the lad to control himself so that he can behave in the company of others in such a way that they catch no glimpse of his feelings, or of his inner being. Only a controlled person can properly adapt. Whoever controls their speech is esteemed. People who talk too much, or give vent to their anger and wrath, put themselves in the wrong, irrespective of whether they were originally in the right or not, or whether they had grounds for anger (according to the Ovambo in Namibia).[260] No matter how important (negative) feelings are, they should not be outwardly revealed. Whoever makes a show of anger is vulnerable and stirs up uncontrollable forces. There are various reasons for this. The Ovambo refer to God. "God walks, he does not run", says one of their proverbs. Others refer to the power of the word. A word spoken in anger cannot be taken back. It attracts the attention of the sorcerers. Words should unite, not divide. How can a word spoken in anger have a healing effect? The controlled person follows the ideal of coolness, speaking like a wise woman who weighs her words. If the word comes from a 'cool', 'white' heart, it makes peace. "The patient man has peace", the Dogon say. "He refreshes, like water".[261]

The centre of strength is seen in human fertility. As humankind is the centre of the cosmos, so the sexual organs are the centre of human beings.

---

part of the subject as the basis of all African ethics, this would be an improper generalisation from conditions among the Bambara. In many respects the Bambara play a special role, which can be transferred to other peoples only with caution, even though they have much in common with their neighbouring Dogon. I have not been able to establish among other peoples that self-control serves spiritual ends; cf. also, H. Baumann, 1980.

[259] M. Ntetem, 1983, pp.97f.; on the upbringing of African children, cf. I. Schapera, 1971; O. F. Raum, 1967.

[260] I experienced this once myself when leading a theological seminar. I had left the room in a bad temper, in order to give the students time to consider what they had done wrong, and to come up with some suggestions. In a little while a delegation from the students came to me in my study. To my surprise, I received from them neither an apology nor an explanation of their behaviour, nor even any proposals. On the contrary, they demanded that I formally apologise, because in my temper I had slammed the door – I was not aware of this – and had left the room in a rage. The students' misbehaviour was no longer the issue. I had shown my bad temper, and so was in the wrong. Accordingly, it was up to me to apologise.

[261] According to D. Zahan, 1979, p. 113.

Sexual symbolism runs right through the whole spectrum of African symbol formation, as we have already seen. In traditional Africa, white can stand for the power of sex and fertility (semen, mother's milk), and then it means the legitimate force of fertility. Otherwise, red stands for fertility and strength. Both aspects are included in this: the idea of the over-riding power of *sexuality*, and the danger which it also contains.

Sexuality is regarded in Africa as something very natural, a gift of the ancestors, a gift from God. People are prepared for it from their youth. Sexuality is not repressed,[262] but has to be channelled so that it does not have a destructive effect. Its rightful use is to be safeguarded. Young people are permitted sexual activity, but the deflowering of a young girl is considered a scandal. In most peoples pregnancy before marriage is regarded as devaluing the girl, but in some as a sign of fertility. Sterility is the greatest misfortune. Polygyny used to be a guarantee of fertility. The woman is seen as a garden, having to bear fruit, so the man has to go in to her as often as possible. This is the only way to guarantee descendants.

Extra-marital affairs occur in Africa, just as they do elsewhere, but in traditional society there are particularly strong sanctions against them. They endanger not just the stability of the marriage but also the health of the man and the birth of the next child. If a woman cannot bear children, that is blamed on extra-marital affairs. She first has to confess her guilt and undergo purification so that she can conceive safely. The special danger in extra-marital sex is based in belief in the ancestors. The ancestors are present in the woman's blood and the man's semen, as we have already seen. If 'foreign' semen comes into contact with the blood of the woman, the ancestors do not recognise it and there is 'strife' in the woman's blood. Illness, infertility and impotence are the consequences.

Homosexuality is considered most reprehensible in Africa, because of the close relationship between sexuality and fertility. Even peoples which tolerate it in puberty disapprove of it for grown men. If it should occur, it

---

[262] Cf. the detailed description of J. Kenyatta, 1968, pp.155ff.; Cf. further I. Schapera, 1971.

186

falls into the area of witchcraft, according to, for example, the Nyakyusa.[263] Among the Ovambo, it is taken as a stroke of fate from God, against which there is no defence.[264] They count homosexuals as women, because they are weak and not brave. Homosexuality occurs in prisons and men's hostels run by the mining companies, of course, and there it is tolerated as a temporary phenomenon. It does not have any permanent consequences, and it is not continued when life gets back to normal.[265]

Like homosexuality, the absence of marriage is not understood in Africa, and is disapproved of by religion. The single person is disobedient to the ancestors, even to God, since he or she destroys the stream of life. That is why Roman Catholic celibacy is unpopular in Africa. The relatively limited growth of the African priesthood is explained by this attitude, which also accounts for the high percentage of those who later leave the priesthood, or secretly or openly break their vow of chastity. Orders of monks are practically non-existent in sub-Saharan Africa. Somebody who doesn't marry can virtually be described as a 'non-person'.

The emotional side of power and fertility is symbolised by 'heat'. Heat comes from the ancestors. There is no fertility without its presence, and so there are no descendants. Heat also signals danger. Therefore sexually active men may not follow certain occupations; if they are allowed to associate at all with men who have dangerous jobs, such as hunters and smiths, it is only when certain precautions have been taken. The heat of sexuality corresponds to the 'heat' of wrath, and makes people susceptible to the machinations of witches and sorcerers, which cannot operate without 'heat'.

---

[263] M. Wilson, 1963, pp.87f. & 196f.

[264] "Sodomy is not deliberate; cowardice is a thing which comes from God", according to an Ovambo saying, quoted by E. W. Smith, 1961, p. 150.

[265] I was told by several sources that there was a people in Zimbabwe which practised homosexuality. They were said to have adopted it in the workers' hostels in Johannesburg. Calling other peoples 'names' in this way is also known in other parts of Africa. It seems to me, however, that it is used more as a strategy to stand out from other societies than to convey accurate information.

187

Wrath is as strong as fertility, and is also part of being human. Not everybody has it to the same degree, some have more, some have less.[266] Legitimate wrath is concerned to restore order to the life of the lineage, the clan and the people. Illegitimate wrath creates disorder and is attractive to witches and sorcerers.

The force of sexuality is located in the sexual organs; among the Zulu the power of wrath is located in the throat, the gullet (wrath, anger = *ulaka*; gullet, the inner part of the throat = *ililaka*). The evil word is the most important instrument of wrath. Yet even the heart can be filled with it.

Justifiable wrath should stir the conscience of others. If a son does not visit his distant father for a long time, and does not occasionally give him pleasure with the gift of a piece of meat, then one day he will dream of his father, or become ill. The diviner will determine the cause: the father is moved to anger.[267] Now the son is conscience-stricken, and sets about appeasing his father with a sacrifice. The killing of an animal is considered a sacrifice of reconciliation. This does not necessarily include the idea of vicarious sacrifice, but means, e. g. among the Zulu, quite simply the restoration of broken social relationships. It will simply give pleasure.[268] The common sacrificial meal is the instrument and expression of social enjoyment.

Wrath, like sexuality, is symbolised by the colour red. It has to have its counterpart: red is only unambiguously positive in interaction with white. Wrath has its place in society, but it has to be contained. Any excess is unhealthy. Therefore those who are justifiably angry must channel their emotions and express them in moderation. That applies as much to those in authority, who always have the privilege of directing anger towards those 'below them', as to those below who have a right to be angry with those 'above them'. They must not show it directly, however, but operate via a

---

[266] A.-I. Berglund, 1967, p. 255, quotes two Zulus as follows: "If men did not have anger, they would not be men. Some people have much anger. Some have little anger. But all people have it, whether it be much or little. It is like the blood. It must be in a man".

[267] For the significance of 'anger' and 'cursing', cf. I. Schapera, 1955, pp.181f.

[268] For the whole of this topic, cf. A.-I. Berglund, 1975, pp.258ff.

188

third party so that neither the superior nor the subordinate will lose face. The indirect course helps cool down the emotion.

Rituals are the special way of channelling wrath and emotions. As we have seen, in the mourning rites of the Nyakyusa a war dance will be performed at a certain point, so that war 'within' is externalised and overcome; the dance is an outlet for the anger.

The Nuba in Sudan have a festival of knuckle-duster fighting known as Timbra, at which the fighters display their strength and courage in order to be accepted into the next age-group. It is the high-point of village life, celebrated at harvest-time, and is an outlet for aggression, something of which they are fully aware. The Timbra have a healing effect on community life. The Nuba are at any rate "proud that in their community it practically never happens that knives, spears, rifles or other weapons are raised against each other. On this point, they feel that they have a significant advantage over their neighbours, who do not have knuckle-duster fights".[269]

The *increase of power* is an important motive for ethical action. It is regarded as legitimate and positive. Unlimited power, on the other hand, is unacceptable, since anything conspicuous or unique is regarded as bad, even evil. In exceptional cases it is acceptable, however, for people who occupy the appropriate positions, chiefs and kings. In extraordinary cases, measures can be taken which are otherwise taboo and produce dreadful consequences. Inverse action leads to the ultimate increase in power, e. g. incest.

The reason why *incest* is placed under the strictest taboo in Africa has little to do with biological considerations, particularly since marriage between cousins is, as we have seen, preferred under certain conditions. The incest taboo appears to be connected with the ordering of life, since incest destroys the hierarchical echelons of the family. If a man has a child by his daughter, he is simultaneously his own father-in-law and the grandfather of the child. His child is also his grandchild. His wife is his mother-in-law, and his daughter is both wife and daughter in one. Order collapses, the law of inheritance disintegrates. A similar confusion exists when a brother and sister produce children. The parents are uncle and aunt to their own child, and the grandparents are in-laws. The order of generations

---

[269] O. Iten, in: W. Raunig, 1980, pp.106f.

comes to a standstill. Life 'marks time'.[270] The African sense of the order of life resists this with all its strength. In the sacral kingship of West and Central Africa, marriage between brother and sister is required, because the exceptional breaking of the taboo increases the king's power.[271] The same blood and semen mingle as with their parents, which magnifies his strength.

Two examples from modern times show how strongly the idea still prevails that inverse action leads to an increase of power, through breaking down incest taboos. When, in southern Africa, a missionary showed a young member of his congregation a new development project from overseas, his reaction was: "If I slept with my sister, I could build that too!" In Nairobi a missionary was confronted with a pastoral problem. Before every important match, a footballer raped his mother, one of the most monstrous crimes in traditional as well as modern Africa.

2. Evil

Transcendental dualism has no part in African religions. The separation of reality into two mutually exclusive areas is unknown. God has no counterpart. Just as God is not thought of as being apart from the reality of the world and human experience, so his action is also not limited to one area, from which another could be excluded. How strongly rooted this thought is, is made clear by the fact that the Nupe, who came to know the devil as an object of belief under the influence of Islam, accord him hardly any significance in their daily life. Satan is a creature of God, not his opponent. He is one of his "ambiguous creatures".[272]

Evil is an anthropological reality, no more and no less. Human beings experience evil and know that people can be evil. As anger is a part of being human, so also are the other evil impulses of the heart. Evil has its origins in

---

[270] On this, cf. the splendid description of such 'confusion and disorder' in a Western context in Thomas Mann: Der Erwählte, 1951, p. 53. [Engl. trans.: 'The holy sinner'. London, 1952.]

[271] On this problem, cf. J. F. Thiel, in: K. E. Müller. (ed.), 1983, pp.367ff.

[272] S. Nadel, 1970, p. 13.

190

human beings themselves. It is enough for the African to know that. The question of evil as such is unimportant, since it contributes nothing to coping with life in practical terms. If you suffer evil, you have to trace the person who is the cause of it. You have to search your own heart or look for the cause in others, including the ancestors. Somebody has caused the evil. Only the otherwise inexplicable and recurrent misfortune, the calamity which surpasses human experience, is ascribed to God himself. That God has the right to harbour such wrath against human beings is accepted without question. It is precisely because you cannot deduce the reason for evil that you know God is involved. Did he not create death?[273] Nothing is outside his domain. God sends the message of death; it is for humans to accept it.

If you go on to ask exactly where evil is located, the answer is almost always the same: in human envy. The reduction of the origin of evil to a common denominator is indicative and confirms earlier observations. Envy is directed at people. It does not know any other line of direction. Here too, human beings and their relations to their neighbours are at the heart of things. Evil is experienced as the destruction of interpersonal relations. It is not tied to an eternal or abstract law. In Africa there is no such law but only the living law of tradition, which determines the present. Common life makes human beings human and anyone violating this prepares the ground for evil. Evil does not exist without people: evil-doers have to bear the consequences, as well as victims.

African culture has been characterised as a 'culture of shame' and contrasted with the 'culture of guilt' of the West.[274] This typology tries to make sense of the phenomenon that Africans are ashamed of an act if it becomes known but if it remains hidden their conscience does not strike them – or so it appears to the overseas observer. Many detailed observations confirm this characterisation. We must understand how it differs from the Western concept of conscience, moulded by Christianity, because this will illuminate the African image of human beings.

---

[273] J. B. Danquah, 1968, pp.132 & 190; cf. above p. 200.
[274] Cf. A. F. Welbourn, 1968.

'Guilt' is recognised in the world religions through law which, applying to everyone everywhere, is oriented to actual deeds. In contrast, African ethics deal with situations. Tribal ethics only apply to the small-scale society, not to those living outside it; strangers within the society are only partially bound by them. Only where the community is actually disturbed, i. e. where the feelings of the individuals in this close circle are hurt, does a deed have an effect – on both perpetrator and victim. Adultery which does not become known counts as not having happened. If the husband should catch the lover in the act, his rights will be violated and his feelings wounded. He will call his wife to account and shout at her for all to hear; the harmony of the house and village will be disturbed. The deed only becomes evil through the consequences. The community will then go into action until peace is restored. It is not guilt that activates the community, because nobody is aware of it. Guilt demands forgiveness. It does not disturb the village environment, but is a matter for the heart. Forgiveness can be expressed in private, and received in prayer. In contrast, shame possesses a public character, it belongs to the 'world outside'. It activates the group and calls for reconciliation. As we have seen in various ways, the 'outward' has primary significance in Africa, and its 'inward' effect is secondary. What is not known has no impact, and so can be regarded as not having happened. But anything that challenges society must be put in order again, by society and not by the individual acting alone. The problem of evil shows that African ethics are fundamentally social ethics, and are understood as such.

The following example may clarify the problem. A mine-worker in southern Africa discovered after his return to his native village that his wife was pregnant. After the birth, he publicly accepted the child as his own, although everyone knew he had been away for months around the time of conception. He secretly wanted to track down his wife's secret lover. After finding him out, the husband went before the tribal court, accusing him of adultery with his wife and of begetting a child. The court did not accept the charge, because he had publicly declared the child was his. This secret investigation was only creating a disturbance, it stated. He had to think himself lucky not to be accused of having brought 'false' charges of adultery against somebody.

A special problem merits attention in this connection. The idea of destiny is practically unknown in Bantu Africa, but is found, variously expressed, in the Sudan belt and among West African peoples. Does this basically change the image of guilt and offence depicted above? Is it now expressed in fundamentally different anthropological terms? Let us return once more to the idea of the Akan peoples. *Kra* or *okra*, as we saw, comes from God, and is also that part of a person that comes from God and indicates his or her relationship with God. It is called "the small bit of the Creator that lives in every person's body".[275] Occasionally it is also expressed as if the *kra* existed independently of the human being, as a pre-existent soul.[276] God gives it leave from the 'home of the souls' or, more precisely, an assignment upon earth, which is to determine the character and individuality of a person – his or her destiny. "We cannot thus be made responsible for our own character or moral failings. If the *okra* does its God-given work on earth, this is called *obra*, i. e. that-which-has-come-into-the-world, the way to live, conduct, behaviour".[277] Is life then determined to such an extent that people tend to be fatalistic? This is not my impression; after all, the idea that the soul must give an account of itself developed precisely among the peoples of West Africa, and hardly anywhere else. What appears to us as a logical contradiction is not seen in this light in Africa.[278] Rather, the idea of destiny reflects the diversity of life's experiences, which cannot be reduced to a common denominator. An element of resignation is certainly involved. 'Our destiny' is unavoidable since it comes from God, a Twi proverb says. This idea is in keeping with the human tendency to plead innocent, but it would not be African if it did not also contain the impulse to play a trick on fate, if only a little

---

[275] Quoted by K. A. Busia, in: D. Forde, 1963, p. 197.

[276] Cf. the reference in A. Ringwald, 1965, p. 304, A130, to Christaller's dictionary: "okra is sometimes spoken of as if it were a personal being distinguished from man himself"; cf. on this whole subject, J. V. Taylor, 1965, pp.52ff & 58ff.; M. Fortes, 1966, pp.21ff.

[277] A. Ringwald, op. cit., p. 58; M. Fortes quotes W. R. Bascom, Social Status, Wealth and Individual Differences among the Yoruba, 1951, pp.22f.: 'The fate of mankind'.

one. The question of whether notions of fate were influenced by other religions (Egyptian?) requires no further investigation here; they are at home in
the more complex societies of West Africa, but not in the simpler societies of
Bantu Africa. This seems to reveal a touch of individualism: even within the
clan, the fate of an individual is a matter for concern. Not so in the traditional
Bantu religions – they could not imagine calling on their own *kra*, guardian
spirit, destiny, or that they could ceremonially cleanse their heads, the
dwelling-place of the *kra*, to express gratitude for unexpected success (*as-
sumguare* = to wash your own *kra*).

3. Bringers of evil – witches and sorcerers

Since E. E. Evans-Pritchard[279] investigated witchcraft and sorcery
among the Zande in the 1930s, research into this phenomenon of African societies has considerably expanded. Hitherto firmly rooted in the nebulous
field of superstition, the underlying social and ethical patterns have been the
subject of so many studies that we can restrict ourselves to the aspects relevant to our inquiry into the image of humankind in African religions.

The difference between witches and sorcerers that is fundamental to
the Zande cannot be transferred to all African societies, but it helps to explain
the phenomenon and will be upheld in what follows. Sorcerers work with
medicines, consciously, and by day. Their purposes are exclusively evil. They
are employed by people to harm others. They use poison and analogous actions in order to bring bad luck to other people. Their power lies in two
things: medicines and the bad consciences of the people they want to hurt.
They have little impact on those who do not fear them. Sorcerers can only
harm people who also desire evil, whose emotional stability is impaired, or
who have already harmed others through sorcery.

Medicines can protect against sorcery. The question is only who has
the better and stronger medicines. In extreme situations, people will not even

---

[278] Attention is drawn to this connection by E. Dammann, 1963, p. 51, 16A.

[279] E. E. Evans-Pritchard, 1978.

flinch from strengthening the medicine through the power of the human body, which has led to cases of homicide. While cannibalism is otherwise unknown in Africa it occurs occasionally within the context of harmful magic, medicines containing human organs being considered the most powerful and effective. This can only be explained within the overall concept of power and the 'analogous unity' patterned on the human body.

The sorcerer represents the evil in people. He (rarely she) harms another person without justifiable anger. In most cases the sorcerer is known (as far as possible, somebody from outside the village is sought), but for fear of revenge he is not expelled from the community. He is avoided if possible, and kept at a 'friendly' distance.

Witches function differently. Usually they are not conscious of this reputation and of their nocturnal mischief. To the amazement of European observers, women (rarely men) accused of witchcraft are often very ready to admit it, even when they have a clear conscience. That is understandable in psychological terms if women are menopausal, which is very often the case. It is also understandable in a society in which this sort of self-incrimination does not lead to social excommunication but to a renewed acceptance after the appropriate ritual. Despite such a possibility, the existence of witches in Africa remains an expression of deep uncertainty and anxiety. Fear of being harmed and the desire to do harm are often only two sides of the same inner mental attitude.[280]

Witches are part of everyday life, like human envy and greed. Witches threaten life, but they also provide relief from coping with everyday problems. They provide a foil for normal ethical life. At the same time, the unfathomable nature of negative experience is explained as being their work.

Witches are described as 'morose' and 'anti-social'. They 'eat alone', they 'pass others without greeting them', they are 'easily offended'.[281] They stare at others with a fixed gaze, they are 'unpleasant', 'sluttish', 'dirty'. But

---

[280] Cf. C. Staewen & F. Schönberg, 1970, p. 107.

[281] L. Mair, 1969, pp.43f.

even demonstrating good attributes can arouse suspicion: excessive friendliness, exceptional diligence, unaccustomed success.

Witches have particular animals as familiars: apes, buffaloes, antelopes, leopards, elephants. These unusual associations with animals and extraordinary properties make encounters with witches a sinister, even 'diabolical' experience.[282]

E. H. Winter has drawn up a witches' profile according to the ideas of the Amba in Western Uganda:

"1. Witches sometimes stand on their heads or rest hanging upside down from the limbs of trees. 2. Witches are active at night.3. When they are thirsty, they eat salt. 4. They go about naked. 5. They can transform themselves into leopards, or they may have leopards as their familiars which will attack people at their command. 6. They eat people. 7. Their victims are invariably members of their own village. 8. The witches in various villages are bound together in a system of reciprocity".[283]

At first sight this seems absurd, the fearful fantisising of a vivid imagination, but there is method in it. Witches do the contrary of what every normal member of Amba society does. They convert the ethical norms into their exact opposites. Healthy Amba are active during the day, not at night. They do not drink salty water when thirsty, never go naked, do not eat human flesh, and are always loyal to the inhabitants of their own village.

This picture mirrors the inverse image of right conduct. It shows that belief in witches contributes to maintaining the moral values of the society, ensuring that nobody steps out of line. It hinders the emergence of a competitive instinct, encourages uniform behaviour, and is repressive. However, indirectly it strengthens people's social awareness.

In African thought there is no contradiction between belief in witches and the perception of a natural cause-and-effect; they are complementary. Causality says how a misfortune happens. But such a simple explanation is not satisfactory because every event in the world has a deeper cause. Belief in

---

[282] H. J. Koloss, in: W. Raunig, 1980, p. 80.

[283] J. Middleton, in: J. Middleton & E. H. Winter, (eds.), 1969, p. 292.

witches answers the question "Why?". Why did something happen to me at precisely this moment? Why did this misfortune befall me, why am I ill, and not somebody else?[284] By being able to name the cause of misfortune, belief in witches contributes to people's emotional stability: it is easier to bear a misfortune if you know the cause, and can then combat it, than if you are at the mercy of a nameless fate and are mystified by an event.

If the belief in witches has a positive value in socio-psychological terms, this must not conceal the fact that, except perhaps among the Zande, it generally has a depressingly negative effect. It is not only restrictive, but also repressive. Monica Wilson has described belief in witches as "standardised nightmares of a group".[285] Among the Pondo in southern Africa, she was able to show how taboo wishes and ideas come to the surface in the belief in witches. In a small-scale society, which allows little room for chance, development or individuality, and in which everybody knows everybody else, the possibility of internal tensions grows in proportion to the closeness of the relationships. In the belief in witches, covetousness, envy and jealousy rise to the surface and poison the life of the community. Belief in witches is the focal point of suppressed cravings and repressed anger. It relies on the power of the evil word. In times of social upheaval, it sometimes spreads like an epidemic. The formation of breakaway groups, thus preserving the existence of a clan torn by dissension, indicates one opportunity for resolving tensions creatively.[286] The much more usual reaction to the increased appearance of witches is their persecution, killing and social ostracism. The appearance of 'witch-snooping' movements offers a further variation of healing the intolerable problems in the village, although the opposite effect is often produced.

---

[284] Cf. E. E. Evans-Pritchard, 1978, chap 2. Deserved misfortune comes from the ancestors; undeserved from the society (= witches), with which people live in a state of tension, whether they realise this or not; W. D. Hammond-Tooke, 1975.

[285] Quoted by J. Middleton & E. H. Winter, 1969, p. 9. For what follows, cf. M. Hunter, 1969, and the same author (= M. Wilson), 1971, pp.35ff.

[286] Describing the Bakossi in Cameroon, H. Balz writes: "Witchcraft in Nyasoso... takes exact account of every bad word spoken by man against his fellowman" (H. Balz, 1984, p. 374). For the whole of this subject, cf. ibid., pp.319ff.; for the division of clans, cf. L. Mair, 1969, pp.115ff.

Where the encounter with witchcraft is channelled by rituals we find the most 'humane' form of dealing with the social tensions that have been condensed into belief in witches.

There is no belief in the devil in Africa. The existence of witches is not a question of 'faith', but of everyday experience. Belief in witches is in Africa an expression of the reality of evil.[287]

4. Defenders of morality – diviners and medicine-men

In African religions and societies the diviner provides a point of contact between the world of the ancestors and the world of the living. Each world is undoubtedly accessible to everyone, yet there are people who have special access to the other world, either through birth and position or through vocation. To the first-named group belong the heads of families at any particular time, that is, the eldest son of the most recently deceased father. He is most closely related to his father, knows him best, and has the position of honour which is appropriate to dealings with family forebears. The *diviner* belongs to the class of those called to deal with the ancestors. No-one is born to be a diviner, even if there is a long family tradition of this calling.

Hearing the call is the most important pre-condition for this occupation. It begins when the ancestors start to 'brood' over a person, as the Zulu say *(ukufukamela)*. As a hen sits on her eggs, and something new comes of them, so the ancestors brood over someone to make them into a new, different person. The signs that the ancestors are calling are unmistakable: frequent and inexplicable dreams, much sneezing, yawning and burping, an ache in the shoulders, sides, upper back and below the neck. Finally, sleeplessness and sleep-walking are signs of the presence of the ancestors, since for them night is day.

---

[287] "The idea of witchcraft is recognition of the reality of evil; the denial of it is a denial of the existence of evil" (M. Wilson, 1971, p. 36). For a treatment of this whole problem and a comparison with belief in witches in Europe, cf. G. Parrinder, 1963; L. Mair, 1969, pp.180ff.; S. F. Nadel, 1970, pp.201ff.

If the signs are clear, you have to find out which ancestor is calling, one from your own family, or one from your spouse's. In the former case you can pluck up courage to put up a fight, because in the end you know your own forefathers. That applies particularly when the ancestors call women. To be married to a diviner is a nuisance. That is why, at least in Zululand, men seldom have a bad conscience about rejecting the call addressed to their wives.

If the call is rejected, the person concerned may become completely well again. But if they experience a bad relapse, nobody will hesitate to give in the second time. Anybody who has accepted the call is obliged to alter their life. Four changes are striking: 1. They do not wash any more, or only with the contents of the stomach of a slaughtered animal. The fluid has a special function, which makes the one called acceptable to the ancestors. It bleaches the hands, making them white like those of the ancestors. 2. Anybody who does occasionally wash must apologise beforehand and then afterwards rub themself with the contents of a gall-bladder. The empty gall-bladder will be fixed in their hair. It shows the ancestors that they are receptive to them and have accepted their call. The ancestors love gall-bladders, since it has only one exit, like a traditional Zulu hut. Its sour contents taste sweet to the ancestors, since for them everything is reversed (inverse analogy). 3. Hair grows long, as do one or more finger-nails. Hair and nails signify life. The growth is an indication that the person is moving to a new situation. The hair of a new-born child is cut; it is no longer a foetus. The hair of a bride is cut; she is no longer a girl. The same is done to a young man after the celebration of puberty; now he is a man. At the end of the period of mourning, the hair of a widow is shaved, as a sign that she is no longer a widow, but may remarry. The hair of novice diviners is also cut at the end of their apprenticeship. They separate themselves from their old lives and belongs to a new fraternity. 4. The man or woman who is called must abstain from using all cosmetics. Cosmetics are meant to make people beautiful and arouse attention. That is exactly what should no longer happen. Whoever is under the direct influence of the ancestors lives dangerously and should be avoided. Instead of normal cosmetics, the novice will rub on white clay or ashes, because white is the colour of the ancestors. Nobody can be a diviner without white colouring.

Apprentices are taught by an experienced diviner. The training serves the purpose of restoring their health and of introducing them to the life and techniques of a diviner. They also have to learn to live in such a way that the ancestors continue to brood over them, without harm to body or soul.

Here is the report of a diviner, describing in detail the experience of accepting a call.[288]

I was very sick, having dreamt much for many nights. The body was painful everywhere, especially the shoulders and sides. It was *izibhopho*. The whole body was in sickness. On a certain day, in the evening, I was sitting in the doorway. Just sitting, there came a beetle (*umzifisi*). It came closer. It was white. It came closer and closer until it was next to me. I heard it saying certain words. It said, 'Stand up! Follow me! Stand up! Follow me! (*Sukuma! Ngilandele!*)' It was saying these words very much, flying around about me. It spoke those words until I stood up. It flew in a certain direction, calling me all the time. I followed it. I walked and walked, following the beetle which was calling me all the time, saying the same words. I simply followed, going in the direction of the beetle all the time. It was flying in front. I was walking behind. I felt strong. The energy returned to the bones. I even followed running. I was amazed, finding myself running but being such a sick man. The beetle flew to a certain pool, all the time saying to me, '*Ngilandele!*' I walked on the stones, entering the pool. I walked on the stones in the pool until I came to the bottom, all the time following the beetle. There I stopped. I looked everywhere, seeing many things. I saw a very great python (*inhlwathi*) coiled on medicines. It was surrounded by many other snakes, big ones and small ones. They were the snakes of our fathers. They were just there, at the bottom of the pool, lying there and looking at me with open eyes. The python had a lamp (*isikethekethe*) on its head. It was shining in the pool, throwing light everywhere and revealing the things there in the pool. There was also a lady there with very big breasts, suckling the children of the python. There were many children of the python. It (the python) put spittle (*amathe*) into the woman. She became pregnant and gave birth, producing the children of a snake. The python said to the shade-snakes, 'Is this the man?' They agreed, saying that I was the man. Then the snake (python) spoke to me, addressing me clearly, 'Did the beetle bring you here?' I agreed. 'What was the colour of the beetle?' I gave the colour of the beetle. It said, 'Did it speak of medicines?' I agreed that it had spoken of medicines, adding that I had also dreamt of medicines. It said, 'The medicines are under my stomach, just underneath me. Just take some medicines.' So I took some medicines, fearing very much. Then it said, 'Smear yourselves with the medicines seeing that you have work (to do).' So I smeared myself with the clay, being naked. Then the snake put spittle on me. I feared very much. I put spittle everywhere. Then it returned, lying on the medicines, leaving me there with the medicines and the spittle. It was hot. Then the python said, 'Look at all these. Do you know them?' I said that I recognised them, seeing all the shade-snakes and the woman with the breasts, just suckling all the time. The python said to me, 'Just take some medicines in the hand.' I took medicines in the hand from under the snake. Then the beetle came to me saying the words as before. I followed it, walking on the stones of the pool. I did not look back, having been told not to look backwards. I walked and walked. I came to the top of the pool, following the beetle all the time, just following it. When it came to the bank of the river it stopped, saying, 'From here I leave you.' It returned into the water. There arose a mist. I found myself on the bank of the river, being naked and having the white medicines of the pool. There was whiteness everywhere on the body. Then I looked in the hand and saw the snake that I took in the pool. I hung it around the neck, its head resting on my head, the body around the neck. I walked home. I came home after walking a very long way. There was much noise, people lamenting very much, simply shouting and screaming (*isililo*) the death lamentation. I said, 'Surely there must be a corpse, somebody having died, seeing that they are lamenting thus.' I came close to the homestead. I called on them saying, 'People of my fathers, what is this noise, my not having heard that there is death in our place?' They said, 'No, there is the corpse of the one that is not. He left here one day in the evening, just walking in the direction of the great river. Since his departure he has not returned. So we are lamenting him, seeing that he did not return.' Then I knew that they were mourning me. I said, 'No, I simply went to the river, being called by a beetle, taking medicines at the river. Even just now I have the medicines.' They came out. They saw me. They were very much amazed, seeing me naked and carrying medicines and with a snake. They said, 'But you were dead. We have heard of them that know (diviners) that you were dead. But now we see you living again. We cannot deny the things that were said. But you are living now, having medicines and carrying this thing. But how is it that you left, leaving no word?'

The symbolism of this wonderful text requires no detailed interpretation; from the point of view of depth psychology, it is clear. I will merely draw attention to a few important points. The great python calls the diviner '*inkosi yamadlozi*', the lord of the ancestors. This means God himself, the

---

[288] Berglund, 1975, pp.140ff.

life-giving creator. To the question why God is not himself present on the earth, the diviner answers that God will not consume everything with his fire, that is why only his image is down there. "He sends his animal". He makes woman fertile. "That is the sign. The sign says that life (*imphilo*) comes from the one above. He made the woman fertile. That is the sign of the woman!" The ancestors make children, but the power of fertility comes from God. The spittle is a symbol for semen. God and the ancestors together bring about fertility.

The great pond is called '*uhlangu*' – the place from which human beings spring, according to Zulu myths. "Reeds are the carriers of water. They go deep down into the earth and cause humanity's conception".

All in all, it is a matter of a birth – the birth of a diviner. This binds the snake and the diviner together. The saliva of the snake is used as medicine.

The whiteness of the various objects is associated with the ancestors. The water is running water and symbolises life, also fertility. Running water means a man's fertility, and still water is a reference to a woman's amniotic fluid. We have here a telling, intense portrayal of death and rebirth. The diviner entered the water and came out again, naked and white like a new-born child. Even black children are light-skinned at birth. "Why are they white at birth? Only because of the ancestors".

After initiation a period of teaching begins, which in Zululand usually lasts two years. The novices themselves decide when it is over, when they are convinced they are mature enough to become a diviner. The hen broods over the egg, but the chick itself pecks open the shell, it is said. A great feast is held, another initiation and finally recognition by other diviners concludes the training.

The diviner is not a charlatan in traditional society, even if everybody knows that there are such characters. Despite the existence of a kind of professional ethic there is a certain amount of rivalry among diviners. There are no known cases of cooperation. The identity of the true diviner is determined by the ancestors, not by human desires. However, the desires of victims and advice-seekers are relevant. Diviners are fully aware of the tensions which exist in the community, and expose them during the enquiry. Their function is often that of a catalyst. They offer people the opportunity not only to talk over the misfortune that has befallen them, but also to put into words more deep-seated cares, the pain of neglect, failings and anxieties, and to discover ways of resolving the situation. Diviners probe for answers or, conversely, confront people with possible solutions. Depending on their tradition and technique, they will have recourse to 'meditation aids', such as bones, stones, etc., or will rely more on questions. Often the two are connected. In West African countries this technique is highly developed. The various forms and constellations of stones produce fixed answers. Divination is not a mechanical exercise or technique, but an intensive form of communication, in which there are patients and doctors or, more precisely, 'therapists'. Alertness and empathy are characteristics of diviners. They encourage people to speak, as psychotherapists do. Because such questioning usually takes place in groups and not in secret, there are group dynamic processes at work. The diviner will seldom give an answer which is not attuned to people's feelings, especially as their conscience has been aroused, perhaps by illness, making them sensitive to the possible causes of the tensions which exist.

Words are not the only means of communication between the diviner and his or her patients. We have already seen how every colour, every ritual and every dream is full of symbolism. The associations which the symbol releases are often more important than the object itself. The same applies to the aids for divination. "If we have these things, then we know that they (the ancestors) are near, and help us with divination. But if they are not near, not even these things will help at all", said a Zulu diviner.[289]

In all this diviners see themselves only as a medium, an instrument of the ancestors. The latter disclose where a spell has been cast, and indicate the way to fight against the power of the sorcerer. They can do this because they see and know more, and are concerned to stand beside their descendants in the struggle against the evil, which takes on a visible form in the person of the sorcerer. This is why the diviner is so respected in traditional society.

---

[289] Ibid., p. 173.

They know the causes of evil and show the way to restoring the old order, the health of individuals and the harmony of the community.

In various peoples the office of diviner is linked with that of the herbalist, usually known as the medicine-man and sometimes as medicine-woman. Their field of activity is then extended, even if the office itself is not basically changed. Diagnosis and the discovery of healing medicine are only different aspects of the one healing procedure. Money corrupts the character, and that applies to diviners and medicine-men as well. Anyone who has power over sickness and health can easily be tempted to abuse it. People also go to the diviner today in order to inflict harm on others. It is this mixture of completely contradictory tasks in one person (sorcerer and healer) which has brought the office and person of the diviner into disrepute. The dislocations of modern life, the profound processes of change brought about in traditional societies by schools, medicine and Christianity, has had the further consequence that the office of the diviner (now generally known as 'witch doctor') has fallen into disrepute and been bracketed with the 'demonic'. The gap has been filled by the leaders of the Independent African Churches. They now carry the biblical title of prophet. B. Sundkler was able to show how strikingly the distinguishing features of the phenomena coincide,[290] so that the characteristics and symbols of diviners have been interpreted in a Christian sense. The symbol remains, but the meaning is changing.

Four main points can be drawn from these parallels:

1. Diviners and prophets must be called. The signs of a calling and setting apart, dreams, illness, repeated belching, 'ecstasy', are no longer, however, signs of the ancestors, but are interpreted as the working of the Holy Spirit. New wine in old wine-skins...

2. The diviners helped their societies. It was their task to improve relations between neighbours. While the ministers of the mission churches sought to restore the relationship with God, the task of the prophets is aimed

---

[290] B. Sundkler, 1964.; on this whole topic, cf. also H. J. Becken, 1972 (bibliography).

at healing, and restoring the social relationships of small groups – be it the new church or the family. The diviner's driving out of evil spirits activated by sorcerers has its counterpart in the exorcisms of the prophets.

3. The diviner worked within the community, initiating healing processes rooted in the group. Today the Zionist churches are, in many respects, somewhat like hospitals with the dynamics of psychotherapy groups. People live together for days at a time, praying together, purifying themselves regularly both internally and externally by means of salt, ashes and ritual bathing in streams and the sea, until healing is achieved. Salvation takes the form of healing – as in traditional religions. The diviner was a medicine-man; the prophet is pastor and doctor in one.

4. In traditional religions the healing process was begun in ritual and accompanied by ritual. Every treatment symbolically transcended the procedure. The same applies to the prophets of the healing churches. Not only do they speak a simple language, rich in images; they translate it into actions (dance, purification, confession) and rites. A new liturgy has been developed, corresponding to traditional feeling. The members of these churches can remain completely African, maintaining the original world of meaning and images, and being led into the modern world in a new group.

5. Guardians of the law – secret societies

The structure of African society, J. Ittmann once wrote, "can be represented as two intersecting lines. The vertical lines are the descent groups of the clans which form the people, with their ... clan chiefs... They watch over the external well-being of the settlement and the people. The horizontal lines interlinking the clans and the settlements are formed by the cultic secret society".[291] In previous chapters we have only looked at the first aspect in connection with the veneration of the ancestors, without describing directly how communities were ruled. To depict the African image of humankind, it sufficed to refer to the patriarchal structures of authority. In acephalous socie-

---

[291] Anthropos, 1957, p. 164.

ties, or those ruled by chiefs or kings, the inner structure remains the same, based on the authority of the 'fathers', of the eldest of the clan and of the clan leader. The eldest member of every family is a potential chief, i. e. a king. Conversely, every sacral monarchy still reflects the authority of the eldest of the clan, who is the mediator between the living and the ancestors, even God.

In relatively homogenous small-scale societies this form of internal authority and of external government is sufficient. However, with the increase in ethnic and cultural contacts which turn small-scale societies into larger ones, the simple forms of government no longer function. New structures have to be developed and new authorities created, at the horizontal level. Where there is still a mythical and religious unity of the people, as expressed in sacral monarchy or in highly organised central government, secret societies are less necessary and less likely to be found. They are apparently a modern phenomenon.

What is the significance of secret societies for the image of humankind? First, they confirm the picture we have found so far: a person becomes a full member of society through ritual. As in initiation rituals, acceptance into the secret society involves dying and rising again into the new life. It teaches obedience, and also the virtues which guarantee its continued existence. However, these values are not binding on all members of society, since the secret society is not identical with the entire people.

In other words, secret societies are a means of reacting positively to the first signs of a pluralist society. The crucial elements are downright contradictory. The secret societies are a kind of secular government, working at night, and so supplementing the 'official' government of the country, which works by day. The secret societies take care that the ethical standards of the village do not lapse. Since in most cases they extend beyond the village – the largest and best-known are found throughout the whole country – they are concerned with the standardisation of ethical standards and their implementation in the whole of the district.

The means used to implement their particular ideas are the same as those of traditional small societies: internal group cohesion through rituals based on the laws of analogy, attachment to animals and their powers, identification with animal symbols. The power of the secret society is established and imposed by oath, threat of punishment, symbolic actions and, above all, by the use of medicines (in the literature usually called sorcery). Secrecy is also an effective means of increasing belief in the external power of the secret society. Even that is not original, since making something taboo always serves this purpose, as we have seen. What is new is the radical bond with the group, setting it clearly apart from other groups. This distinguishes secret societies from initiation schools, which only enable a temporary distancing since their purpose is re-entry into the whole community.

The selection of those who can be accepted is also new. Only the free-born can become members, and not strangers, slaves or freed slaves, or those who have come from another village. In some secret societies, only rich villagers can join, because the 'entry fee' is so high that poorer people cannot afford it. This entry fee may initially appear a great sacrifice, but in the long term it is a good investment, because the members know how to look after each other very well. Secret societies are our 'bank', according to an apt modern comparison.[292] Social aspects alone are no longer decisive, as in the initiation schools which follow the rhythm of life; here economic interests push to the fore.

Religious elements are not entirely absent, but they do not play a prominent role, as the ancestor cult otherwise does. Secret societies did not emerge from religion, but were often taken over from other peoples; they only associate themselves with a few religious elements, such as certain symbols, belief in spirits, notions of the soul, and masked dances. Belief in demons finds as little place here as in the rest of Africa.[293] Since medicines without sacramental force are hardly conceivable in Africa, they indirectly

---

[292] J. Ittmann, 1953, p. 175.

[293] This has been proved conclusively by H. Balz, 1948, chap. 3, in opposition to J. Ittmann. Reference is made in his argument to two secret societies which serve festivals (*Ahon*) and the maintenance of order (*Mwankum*). I am indebted to this work for important insights. For the study of secret societies, the following is still fundamental: D. Westermann, 1921, pp.228ff. Cf. also J. Ittmann, 1935, & 1957; G. Parrinder, 1961, pp.127ff.; C. Geary, 1976, pp.106ff.

bring religion into the secret societies.[294] Altogether, religion seems to have been removed from the centre to form part of the cultural superstructure. Today modern Africans regard secret societies more as part of the cultural heritage of their people, and even adherents of a revealed religion, i. e. Christians or Muslims, can belong.

Secret societies claim to reflect the ethical pattern of traditional society and to preserve it. That is generally correct, yet with one important qualification. You are born into the family, clan and traditional society with their necessary concern for the well-being of all. Now you can, indeed must, choose between competing groups. That also applies even when the decision to join a secret society, or the refusal to do so, is occasionally made under pressure. In addition, fears of competition are mobilised. Once you have opted for a group, the internal group pressure is much stronger than that of the natural group. But it does not cover the whole of life any longer. Life is compartmentalised.

The new tie is established by a covenant, often sealed in blood. Since membership of the group is no longer a matter of course, it requires this additional means of reinforcement. The concept of the covenant thereby takes on a central significance, both ethical and legal. Yet this does not make it a central theme of African religiosity in general.[295]

The Mau Mau movement showed for East Africa what significance such a secret society can have, albeit temporarily, in this case for the development of a state.

In the preceding chapters, I have referred where possible to both sexes in describing the image of humankind reflected in African religions. Yet the general impression cannot be resisted that African societies are male dominated. This also applies in matrilineal tribes, even if women have a different position there from in patrilineal societies.

---

[294] On the question of medicine and religion, cf. E. B. Idowu, 1973, pp.197ff.

[295] E. B. Idowu, in: C. G. Baëta, 1968, p. 434; for the concept of covenants among the Kikuyu, cf. C. Ndanyu, Conception of Covenant in African Traditional Religion and Customs, with Special Reference to the Gikuyu of Kenya. Diss. theol., Heidelberg, 1987.

For this reason, it seemed relevant and necessary to insert a special chapter here on the position of women, based on a paper written by my wife. While largely reliant on secondary source material, she also draws on our years spent living in Africa where she had close contacts with African women.

6. WOMEN IN AFRICAN RELIGIONS
(by Renate Sundermeier)

I. Cultic roles

1. Images of women in the African pantheon of gods

At first sight, it is disappointing that there are no spectacular images of Goddesses, like those we know from other cultures. And yet in the African heaven there is often a woman or a feminine principle in a prominent position when it comes to creation, or fertility, or rain, thunder and lightning. In this connection, in many peoples, there appears to be a divinity who is either feminine or androgynous, or else the creator-god is wedded to the earth or the primeval mother. An example will illustrate this.

Among the Fon in Benin, there is the bisexual creator divinity Mawu-Lisa, commonly described as a Janus figure: one side is feminine, her eyes are the moon (Mawu), and the other is masculine, his eyes are the sun (Lisa). In addition, in one interpretation Mawu means earth, and Lisa means heaven, and the eclipse of the moon is the sexual union of both. Mawu is the personification of fertility, motherhood, forgiveness, gentleness. Lisa is power, might, tenacity. Apart from that, Mawu-Lisa guarantees the rhythm of day and night. The feminine element is night, freshness, quietness, joy; the masculine is day, heat, work. Human life and characteristics are thus foreshadowed in the deity. The divinity leaves its imprint on life and preserves the balance between extreme opposites. Since it represents the ideal twin, among the Fon the birth of twins of opposite sexes is regarded as the ideal kind of birth, whereas, among many other African peoples, twins, or at least the second child, have reportedly been killed soon after birth, to prevent misfortune. Perhaps it is no coincidence that among such societies I have found no dual divinity, whereas I have found the same respect for twins in those peoples where there are both masculine and feminine creator-gods, e. g. the Yoruba and the Dogon.

The extent to which divine, thus ideal, circumstances can be transferred to earthly relations is shown by the fact that the chief of the Fon is still addressed by the honorific title 'Two in One', although it reportedly has been a long time since the reign of a pair of twins of opposites sexes, who had to be treated exactly the same. Two people were even appointed to every title and office in the chief's court, one a man, one a woman. Dual nature is here equated with perfection, wholeness and worth.

In many parts of Africa, among the West African peoples as often as among the Bantu of Central Africa, we find figurines analogous to the bisexual creation principle, figures with breasts and a phallus as well as other sexual symbols, which are clearly linked with the tradition of creation myths. Among the Dogon in Mali, a symbol of this sort is found in connection with the loft, namely, an inverted basket with a round opening at the bottom and a square upper surface, which is still made today. In the original form of this loft, the so-called 'heavenly store', there were also steps on the four sides. The treads were feminine; each bore a prototype of the 'original couple' of everything created, God's unique gift. The risers were masculine. Treads and risers are one, but are distinguished from each other as the masculine and feminine principle.

In some peoples, even the names of the genitalia indicate the close conceptual link between the creation myth and the human community. Among the Lobedu of South Africa, the name of the female sexual organ is 'the place of the gods' and the name of the penis 'the support of the village'. On one hand, sexuality extends into the religious sphere, and on the other, it consolidates relationships of daily life in the here-and-now.

So we see that, when it comes to envisioning God, women have their place in the myths of creation. Myths stimulate everyday ideas and experiences, just as human life inspires mythical concepts.

2. The role of women as divine queens

Here and there in Africa we find the institution of the divine king, among the Bantu, the Loango in the Congo (Zaire), the Shona in Zimbabwe, and among the peoples of West Africa, e. g. among the Twi in Ghana. In this case, the queen mother, who is not always the biological mother of the ruler, regularly receives great honours, even if she is not considered divine in every case. Both trace their origin back to the heavenly divinities. The life of the divine king is rooted in ritual functions, because he is the mediator between human beings and the deities, his ancestors. The apotheosis of his life is the ritual sacrificial death at the end of a specific period of rule. Among the Shona, the chief wife of the king had to play the active leading role, but also a passive role, in the ritual death of the king. After he had ruled for four or five years, she was commanded by the most senior councillors to strangle the king. After the passage of a further year, she herself, or the king's favourite wife, when they were not the same person, was first of all robbed piece by piece of her adornment, then strangled as well, and laid to rest in the same grave beside the king. Underlying this second death is the desire that the dead ruler should have his beloved wife with him in the next world. The killing of women was also customary, however, as the ultimate gift of subjects in some peoples which did not have divine kingship. Among the Lunda in the Congo and the Kwanjama-Ambo in Namibia several women were strangled and buried beside the dead chief, as well as a living young girl, bound hand and foot. What is surprising is that these are matrilineal peoples.

I should like to look more closely at a people in which a woman holds the strongest cultic position as the divine queen. Significantly, this has to do with its rain ritual. Once more the analogy, rain – fertility – woman is clear. The rain queen of the Lobedu in South Africa is not primarily the ruler, but the rain-maker, and the appearance of rain is the highest divine justification

211

for her high office. The men are dependent upon her ability to make rain, and to deprive the enemy's region of rain. Because she can do this her neighbours are very friendly, and even pay tribute to her. In exchange for the rain, the queen's subjects present her with maidens, who are known as 'the queen's women'. The queen passes some of them on to high-ranking vassals or to allied chiefs. The analogy is obvious: her subjects receive the fertility of the land in rain, and give fertility in the form of women. The rain queen herself is not married, but is expected to have children by a 'secret partner', proving that she really is in perfect physical condition, as is expected of divine kings.

It is believed that the queens are so closely linked to nature, or, in African terminology, to their divine ancestors who give rain through them, that they can influence the rain through their emotions alone, without any ritual. The fact that the rains came much too late in 1934 was explained as being due to the anger of the queen over her daughter's affair with a commoner.

Right at the beginning of her reign the queen must prove that her ancestors have really entrusted her with the office. If drought and famine occur later, it will be ascribed to other, contrary powers. A rain-doctor, working with the queen, has to expose these hostile powers and render them harmless. If he discovers, for example, that the ancestors of the queen 'tie her hands', he will conduct ceremonies at the shrine of the royal ancestors. What the queen really does in order to make rain is a closely guarded secret. Shortly before her death, she confides this to her designated successor alone. The ingredients of the rain medicine are guarded in earthenware vessels at a place to which only a few people have access. The principle of analogy, which has a dominant role in all African rites, is easily recognisable in many ingredients. They include a climbing plant, containing a lot of water, the feathers of a 'lightning' bird, sea water, black and white mussels, white because that is the colour of the ancestors and water, and black, the colour of thunder clouds. Beside the vessels, there are horns containing a powder, whose smoke, when burnt, rises to form rain clouds. The most important ingredient of rain medicine, namely the skin of the deceased rain-queen, is never mentioned. Among other peoples who venerate their kings as divine, the skin of the dead king is also used for cultic purposes. If we apply the principle of analogy to the rain-queen the explanation could be as follows: as snakes shed their skins, but still live on, the institution itself lives on and is renewed, in spite of the death of this rain-queen.

Because of her sacral character, the queen is subject to certain restrictions, as is generally the custom with divine queens. She must not come into contact with ordinary subjects, and her freedom of movement is very restricted. One of her names is 'she who stays in the hut'. The divine nature of the queen entails the belief that she is without physical deficiency, not susceptible to illnesses, and not subject to natural death. It is believed that she can only die of her own free will. Her ritual suicide must not take place when she is still young and strong, as we saw in other cases, but is connected with the fourth circumcision ceremony of the youths, which takes place at irregular intervals of several years. She must see the young men go away, but not come back, it is said. An analogy of the number four with the seasons is suggested, and thus with the fulfilment of the cycle of the year. However, this cannot be proved. The changing seasons do not have such a pronounced effect on daily life in Africa as they do in a more temperate climate.

The above shows that women can play a very important cultic role. The number of examples could be extended, but in the end one thing is clear, and that is: for ordinary women, who are not from a royal family, or are not the wives of a chief, the chances of playing a leading part in ritual are small indeed.

3. Other roles for women in ritual

Now I should like to examine to what extent the average woman can play a cultic role at all. It is an established fact that, for all the significance of the ancestor cult throughout Africa, there is little veneration of female ancestors. It occurs, if at all, in the family. Male ancestors will be always be invoked in matters of importance for the whole people. That reflects everyday life. A woman's place is in the home. Usually men have the final say in matters concerning the whole community. To intercede for members of your own family, you set apart a goat for the deceased grandmother, who perhaps had

213

been particularly fond of the family member concerned, or you perform a ritual with a piece of pearl jewellery which belonged to her. However, women can become dreaded avenging spirits if they die during pregnancy. In such cases, the cause of death is accepted as being that their husband mistreated them. Together with the spirit of the unborn, they will haunt the husband's family. Women are actively involved in the veneration of the ancestors, mainly as the wives of their husbands, i. e. in a subordinate position – collecting wood for the ancestral fire, or among the Herero as 'guardians of the fire' (*ondangere*). If they themselves are the head of the household, or are old enough to approach the ancestors themselves, they can also be the chief officiant.

Some women in matrilineal societies play important roles in traditional rites. For example, among the Bemba female guardians keep watch over the sacred relics. Otherwise women are only involved, to my knowledge, with respect to fertility in the widest sense. For example, among the Lobedu, a single annual sacrifice for the ancestors, the harvest beer, is prepared by elderly women and girls who have not yet reached puberty. That is very important: old women and young girls. This example points to something running through all religious practices in Africa – the ritual impurity of women during their years of menstruation. This is the fundamental reason why women are widely excluded from performing rites.

African men have strangely ambivalent feelings towards women. On the one hand, they protect, even honour them as the source of fertility, and the guarantee that the chain of life is not ruptured – the most important point for all African philosophy – and the result is, at least for aging women who have fulfilled their role as wives and mothers to the satisfaction of the clan, a respected, assured place in the family circle. On the other hand, there is a mythical fear of impurity caused by menstruating women, which would bring illness and death. This explains all the taboos connected with menstruation. As already noted, the general exclusion from ritual can be offset by high birth or the high rank of a woman's husband. Furthermore, they are not allowed to collect medicines, or sleep with their husband during their period, because through the woman's blood the husband comes into contact with the

214

woman's ancestor world which is alien and harmful to him; they are not even allowed to cook food at this time. Among the Dogon of Mali, menstruating women are completely banned from the village and must remain in huts some distance away. They must avoid the paths in general use, and wash themselves in special places. These particularly strong taboos are based on the special form of the creation myth among the Dogon. Among the Zulu, women may not even enter cattle kraals. The cattle are closely linked to the ancestral world of the master of the kraal.

The core of the problem is this: blood, when it has left a living organism, loses its positive meaning as the life-force, which stands for everything that is good and brings healing, and is converted into its opposite, becoming impure and dangerous. For this reason, corpses are also unclean. Even after childbirth, which in itself is an experience of great joy, women are impure because of the blood loss and must undergo purification rites before taking up normal life again. The initiation rites for young girls must also be seen in close connection with the dangerous nature of menstrual blood. Among the Pondo in South Africa, the rites are for the protection of women themselves. During the rites, the young girl is placed under the protection of male ancestors, which is why these rites must always take place in the paternal kraal. If the ceremony is not performed because of the expense involved, and illness later befalls the young woman or her children, the rites will be carried out immediately. There is fear of poison through impure blood.

To sum up: because of the social position of women and their ritual impurity, women are generally excluded from important religious practices. This practice is a little less rigid in matrilineal societies, where they are more esteemed. Ritual impurity has consequences for the everyday life of women.

4. Women in witchcraft and magic

Even greater than the danger of being made impure, which can be countered with the help of taboos and purification rites, is the danger from witches and sorcerers. The distinction is generally this: witches work with the help of their intrinsic powers or with the help of obedient spirits, while sorcerers use medicines, which can possibly be detected by an autopsy. It is generally accepted that witches and sorcerers do harm because of envy and resentment. The more fundamental reason for belief in witches is not being able to find a cure for every illness, nor a remedy for bad luck and misfortune. The same justification is provided for belief in spirits, which we will discuss later. Monica Wilson calls belief in witches and sorcerers 'standardized nightmares of a group', emphasising that there are no individual ideas about the existence of witches, and that the group recognises them by what they have been taught. Witches are the complete antithesis of the ruling moral code and, since in Africa external and internal things are never separated from each other, this is also shown in their behaviour.

In principle, witches can also be male. With the exception of the Lugbara of Uganda I have not found a people where witches are only men, but there are many in which only women are suspected of being witches.

The Nupe in northern Nigeria have an entire organisation of female witches, allegedly headed by the well-known leader of the market women. This assumption can be explained by the fact that the Nupe women are generally so successful in trading that their husbands have become completely dependent upon them. This is a case of social envy on the part of the potential victims, a confirmation of the nightmare theory. The neighbouring Gwari people, whose womenfolk are not nearly so successful, has no gender distinction for witchcraft. Among the Pondo in South Africa, too, only women are cast as witches. They have sexual relations with the spirits of their hearth, who have pale skin. When you consider that the land has been settled by whites for hundreds of years and that sexual contact with them used to be taboo, at least for the black men, and if you know that the Pondo continually have contact with sexually taboo people in their large family compounds, it is understandable that Pondo men have sexual nightmares.

Morton Williams has put forward the following theory concerning the Yoruba in southern Nigeria: the infant mortality rate of 40% is responsible for their belief in exclusively female witches. The men suspect their wives of causing this – it is assumed that witches and their familiar spirits gorge themselves on the flesh of their victims – and wives suspect their co-wives and mothers-in-law.

There is usually a combination of motives. In recent times, when the authority of the chief to persecute and punish witches has been largely withdrawn, court statistics show that, in 24% of all cases involving an accusation of witchcraft, the two wives of one man are the plaintiff and the defendant respectively. So jealousy is a further motive. It may be assumed that, with the gradual decline in polygyny, the figures have already changed. All the same, such a figure says something about the strong psychological pressure on women in such marriages, something which many anthropologists do not want to accept.

The view is also widely held that people, and principally women, become witches without any blame being attached to them. They are compelled by a spirit, which continually brings misfortune upon them or their children. Of course they can try to transfer the spirit to an animal through ritual, but if that doesn't work they have to take up witchcraft. In any case, a public confession of guilt can then help. The essential part of being a witch can be inherited or absorbed with your mother's milk. In this case, a person has hardly any freedom of choice in the face of the evil in the world. So in these societies witches are not subject to any strong moral judgement.

To sum up: inexplicable blows of fate, sickness, or the frustration of failure induce people to search out who, or what, is responsible, so as to tackle the problem at the root.

5. Possession

As we have seen, women do not generally have a strong cultic position. There is, however, a kind of back door through which they can be admitted to religious practices, and that is possession. It is estimated that 95% of the cases of possession involve women. The medical diagnosis is called 'hysterical dissociation'. Situations of stress are responsible for possession, and African women have certainly always had plenty of that. We should also see possession as a coping mechanism. A long-term stressful situation, i. e. infertility, very frequently leads to possession. If an African woman cannot fulfil expectations regarding her role as wife and mother, she is a nobody in traditional society. There is no other role open to her, unless it be the 'negative' one of prostitution. If a woman tries to find a way out of a stressful situation, or if she urgently needs attention, different societies offer their own solutions. One of them is possession. It allows the woman to escape from an unbearable situation, at least temporarily. Evil spirits and demons are driven out during a solemn ceremony to the approval of a large gathering. We do not need to concern ourselves further with this form of possession, which does not merit cultic status. However, those possessed by the spirits of the ancestors or manifestations of the divinities have a respected position, at least when they speak officially. The following historical example shows how great the power of a medium can be.

Mbuya Nehanda was a medium of the creator-god Mwari, who led the Shona in Zimbabwe in a rebellion against white occupation. Although initially successful, it was put down in 1897 with much bloodshed. She herself was executed in 1896 by a British firing squad. Before the uprising she had already become famous as a medium; local chiefs sought her advice on tribal affairs. The rebellion called for a charismatic leader. Nehanda promised her followers invulnerability, even immortality, an idea which appears again and again in 'holy wars'. The relevant formula is: the bullets turn to water. (cf. Maji-Maji uprising in Tanzania). Nehanda instructed her followers not to enrich themselves with the goods and chattles of the whites. They first obeyed – the booty piled up in Nehanda's kraal. Then they broke the command. The Africans attributed the failure of the rebellion to their disobedience, and not to Nehanda's misjudgement of the situation, or to the large contingent of troop reinforcements assembled by the government.

A century later, a medium from the Hurungwe tribal area of northern Zimbabwe, hosting the spirit of Mbuya Nehanda, warned the Zimbabwean prime minister to make amends for offending ancestral spirits through his lack of contrition for brutal repression by the army. Reportedly he became deeply anxious. Ndebele mediums from southern Zimbabwe had condemned him since the mid-80s (source: The Times, London, 9.3.98).

To sum up: in Africa possession does not always mean something negative, often being seen as the gateway to greater insights and powers which can be used in the service of the community. The assumption behind this is that possession is an indication of certain characteristics, the stamp of credibility, so to speak, for future mediums, healers and diviners. Unwanted possession is healed through exorcism by experts who have usually been possessed themselves at some time. An initiation ritual serves as a kind of ordination to the service of the ancestors or the gods. Women are apparently more disposed towards such phenomena than men. Their 'credibility' is unchallenged, even if they are of an age when they are still ritually unclean.

II. Signs of change

In the following pages, I will attempt to show how the role of women in their religious practices and ideas reflects economic and social change. Even if the process is still in a state of flux, certain phenomena and tendencies can be perceived.

Change in Africa is particularly at the expense of women. In spite of great progress towards professional success, emancipation and social recognition, the majority of African women have lost their status and security. Their work is usually the conventional drudgery which does not earn money, and even when they have a job outside the home, their work is the worst paid. That can be proved by a few figures. Women have built 50% of the roads in the mountain kingdom of Lesotho, and 80% of the hospitals, schools, kindergartens and roads in the rural areas of Kenya. 60–80% of work on the land in Africa is done by women. Yet only 10% of economically active people are women, because usually they have to work in 'Food for Work' programmes or with uneconomic methods. A further heavy burden on women consists of the way in which family life in the extended family is frequently disrupted by urbanisation and the system of migrant labour, so that they lose the social security and high status which in traditional society is their reward in old age for all their trouble and privation.

1. In their insecurity and fear of life, women with the background of traditional religion attempt to find relief from the pressures and burdens weighing on them by escaping into traditional patterns of thought and behaviour.

In the different countries of Africa the following may be observed. Among e. g. the Yoruba, Bete and Ashanti, middle-aged women stream to the shrines of spirits in order to combat witchcraft, accuse themselves of being witches, and gladly make amends for it. Self-accusation of a somewhat grotesque kind is reported from Zimbabwe. It is a matter partly of confessing to deeds which can be shown not to have happened, such as cannibalism. Following modern witch-hunts by West African brotherhoods, conversations of anthropologists with 'convicted' women have revealed that a large number of these women actually considered themselves to be guilty. Some said that they did not know they were witches, but accepted this as a fact. Others asserted that they became witches against their will and were now happy to be 'liberated' from this pressure through confession and paying a fine. The medical diagnosis in these cases might indicate menopausal depression, but a scientific explanation will not help the women. In this emotional crisis, they need attention. Ultimately punishment also leads to renewed acceptance. So turning to the ideas of traditional religion has a liberating function in the end. Outsiders can only speculate how heavy the burden on such women must be when they go to such lengths to cast it off.

2. Women in the mainline Christian churches turn to women's groups for help in coping with the insecurity of their lives.

The South African women's church organisations will serve as an example of this. They usually go under the name of '*Manyano*'. Just the formal terms of address ('Mrs Matsebathlela', 'Madam President') is a step towards coping with their everyday life, because in their places of work women are often addressed by their function ('Cook', 'Nanny'). The meetings begin with short Bible readings and extempore prayer. Gradually a gentle sighing and weeping starts, until a woman begins to shake violently. The spirit possesses her. She now begins to speak, while the other women listen intently. The speaker reaches greater heights of emotion, wails and cries out her troubles from the heart. One women follows on from the other until a catharsis is achieved, and their feelings are relieved. Apart from the shaking, there are other elements known to traditional religions. Dreams with stereotyped contents are frequently narrated, the significance of which is an indication of the dreamer's identification with the group, e. g. that the Manyano membership card must be shown at the gates of heaven. Then there are dreams of a call, reminiscent of the dreams which a diviner has when she is called in the traditional religions.

The second part of the meeting activates the women's delight in social involvement. Collections and sales of work are organised to support church finances and visiting services to old people, the sick and prisoners. It makes them proud and happy, and strengthens their feeling of belonging, when they are successful as a group. This undoubtedly contributes to the emancipation of the women.

The women also proudly keep a firm eye on the high moral standards of their group. Members who contravene the rules of the Manyano, e. g. who drink alcohol, dance, swear or brew beer, have sanctions imposed upon them, of which the most severe is to lose the uniform which all the Manyanos wear at meetings. The uniform is a basic part of membership. On the death of a member, her uniform is laid upon the coffin, and carried with her to the grave – a clear indication of the strength of the community feeling which has always distinguished Africans, and which survives beyond death. The strict observance of rules and regulations, which the woman have imposed upon themselves, is a reaction to the general uncertainty about the rights and norms of modern society and to the incomprehensible European administration of justice. A woman put it like this: "European laws tell you what not to do, but they do not tell you what you must do". The fact that guilt is forgiven and forgotten after repentance and confession is an essential hallmark of the group – and distinguishes it from similar organisations of white churches. Anyone who makes a public confession can be reinstated as a full member of the group. She is not condemned to isolation and loneliness, and does not fall by the wayside.

3. The Independent Churches offer a new sense of belonging to women who have been uprooted.

The whole of sub-Saharan Africa since the end of the last century has increasingly seen the emergence of breakaway churches and small independent church groups in recent decades. The reasons for this must be briefly outlined here, since they throw light on the problem:

- The racial barriers that Europeans set up exacerbate separatist tendencies among black people.
- There are too few positions to accommodate black leaders in the mainline churches.
- Being cut off from their roots, Africans feel a great longing for a church 'people' with a spiritual leader modelled on the tribal chief.
- The mainline churches have not succeeded in transplanting the Christian message to fit in with the African heritage.

Women are particularly well represented in the Independent Churches, not simply as members seeking healing but also in leadership circles, as deaconesses, as mediums or prophetesses, and even as founders and leaders of new Independent Churches.

Many thousands of small groups which meet on Wednesday afternoons and Sundays provide enough space for people to receive healing if they feel they are physically or spiritually ill – no sharp distinction is made between the two. They can then assist other members of the group in healing rituals. That may take the form of a group meeting by the sea in the early morning. After prayers and hymns, the leader of the group takes a sick woman by the hand, goes a little way with her into the sea and immerses her several times in particularly strong rolling breakers. The purifying sea carries away evil. The patient, who is now completely beside herself, twitching, screaming and rolling on the ground, is handed over to two other women in the group who look after her until she is calm again. They help her put on dry clothing, kneel

222

down with her in the sand and pray with her. In this way members of the group take turns as helpers and patients.

The groups contain particularly large numbers of infertile women or women who have suffered miscarriages. Lack of children is still considered to be the greatest misfortune. The belief that a demon is responsible is widespread. The prophetic healers take this seriously. In fact, on the pattern of the traditional healers, they believe that a spirit, in this case the Holy Spirit, gives them power to cast out demons.

The issue here is not whether massive psychological influence can relieve suffering when there is a corresponding expectation of healing. It is just to note that women longing for visible signs of healing are apparently brought relief from their suffering when they are healed with the support of a group.

Women in the Independent Churches can also fill prominent positions, irrespective of their birth and social position, in contrast to the traditional religions. Ma Nku, whose followers have firmly established themselves with an enormous church building in a Durban township, Dolosina and Lucy Mofokeng are three prophetesses and founders of churches which have spread beyond city and tribal boundaries. A particularly notable example is Alice Lenshina Mulenga, a Bemba woman from Zambia, who from 1954 took on the role of a prophetess. Because of the particular circumstances of her activities even European newspapers took up her story. In 1963, during Kaunda's struggle for Zambian independence, the members of her *Lumpa Church* were not prepared to vote for a secular party, because they believed that their Church represented the Kingdom of God already made visible on earth. Hundreds of believers were killed in an armed struggle, and Lenshina was taken prisoner. 'Mama Lenshina' also had a history of a call, which had many points of similarity with the history of the calling of a traditional diviner. Even her methods were basically the same as those of a traditional healer.

In contrast to the traditional religions, the Christian religion offers a broad cross-section of African women help in coping with the present and also considerable help in their emancipation. Women, in particular, seek and find a way of life in Christianity. In her book, *Black Women in Search of God*, Mia Brandel-Syrier writes the following, which could apply to the whole of Africa. "Faced with the problems of a new and bewildering world, they fight their way through with well-nigh superhuman courage and dogged persistence. They won't give up .... Better than their menfolk are they able to weather the storms. Like all women the world over, they have stronger, deeper roots. And it is to these strong, sensible, enterprising women, that African Society owes whatever there is of sanity and sense" (p.28).

7. Social transformation

There is still no generally accepted, water-tight theory of social change. Some say it is due to external and some to internal causes, and this question has not yet been resolved. A similar debate exists in the field of social and cultural anthropology. There are still those who support Malinowski, according to whom culture can be compared to a tightly meshed net, the whole of which moves when only one loop is pulled. Others maintain that it is easy to change single aspects of a culture without affecting the other aspects to any great extent, since it is the resistance of most aspects of a culture that makes change in one sector possible at all. Only that way can the existing culture survive as a whole, while allowing for change and the integration of what is new.[296]

In the 1930s Godfrey and Monica Wilson turned their attention to the questions of social change in East Africa (their work was not published until 1945), emphasising the importance of the change in scale of societies, a concept that has since been taken up by a number of social anthropologists.[297] Since the values, morals and symbols of African religions in fact relate to small-scale societies, as we have seen, this observation is relevant because we can more easily demonstrate changes with its aid. However, the social transi-

---

[296] On social change and on the following passage, cf. P. C. Lloyd, 1969; M. J. Herskovits, 1962; G. & M. Wilson, 1968; M. Wilson, 1971; L. Mair, 1972; K. E. Bleyle, 1981.
[297] Cf. L. Mair, 1972, pp.269ff.

tion from micro to macro-structure is only a frame of reference and should not be considered the sole cause of changes. The reasons for this shift in scale are known and need not be spelt out here in detail: colonialism and the gaining of statehood, population growth and urbanisation, new educational systems and means of mass communication, the emergence of parties, and the impact of new religions. Finally, there are the economic and ecological changes (e. g. in the Sahel), since natural catastrophes have a more serious effect in politically unstable states than in those with healthier political and social structures. The unity of the traditional living area and the comprehensive nature of the previous order of life were profoundly disturbed by the integration of various peoples into the larger entity of the state. It meant a basic increase in outside contacts with people of other ethnic groups, and other types of society and social strata. Small-scale societies live with limited, but intensive, contacts which become looser as outside contacts increase. This leads to a certain degree of anonymity and at least partially challenges the previous security provided by the group. The still smaller group, i. e. the nuclear family, gains in significance, while links to the clan and people become looser.

This has the following consequences. The unity of the the territory matched the actual or perceived unity of the people, as we have seen. They all had a common origin and so were responsible for one another politically and socially. Thanks to their economic interdependence everyone shared in prosperity as well as in poverty and need. Wealth was permitted only on the basis of birth and status; it went to the family, not the individual. The pattern of life was based on uniformity, even in matters of morality, conduct and religion. There was strict group cohesion, serving the unity of the community. The intrusion of Western economics is changing that fundamentally. It is premised on a larger area of activity and there is less sense of group identity. Individual effort is required. Work is not aimed at subsistence alone; it is no longer a community activity, but is becoming individualised. It enables people to get on in life. The individual can gain – or lose. The group provides support only in a limited way. Anyone who wants to succeed must break their family ties and look after themself. This is the only way to amass capital and re-invest.

225

You cannot at one and the same time save money and share it with the members of the family, which was traditionally an obligation.[298]

The effect of this pressure to perform is visible in modern African society. Psychological tensions are increasing, which would be diagnosed as requiring psychotherapy elsewhere, but which in Africa are expressed in an evident intensification in the belief in witches, and in spirit possession. Instead of respecting their neighbours, people are beginning to fear them.[299]

In traditional society a person is born with a certain status and with increasing age grows into a higher one, accompanied by community rites. However, other rules apply at school, at university and in business life. They require personal achievement. Now what counts is individuality. Bribery, corruption and the desire for a title denoting status are gaining ground.

Traditional religion cannot provide guidelines for the new situation, nor a guaranteed moral pattern backed by sanctions. That is asking too much of it. The consequences for society can be serious, when sanctions no longer have any effect and a moral identity has not yet been found. Moreover, if the small-scale society is stripped of its ancestral land, the traditional pattern of behaviour with its positive values and sanctions no longer functions at all. In extreme cases everyone may be left to fend for themselves, in a merciless struggle for survival.[300]

Small-scale societies offered no possibilities for choice. What had to be done, what everybody had to do, was laid down in principle. Even the choice of a marriage partner was ultimately a procedure arranged by the extended family, although some peoples did allow a certain amount of scope for a limited 'pre-selection' on the part of the young man consenting to marriage. The mobility of individuals in new societies, the opportunity to choose from a

---

[298] Cf. V. Turner, 1968, p. 23. The question of the mutual influence on each other of African culture and Western economics is treated in more detail by M. Büscher in his Freiburg dissertation, completed in 1987. This includes a fuller bibliography on the subject; cf. also W. Schulz-Weidner, 1964.

[299] M. P. Parin, (et al.) express this in an overstated form which is entirely appropriate for these times of social change, summing up the ethical problem in the title of their book, *Fürchte deinen Nächsten wie dich selbst*, 1971, [Fear your neighbour as yourself].

[300] Cf. on this subject C. M. Turnbull, 1973.

host of new occupations,the emergence of political parties and new groupings – all this not only offers a broader range of decision, it demands it. Without question, that offers greater scope for the individual, guaranteeing 'freedom' in the Western sense, but at the same time it has the effect of isolating the individual. While individuality was not esteemed in the past, it is now part of the burden of modern life. The traditionalist can only outweigh it by finding a new group identity, as offered by the major religions, parties, unions and secret societies.

The comprehensive nature of the small-scale society implies a particular concept of time, as we have seen. The basis of its own identity lies in the past. Time grows into it, and is its actual reservoir. The complexity of the large-scale society, geared to expansion, means that identity is always only an aspiration. Modern economics sees the Golden Age in the future, not in the past. The real time factor is the future, not even the present. In the small-scale society people could enjoy living in the here-and-now; in fact, prosperity was based on the idea that all could share in it right away. Anybody who was legitimately rich was allowed to exhibit his or her wealth.[301] In contrast, Westerners have proclaimed a gospel of work, emphasising the virtues of economy, a modest lifestyle and an industrious attitude. The new approach focusses on planning and future prospects; it considers individual competition unavoidable and prefers the nuclear family because it is cheaper.

One single religion permeated the life of the small-scale society. Religious plurality was unknown until the introduction of Islam and Christianity. Now people are no longer born into a religion. They can, indeed must, opt for a particular one. The choice of religions on offer is becoming more extensive; at the same time, this means that religion no longer covers the whole of life, but is limited to certain areas. Secularisation is growing, because religion

---

[301] "The successful West African tends to symbolise his achievements by conspicuous leisure. The wealthy farmer sits in his compound, directing activities at his farm by mainly occupying himself with involvement in the public affairs of his community. Younger or less affluent men consider it an honour to carry the loads of one whose eminence had brought so much prestige to the whole of his descent group", P. C. Lloyd, 1969, p. 45.

227

does not occupy every new-found area of free choice; religious ties are dissolving.

In the early years of mission the decision for Christianity was in many ways a decision for schools, for the new education, for the West, and against tradition. So the churches were at first representatives of modernity, and their members were open to new things. Through church membership, outsiders and slaves belonging to the underclass of a small-scale society anticipated rising in society, something they could not aspire to normally because of their birth. While mission churches offered people in the radically changing situation in Africa a space where they could encounter the new in a secure setting, they were also a springboard for modernity. The majority of the educated classes and the new elite of Africa belong either to Christianity or, a more recent trend, to Islam. So the churches have become symbols of the modern large-scale society; their members are the elites of the new states, and they represent the new educated middle class. Apart from the small rural congregations, they no longer offer the 'warmth' of the small-scale society, the feeling of belonging, and are therefore under pressure to fragment, whether through individual members leaving to start new church congregations, or large dioceses having to be divided into smaller ones, often on the lines of the old tribal boundaries. There is a recognisable trend towards 'tribal' churches. Societal development patterns are counteracting theological ideas about church unity.

Nowadays the Independent Churches must be seen as the real intermediaries between the traditional small-scale society and the complex large-scale society. They are a 'substitute for the kraal',[302] and they also provide bridges to modernity. Contrary to what was assumed in earlier research, they are not a throwback to 'heathen' society. (B. Sundkler) nor are they to be interpreted only as nativistic movements. They have taken over the place which

---

[302] Cf. the essay by T. Sundermeier with this title, 1973c. The literature on African Independent Churches is immense. A detailed survey of the literature is contained in K. E. Bleyler, 1981. For later publications, cf. the appropriate headings in the Ökumene-Lexikon, 2nd ed., 1986, and in the Lexikon missionstheologischer Grundbegriffe, 1987.

mission churches originally occupied as pioneers of the modern world.[303] They see this role in a different light from the mission churches, however, because they feel completely at home with African thought and symbolism. They offer their members two things: a place where they feel secure, i. e. a home, and at the same time a pattern of behaviour borrowed from the modern world. In this way they stabilise their members, helping them to come to terms with the multicultural, multistrata and economically highly complex society, and to remain (or become) mentally balanced. They are 'healing churches' in the fullest sense of the term. The small groups are manageable; the members' contact with each other and with their leaders is intensive. They emphasise spiritual healing; they give ritual form to their community; and they show their inner faith in dress and outward symbols drawn from both Christian tradition and traditional religion. To underline this, I have selected the following extract from the church laws of the *Lumpa Church* of Lenshina Mulenga in Zambia.

1.   "Lumpa Church is an organisation in which to worship God and his son Jesus Christ. It is not an organisation to make unruly behaviour with the laws of the country.

2.   In this organisation there shall be no racial discrimination, white and black men and women shall be Brotherhood and love each other.

3.   Every Christian must not be in the following habits: (a) Back-biting (b) insult (c) lies (d) pride (e) boasting (f) hatred (g) anger (h) harsh (i) false witness (j) selfish (k) rudeness (l) cunning (m) stealing and etc. He must be sincere, kind, trustworthy, love, patient and truthful.

4.   Every Christian must keep away from the following: coveting, witchcraft, stealing, adultery, sorcery, witches, drunkenness, bad songs and all primitive dances.

5.   Every Christian must have good manners of the public and in private, that is when eating, going to bed, getting up, starting work, at the end of his work, at happiness, at the time of sorrow, when in difficulties and when on a journey a Christian must first pray to his God.

6.   At a Christian wedding there should be no beer provided and no primitive dances be allowed. The couple when married are bound by the Christian law that they shall never be separated until death separates them.

---

[303] So far as I know, H. W. Turner was the first to draw attention to this in 1969.

7.   The duties of every Christian is to see that he goes to Church for worshipping in each day that the congregation takes place.

8.   A widow must not be forced to marry another man, they must only tie a white bead on her hand. If she wishes to marry she can do so according to her own wish.

9.   A Christian must not be a polygamist.

10.   A Christian must not take part to eat food prepared for the mourner and at the mourning feast it must not be prepared.

11.   During the time of prayers, there should be no smoking of cigarette, pipe or snuffing, and no one shall enter in the Church with cigarette, tobacco or snuff.

12.   If a man has taken some beer drink he shall not enter the Church for worship even if he has taken very little drink. Who does not obey these laws is the one that God also does not like. The Almighty God says do not practice witchcraft, keep my love. Anyone who practice witches, he will at the end of the days suffer and be punished".[304]

This example of the church law of an Independent Church shows which virtues are given priority, namely those of personal relationships, in which Christian and African ethics coincide. They clearly reflect the ideals of an African small-scale society (paras. 3 and 4). But the old ideal is translated into action in a renewed form and in different circumstances. The Independent Churches provide a place in which to practise them and put them to the test. They seek to help people find the key to modern society without entirely giving up the character of African communal life. However, those things that hinder progress, i. e. wasteful ways of behaviour (alcohol, tobacco and polygamy), are forbidden (paras. 4, 9, 11) Whoever are members of this Church and follow its commands will not only have their reward in Heaven, but will be well rewarded by their employers, since they work conscientiously, faithfully, honestly and with motivation. They will follow the gospel of work which the missionaries preached. There is a desire to work and to get on, knowing that success is not a matter of fate, but the result of real commitment. But, in a hostile world, people also need harmonious relationships in their own groups. In general they keep out of politics, even if the congregations have introduced modern forms of community life and often 'democratic' ground rules. In a detailed study carried out among members of the

---

[304] J. V. Taylor & D. Lehmann, 1961, pp.253f.

African Independent Churches (AIC) and the mission churches in Durban, South Africa, G. C. Oosthuizen inquired about their attitudes to the state, work, economic ideals, the authorities and families. He came to the following conclusions:

"No more do age and occupation groups predominate, now it is individual freedom. Leadership opportunities have arisen; this is a radical new type of social arrangement – a new society is developing and a new world-view. A work philosophy is developing... In many of the African Independent Churches standards of living and health conditions have improved, through using their incomes with care; they meet the problematic modern issues with confidence, longsuffering and adaptability. Many employers give preference to members of the AI Churches. This accounts for the upwards mobility of many of their members.... In general their lifestyle is more simple, also their clothing... Among the AIC members, the feeling towards church members is often stronger than towards relatives. For example, nearly half of the respondents felt no special obligation that money earned by a young man should be shared with an unemployed first cousin, while no less than two thirds of the EC (= mission churches) felt such a duty to assist... Over the weekends very few will simply sit and rest. They will either work in their gardens, earn extra money or combine rest and other activities in order to earn some extra money... The whole AIC movement is thus a movement towards adaptation to a modern secular society without discarding the deep religious disposition which was basic to the traditional African world. Progress here goes hand in hand with religion – a religion that inculcates a positive disposition towards development".[305]

Unfortunately we cannot delve further into the effects of social change on African traditional religions and on their image of humankind. These are only the broad outlines of the adaptations necessitated by the transition from a small-scale to a large-scale society. African Independent Churches are among the significant phenomena through which Africans display their ability to face what is new and yet remain true to themselves. Precisely religion is proving to be the only power that can bind together heterogeneous elements

---

[305] G. C. Oosthuizen, The African Independent Churches and the Modernization Process, unpublished lecture, 1987.

and also preserve people's humanity and their African identity. While Westerners, because of their religious tradition, are only interested in dominating their natural environment, Africans have developed a culture of adaptability in their religion. The signs are that, in spite of all the political difficulties and domination, they will successfully adapt to new circumstances, technical progress, scientific thought and modern economic conditions, without giving up their time-honoured humanity. In the words of J. Ki-Zerbo: "In the course of its long history sub-Saharan Africa has assimilated the good that has been introduced from outside, including religious influences. Our brothers and sisters on the other side of the Atlantic, transported there by the slave trade, have for hundreds of years maintained their creative drive and their own temperament in a hostile environment... Consequently, we say, 'Yes' to the modern, technological age but, above all, 'Yes' to the African way of life. 'Yes' also to universal knowledge, but 'Yes' to African consciousness, too. And if a young African intellectual were to ask for all that to be summed up in one sentence, we would have to answer him in the words of the philosopher: 'Become what you are!'"[306]

---

[306] J. Ki-Zerbo, 1978.

232

CONCLUSION:
DIALOGUE WITH TRADITIONAL RELIGIONS?

Interreligious dialogue is conducted today at three levels: 1) at conferences of representatives of various religions; 2) in local congregations; and 3) occasionally in university theology faculties. At the first level, there are no representatives of traditional religions. The immediate reason is that they cannot be represented by any umbrella institution or association, and the individual African religions have hardly any spokespersons. The office of priest, where it exists at all as a separate calling (mainly in West Africa), rarely involves teaching. Moreover, the teacher-elders among the Chagga are atypical, and are more concerned with passing on traditions than with specifically religious instruction.

At the level of the local African congregation, a relationship of dialogue is developing only very slowly with representatives of traditional religions, because they feel forced onto the defensive by aggressive mission, and are made to feel that their culture is inferior. On the other hand, church communities regard traditional religion as a hidden threat, because it is known to have the power of infiltrating a congregation and assimilating parts of it. Only within the framework of a growing national consciousness, in which Africans are seeking to understand their own roots and cultural traditions, are theologians beginning to study traditional religion. Concerned for the indigenisation of worship and theology, these are the people who speak up for traditional religions at the dialogues organised by ecumenical organisations such as the World Council of Churches.

At the level of interreligious theological dialogue at universities, traditional religions are in fact hardly ever mentioned, except in academic articles or at the occasional conference.[307] The reason is that they have no elaborate doctrines, and are unfolded in ritual rather than in discourse. Recent research has only just begun to reveal the riches of primal religious conceptualisation

---

[307] H. Bürkle (1977) provides an exception to this.

233

but this is not a sufficient explanation for the neglect. The more fundamental reason lies in the deep-rooted prejudice that traditional religions differ essentially from the 'higher religions'; according to the German philosopher Hegel (1770–1831) they are not worthy of the name of religion, because people (he meant the Europeans of his time) would have to forget virtually all the concepts and ideas they had learned if they wanted to explore and understand these religions.[308] To this day, the prevailing view of indigenous cultures, whether expressed openly or not, is that they are 'magical' rather than religious in the Western sense of the word. This must be the entry point for academic dialogue with traditional religions. Only when relations between traditional and world religions are freed from the encrustations and prejudice of the past, and placed on a new footing, can real dialogue begin. This should, however, be a dialogue in community, arising out of 'conviviality' (German *Konvivenz*), in the deeper sense of living together. And it should take place in Africa, not in Europe.

In order to understand the differences and similarities between traditional and world religions, let us attempt to sum up the previous chapters.

No known small-scale society is without religion. Whether the society has contributed causally to the existence of the religion, or whether the religion has produced a particular form of society is something which cannot be answered objectively today. Any attempt to do so will be biassed by the stance of the particular writer. For us, the only important thing is to realise that traditional religion and society interlock: religion is a constituent element of a society, just as a society shapes the symbols and ideas of a religion. Religion sustains society; society provides the setting in which religion can develop. 'Primary experience of the world' and religious experience are two sides of the same coin, and that means – in theological language – that experience of God and of the world belong together, and are intimately related.

The ways in which these societies cope with reality reveal the connection between people and their surroundings, between the present and the past,

---

[308] Thomas Knox, A Layman's Quest (1969) deals with Hegel's lectures and writings on philosophy of religion.

234

between the visible and the invisible, with the help of analogy. Important existentially and epistemologically, it is translated expressively and instrumentally into ritual. This coping with the world is committed to the "elementary experience of the senses".[309] It reflects what I call the *primary religious experience*. This is a fundamental experience, which grips us from outside ourselves; it is not self-induced. Because this experience is fundamental, it leaves its mark on all aspects of society, determining the way people perceive and fashion the world. It is also fundamental in that it makes a total claim, and permeates a person's whole life. In a small-scale society, religion is inescapable.

Here, as everywhere, religion is revealed in cultic acts. It determines the ethics of the group and of the individual. It conveys knowledge and is itself conveyed in ritual and word, i. e. it gives names to objects, and can be handed down. Like primary experience of the world, primary religious experience finds its main principles of knowledge and form in analogy. It is condensed in symbol and is given visible expression in ritual. Primary religious experience is informed by the life-cycle and the annual cycle of nature. Since it enables people to measure the extent of space and time, it exalts the social shape of the world in celebration. In reverence for the neighbour, the environment, and God, who is understood as the One with many facets, and in respect for continuity from one generation to another, it is a chorus of praise and thanksgiving for life. It seeks to strengthen, stabilise, preserve and increase life, and also to prevent any danger to it. The members of the working group, Christian Interest in Traditional Religions and Cultures, at a pioneering ecumenical consultation[310] were right in finding the elements of this religious experience in all religions. Yet how are these to be judged? Not as 'survivals' (E. Tylor), being overtaken by the progress of civilisation. They are basic experiences, which are vital components of all religions.

---

[309] A. Portmann, 1950, pp.413ff. & 435.

[310] The Inter-Faith Consultation of the World Council of Churches, held in Chiang Mai, Thailand in 1977; cf. the report by S. J. Samartha (ed.), 1977.

Religion does not proceed from the 'primitive' to a higher stage. The Darwinian idea that evolution always moves by small steps from the lower to the higher, and is irreversible, must be ruled out. Instead, religious experience varies with experience of the world, so that the new is always integrated into primary experience and adapted to it. I call the new element the *secondary religious experience*. As the small-scale society is challenged and changes into a large society, people have to find a new manner of coming to terms with the world. The previous, traditional way will no longer do. In the religious sphere, this alteration is sensed, predicted and initiated by seers, prophets and reformers.

The larger society gives people greater scope for decisions and choice. The individual gains space and freedom, as we have seen. This likewise means that religion no longer covers all spheres of life, that the realm of the profane grows and secularism becomes possible. Secondary religious experience is therefore characterised by individualism. The mythical, analogous way of thinking is expanded by conceptual rationality and the symbol is interpreted according to individual inclination. What has been experienced through sensation and intuition is now pervaded by theoretical ideas; religion is reduced to a system, and can be handed down as doctrine. Ritual enactment is no longer sufficient; secondary religious experience appeals to the intellect, demanding belief. The validity of secondary religious experience is not confined to the small group; it lays claim to universal validity. That is the basic reason why it is designed for expansion. Weight is attached to the notion of truth, which was not at issue in primary religious experience. The latter is immediately credible and can be experienced at first hand in society. It is non-missionary, whereas secondary religious experience forces its way onto the world stage as 'true religion'.

Secondary religious experience does not simply replace the primary once and for all. It is premissed on primary experience, which provides the presuppositions for understanding the new. Primary and secondary religious experiences can be clearly distinguished, but cannot be pitted against each other. Each is of equal value in coming to terms with its own world. The history of religion does not proceed with regular steps from primary to secondary religious experience. Rather, we can discern a complex, dynamic and diverse scenario with three phases. Secondary religious experience does not simply leave primary religious experience behind; it is integrated into it so that something new arises. This new, third 'experience' is not identical with either of the other two religious experiences, neither can it be regarded as a simple synthesis. The new religious experience is mediated through prophets, charismatics, founders of religions and reformers, and each time it establishes a fresh norm by which the pre-existent religion is absorbed or rejected. Depending on the case, the integration can be firm or flexible; the rejection can be more radical or more tolerant. The problem of syncretism is inherent in this process. It cannot simply be avoided, because every religion has a tendency to claim absolute validity, and so seeks to restore the primary religious experience on a new level within its comprehensive claim. The more the existing local traditions of the primary religious experience are appropriately and convincingly integrated into the new, the more successful the latter will be in advancing this claim. So every religion which comes into existence in this way is 'syncretistic' as soon as it reaches its goal and becomes a 'popular religion'. This applied to the Israelite religion and the way it adopted Kenite, Canaanite and other religious material into its central rituals and beliefs (Passover, temple worship, the name of God, etc.). Christianity, too, integrated pre-existent rituals into the Christmas and Easter festivals when it gained a foothold in Greece, Rome, Britain or Ireland. We can say, by and large, that pre-existent religious practice is more to be classified as priestly and conservative, upholding recognised modes of behaviour and offering humanity shelter through rites of reconciliation. By contrast, the new, the secondary religious experience, is closer to the prophetic, breaking through the encrusted shell of the status quo, and seeking to lead the way into uncharted territory.

So every 'national' and world religion builds upon the synthesis of two religious experiences, and is shaped by the living, open process of integrating them both. This insight into the history of religion, whose goal is unknown and indefinable, has wide-ranging consequences for interfaith dialogue. Dialogue with traditional religions, which largely resemble each other in their

237

basic structure, is for a Christian like a dialogue with his or her own past. By this, I do not mean a kind of romantic trip 'back to the roots', but an elementary inquiry into what constitutes the basis of all religions, and preserves people's humanity. Dialogue with traditional religions looks for what is right and good and worth preserving in all religions (I Thessalonians 5:21), without falling prey to unacceptable reductionism, or advocating an unhistorical phenomenology of religion. Dialogue can open our eyes to forgotten structures in our own religion, and will make us cautious about jumping to conclusions about 'syncretism'.[311] Moreover it will teach us to show new understanding for the traditional rites adopted in faith, and to devote much closer attention to new forms of church and theology in Africa and Asia. Our eyes will then be opened to the basic experiences and options which have such a profound influence on our lives.

I will explain what I mean with a firsthand example. Pastoral theology was one of the subjects I taught at Lutheran Theological College in Umpumulo, Natal, in South Africa. One of the central problems of African churches is church discipline, illustrated by the participation of church members in traditional community rites, which are hard to escape. Mourning rituals are regarded as dangerous, because there 'pagan' customs are said to be particularly enduring, and the first commandment seems to be seriously violated by belief in the ancestors. In a course on hospital pastoral work we were discussing the phases of mourning when I became aware that the students were listening with more than usual intentness. They were very keen to explore the consequences of their new insights. It was only later that I realised the reason for this. A detailed comparison of the mourning rites of different peoples showed that their sequence corresponded exactly to the phases of mourning which, according to psychologists, every mourner goes through.

Later, I looked at our mourning rites in Germany. Not only did I find parallels with Africa, but to my great surprise my African experiences opened the door to understanding the rites of Theravada Buddhism, which belie the

---

[311] For W. Pannenberg's sympathetic interpretation of syncretism, cf. his: Basic Questions in Theology, London, 1970–71, vol. 2, pp.85ff.

theory that it is non-ritualistic. Numerous discussions with missionaries, colleagues and Buddhists about these correlations showed me that there was a new area of research here for the history of religion, and also for interreligious dialogue. Elementary facts of human existence are expressed in traditional religions and their rituals, involving both spiritual and social components of what it means to be human. For example, rituals accompany people through life and focus on the fixed points of the life-cycles, giving rhythm to life as well as to the cycle of the year, and making repetition possible. They thereby mediate a basic experience of familiarity and reliability, lessening the tensions of life and fostering social integration, because they expand the experiences of the individual into communal experiences. If it is an elementary function of religion not only to keep alive the longing for home, but also to convey a total experience of being at home, then dialogue with African religions can open our eyes to the fact that we from the North must also regain the feeling of being at home in our congregations; and it can show us how.

Then we will not find ourselves in a theological no man's land, leaving it to anthropologists, sociologists and psychologists to write the agenda; instead we will practise genuine theology. Primary religious experiences, as encountered most clearly in the traditional religions of Africa, are about the preservation of life and humanity, and are, in theological terms, applications of the 'first law used'; they belong to the realm of God's creative work. The search for the work of Christ in other religions, in liberation movements, in the secularised world, etc., has proved fruitless, since every happening in the secular realm is ambivalent and cannot be clearly identified as the work of Christ. Traditional religions can also help us to anchor the concern for interreligious relations and dialogue of the World Council of Churches in the first article of Christian faith, i. e. belief in God. The contribution of indigenous beliefs and traditional spirituality would be stimulating for all partners in dialogue. Few theologians have taken up the challenge so far. An exception is C. H. Ratschow with his study of baptism (1983), in which he shows the relevance of the interreligious perspective for his theology. The discussion on the African concept of God sparked off by H. Rücker (1985) goes even fur-

239

ther: he introduces categories drawn from the African experience into a fundamental God debate. R. Grainger (1974) and W. Jetter (1978) have contributed to our understanding of ritual.

These first attempts illustrate the genuine need for dialogue with traditional religions. Let us hope that men and women representing them, plus Christians from an indigenous religious and cultural background, can be encouraged to bring their insights and spirituality into all levels of interreligious dialogue.

Bibliography

Aarni, T. (1982): The Kalunga Concept in Ovambo Religion from 1870 Onwards, Stockholm.

Abegg, L. (1949): Ostasien denkt anders, Zurich.

Adegbola, E. A. A. (1963): Ethik und Stammesreligion, in: H. Bürkle, 1968, 236–254.

Arens, W. (ed.) (1976): A Century of Change in Eastern Africa, The Hague.

Ardrey, R. (1966): Adam und sein Revier, Vienna.

Arinze, F. A. (1970): Sacrifice in Ibo Religion, Ibadan.

Aschwanden, H. (1976): Symbole des Lebens. Bewusstseinsanalyse eines afrikanischen Volkes, Zurich.

Asmus, G. (1939): Die Zulu, Essen.

van Baaren, Th. I. (1964): Menschen wie wir. Religion und Kult der schriftlosen Völker, Gütersloh.

Bacom, W. (1972): Yoruba Religion and Morality, in: Les Religions africaines comme source de valeurs de civilisation. Colloque de Cotonu 16–22 août 1970, Paris, 50–64.

Baëta, C. G. (ed.) (1968): Christianity in Tropical Africa, Oxford.

Balz, H. (1984): Where the Faith has to Live. Studies in Bakossi Society and Religion. Part I: Living together, Basel.

(1985): Ndie. Das Dorfahnenfest der Bakossi. Probleme des Dialogs mit der Religion einer schriftlosen Kultur (unpublished paper).

(1995): Where the Faith has to Live: Studies in Bakossi Society and Religion. Part II: The Living, the Dead and God, Berlin.

Bamunoba, Y. K./Adoukonou, B. (1979): La Mort dans la vie africaine, Paris.

Bartle, Ph. F. W. (1983): The Universe has Three Souls. Notes on Translating Akan Culture, in: Journal of Religion in Africa, 85–114.

Baumann, H. (1936): Schöpfung und Urzeit des Menschen im Mythos der afrikanischen Völker, Berlin.

(1980): Das doppelte Geschlecht, Ethnologische Studien zur Bisexualität in Ritus und Mythos, Berlin, 2nd ed.

Beattie J./Middleton, J. (eds.) (1969): Spirit, Mediumship and Society in Africa, London.

Becken, H. J. (1972): Theologie der Heilung. Das Heilen in den afrikanischen unabhängigen Kirchen, Hermannsburg.

Berglund, A. I. (1975): Zulu Thought – Patterns and Symbolism, London.

Bettscheider, H. (ed.) (1978): Das Problem einer Afrikanischen Theologie, St. Augustin.

241

Bleyle, K. E. (1981): Religion und Gesellschaft in Schwarzafrika. Sozial-religiöse Bewegungen und koloniale Situation, Stuttgart.

Bosch, D. (1973): God in Africa, Missionalia, 3–21.

Brandel-Syrier, M. (1962): Black Women in Search of God, London

Breuer, E. (1925): Züge aus der Religion der Herero. Beiträge zur Hamitenfrage, Leipzig.

Brinkschulte, B. (1976): Formen und Funktionen wirtschaftlicher Kooperation in traditionalen Gesellschaften Westafrikas, Meisenheim.

Bruwer, F. P. (1963): Die Bantoe van Suid-Afrika, Johannesburg.

Bürkle, H., (ed.) (1968): Theologie und Kirche in Afrika, Stuttgart.

(1977): Einführung in die Theologie der Religionen, Darmstadt.

Büscher, M. (1987): Afrikanische Weltanschauungen und ökonomische Rationalität. Geistesgeschichtliche Hintergründe des Spannungsverhältnisses zwischen Kultur und wirtschaftlicher Entwicklung im Kontext Schwarzafrikas, Diss. oec., Freiburg.

Busia, K. A. (1963): The Ashanti of the Gold Coast, in: D. Forde, 190–209.

(1968): Ahnenkult, in H. Bürkle, 109–116.

Buthelezi, M. (1976): Theologie im Konfliktfeld Südafrikas. Ed. I. Tödt, Stuttgart. (lecture published only in German)

Colson, E. (1969): Spirit Possession among the Tonga, in: J. Beattie/J. Middleton, 69–103.

Dammann, E. (1963): Die Religionen Afrikas, Stuttgart.

Danquah, J. B. (1968): The Akan Doctrine of God, London, 2nd ed.

Davidson, B. (1969): The Africans, London.

Dickson, K. A./Ellingworth, P. (ed.) (1969): Biblical Revelation and African Beliefs, London.

Donner-Reichle, C. (1977): Die Last der Unterentwicklung. Frauen in Kenia, Berlin.

Doob, L. W. (1966): Communication in Africa. A Search for Boundaries. New Haven/London.

Douglas, M. (1963): The Lele of Kasai, in: D. Forde, 1–27.

(1970): Purity and Danger. An Analysis of Concepts of Pollution and Taboo, Harmondsworth, 2nd ed.

(1975): Implicit meanings. Essays in anthropology, London.

(1981): Ritual, Tabu und Körpersymbolik. Sozialanthropologische Studien in Industriegesellschaft und Stammeskultur, Frankfurt.

Durkheim, E. (1968): Elementary Forms of the Religious Life, London (1915), 6th ed.

Dymond, G. W. (1950): The Idea of God in Ovamboland, South-West Africa, in: E. W. Smith, 135–155.

Elias, T. O. (1962): The Nature of African Customary Law, Manchester, 2nd ed.

Evans, H. T. (1950): The Akan Doctrine of God, in: E. W. Smith, 241–259.

Evans-Pritchard, E. E. (1965): The Position of Women in Primitive Societies and Other Essays, in : Social Anthropology, London.

(1967): Nuer Religion, Oxford, 3rd ed.

(1978): Hexerei, Orakel und Magie bei den Zande, Frankfurt.

Field, M. J. (1969): Spirit Possession in Ghana, in: J. Beattie/J. Middleton, 3–13.

Firth, R. (1975): Symbols, Public and Private, London, 2nd ed.

Fischer, E. (1967): Der Wandel ökonomischer Rollen bei den westlichen Dan in Liberia, Wiesbaden.

Fleischer, L. (1977): Zur Rolle der Frau in Afrika. Heirat, Geburt und Krankheit im Leben der Hausa-Frauen in Nigeria, Bensheim-Auerbach.

Forde, D. (1963): African Worlds. Studies in the Cosmological Ideas and Social Values of African Peoples, London/New York, 4th ed.

Fortes, M./Dieterlein G. (ed.) (1965): African Systems of thought, London/New York.

(1965): Some Reflections on Ancestor Worship, in: M. Fortes/G. Dieterlein, 122–144.

(1966): Ödipus und Hiob in westafrikanischen Religionen, Frankfurt.

(1967): Institutionen in primitiven Gesellschaften, Frankfurt.

(1975): Strangers, in: M. Fortes/G. H. Patterson (ed.): Studies in Social Anthropologies (Festschrift I. Schapera), London, 229–253.

Friedli, R. (1986): Reinkarnation in negro-afrikanischen Eschatologien, in: W. Breuning (ed.): Seele. Problembegriff christlicher Eschatologie, Freiburg.

Fuchs, P. (1980): Die Hadjerai (Tschad), in: W. Raunig, 83–94.

Geary, C (1976): Die Genese eines Häuptlingstums im Grasland von Kamerun, Wiesbaden.

Gluckmann, M. (1956): Custom and Conflict in Africa, Oxford.

Gölz, F. (1963): Der primitive Mensch und seine Religion, Gütersloh.

Grainger, R. (1974): The Language of the Rite, London.

Greschat, H.-J. (1980): Mana und Tapu. Die Religion der Maori auf Neuseeland, Berlin.

Griaule, M. (1963): The Dogon of the French Sudan, in: D. Forde, 83–110.

(1973): Conversations with Ogotemmêli. An Introduction to Dogon Religious Ideas, London (3rd ed.).

Grohs, G. (1967): Stufen afrikanischer Emanzipation. Studien zum Selbstverständnis westafrikanischer Eliten, Stuttgart.

Guillebaud, R. (1950): The Idea of God in Ruanda-Urundi, in: E. W. Smith, 180–200.

Gutmann, B. (1909): Dichten und Denken der Dschagganeger, Leipzig.

(1932–38): Die Stammeslehren der Dschagga, München, 3 volumes.

Häselbarth, H. (1972): Die Stammeslehren der Toten in Afrika. Eine theologische Deutung der Todesriten der Mamabolo in Nordtransvaal, Gütersloh.

243

Hammond-Tooke, W. D. (1974): (ed.): The Bantu-Speaking Peoples of Southern Africa, London.

(1975): The Symbolic Structures of Cape Nguni Cosmology, in: H. G. Whisson, M. West, 15–33.

Harjula, R. (1974): God and the Sun in Meru Thought, Helsinki.

Harris, W. T. (1950): The Idea of God among the Mende, in: E. W. Smith, 277–297.

Hebga, M. P. (1979): Sorcellerie, Abidjan.

Herrmann, F. (1961): Symbolik in den Religionen der Naturvölker, Stuttgart.

Herskovits, M. J. (1962): The Human Factor in Changing Africa, New York, 2nd ed.

Horton, R. (1967): African Traditional Thought and Western Science in Africa, 50–71, 155–187.

(1971): African Conversion, in: Africa, 85–108.

(1975): On the Rationality of Conversion, in: Africa, 219–235, 373–399.

Hountondiji, P. J. (1983): African Philosophy. Myth and Reality, London.

Huber, H. (1980): Religiöse Aspekte einer westafrikanischen Savannenbauernkultur (Die Nyamde in der Volksrepublik Benin), in: W. Raunig, 49–59.

Hunter, M. (1969): Reaction to Conquest. Effects of Contact with Europeans on the Pondo of South Africa, London, 3rd ed.

Idowu, E. B. (1962): Olódùmarè. God in Yoruba Belief. London.

(1968): Afrikanische Gottesvorstellungen, in: H. Bürkle, 73–84.

(1973): African Traditional Religion. A Definition, London.

Ikenga-Metuh, E. (1987): Comparative Studies of African Traditional Religions, Onitsha (Nigeria).

Iten, O. (1980): Die Nuba (Sudan), in: W. Raunig, 95–109.

Ittmann, J. (1935): Kameruner Geheimbünde, in: Ev. Missionsmagazin, 305–311.

(1939): Die Tierwelt des Kameruner Waldlandes im magischen Gebrauch, Ev. Missionsmagazin, 151ff.

(1955): Gottesvorstellung und Gottesnamen im nördlichen Waldland von Kamerun, in: Anthropos, 241–260.

(1957): Der kultische Geheimbund djengú an der Kameruner Küste, in: Anthropos, 135–176

(1963): Von den Grundlagen der Welt- und Lebensanschauung in Süd-Kamerun, in: Anthropos, 661–676.

(1971): Die Sprichwörter der Kandu (Kamerun), Berlin.

Jahn, J. (1958): Muntu. Umrisse der neoafrikanischen Kultur, Düsseldorf.

James, E. O. (n. d.): Das Priestertum, Wesen und Funktion, Wiesbaden.

Jeffreys, M. D. W. (1952): Confessions by Africans, in: Eastern Anthropologist, 42–67.

Jetter, W. (1978): Symbol und Ritual. Anthropologische Elemente im Gottesdienst, Göttingen.

Junod, H. A. (1962): The Life of a South African Tribe, vol. I and II, New York, 2nd ed., (Repr. 1912).

Kagame, A. (1956): La Philosophie Bantu-Rwandaise de L'Etre, Brüssel.
(1976): La Philosophie Bantu Comparée, Paris.

Kenyatta, J. (1968): Facing Mount Kenya. The Tribal Life of the Gikuyu, London, 4th ed.

Kilson, M. (1967): Women in African Traditional Religions, in: Journal of Religion in Africa, Leiden.

King, N. Q. (1970): Religions of Africa. A Pilgrimage into Traditional Religions, New York/Evanston.

Kirchgässner, A. (1959): Die mächtigen Zeichen. Ursprünge, Formen und Gesetze des Kultes, Basel/Freiburg.

Kiwowele, J. B. M. (1980): Welterfahrung und Gotteserfahrung. Ein Diskussionsbeitrag aus afrikanischer Erfahrung, in: T. Rendtorff (Ed.): Europäische Theologie. Versuche einer Ortsbestimmung, Gütersloh, 119–124.

Ki-Zerbo, J. (1978): L'Histoire de l'Afrique Noire, Paris.

Koloss, H. J. (1980): Götter und Ahnen, Hexen und Medizin, zum Weltbild in Oku, in: W. Raunig, 69–82.

Kossodo, B. L. (1980): Die Frau in Afrika. Zwischen Tradition und Befreiung, Vienna.

Krige, E. J. (1943): The Realm of a Rain-Queen, London.
(1965): The Social System of the Zulus, London, 3rd ed.

Kronenberg, A. (1972): Logik und Leben. Kulturelle Relevanz der Didinga und Logarin, Sudan, Wiesbaden.

Kudadji, J. N. (1976): Does Religion determine Morality in a Pluralistic Society? A Viewpoint, in: Religion in a Pluralistic Society (Festschrift C. G. Baëta), Leiden, 60–77.

Kuper, A. (1982): Wives for Cattle. Bridewealth and Marriage in Southern Africa, London/Boston.

Leakey, L. S. B. (1952): Mau-Mau and the Kikuyus, London, Methuen.

van der Leeuw, G. (1956): Phänomenologie der Religion, Tübingen, 2nd ed.

Lévy-Bruhl, L. (1956): Die Seele der Primitiven, Darmstadt (repr. 1930).

Lévy-Strauss, C. (1963): Totemism: trans. by R. Needham. Boston & London, 1964.

Lienhardt, G. (1963): The Shilluk of the Upper Nile, in: D. Forde, 138–163.
(1967): Divinity and Experience. The Religion of the Dinka, Oxford, 2nd ed.

Little, K. (1963): The Mende in Sierra Leone, in: D. Forde, 111–137.
(1974): Urbanization as a social progress. An essay on movement and change in contemporary Africa, London.

Mair, L. (1969): Witchcraft. London, Weidenfeld & Nicolson.

(1971): Marriage, London.

(1972): An Introduction to Social Anthropology, London, 2nd ed.

Manus, Ch. U. (1986): The Concept of Death and the After-life in the O. T. and Igbo Traditional and Religion, Missiology, 41–56.

Maquett, J. J. (1971): Herrschafts- und Gesellschaftsstrukturen in Afrika, München.

Marwick, M. G. (1965): Some Problems in the Sociology of Sorcery and Witchcraft, in: M. Fortes/G. Dieterlein, 171–191.

Mawinza, J. (1974): The Human Soul, Life and Soul-concept in an East African Mentality. Based on Luguru, Rome.

Mbiti, J. S. (1990): African Religions and Philosophy. Oxford, 2nd ed. (1st ed. 1969).

Menkiti, I. A. (1979): Person and Community in African Traditional Thought, in: R. A. Wright (ed.): African Philosophy. An Introduction, Washington, 2nd ed.

Mercier, P. (1963): The Fon of Dahomey, in: D. Forde, 210–234.

Middleton, J. (1967): Magic, Witchcraft and Curing, New York.

(1969a): Spirit Possession among Lugbara, in: J. Beattie/J. Middleton, 159–170.

(1969b): Witchcraft and Sorcery in Lugbara, in: J. Middleton/E. H. Winter, 257–276.

(1969c): Lugbara Religion, Ritual and Authority among an East African People, London 3rd ed.

Middleton, J./Winter, E. H. (ed.) (1969): Witchcraft and Society in East Africa, London 2nd ed.

Möller, H. J. (1972): God en die voorouergeeste in die lewe van die stedelike bantoe, Pretoria.

(1973): Magie by die stedelike bantoe, Pretoria.

Mönning, H. O. (1967): The Pedi, Pretoria.

Mühlmann, W. E. (1964): Chiliasmus und Nativismus. Studien zur Psychologie, Soziologie und historischen Kasuistik der Umsturzbewegung, Berlin, 2nd ed.

Müller, K. E. (Ed.) (1983): Menschenbilder früher Gesellschaften. Ethnologische Studien zum Verhältnis von Mensch und Natur. Gedenkschrift H. Baumann, Frankfurt.

Mulago, V. (1968): Die lebensnotwendige Teilhabe, in: H. Bürkle, 42–53.

(1971): Symbolism in the traditional African religions and sacramentalism, in: Ecclesia Catholica, 164–203.

Nadel, S. F. (1967): A Black Byzantium. The Kingdom of Nupe in Nigeria, London, 6th ed.

(1970): Nupe Religion, Traditional Beliefs and the Influence of Islam in a West African Chiefdom, London, 2nd ed.

Needham, R. (1967): Right and Left in Nyoro Symbolic Clarification, in: Africa, 425–453.

Newell, W. H. (ed.) (1976): Ancestors, The Hague/Paris.

246

Nketia, J. H. K. (1963): Geburt, Pubertät und Tod, in: H. Bürkle, 236–254.

Nkwi, P. N. (1976): Traditional Government and Social Change. A Study of the political institutions among the Kom of the Cameroon Grassfields, Fribourg.

Ntetem, M. (1983): Die negro-afrikanische Stammesinitiation. Religionsgeschichtliche Darstellung, theologische Wertung, Möglichkeit der Christianisierung, Münsterschwarzach.

Nürnberger, K. (1975): Der afrikanische Hochgott unter dem Aufprall der christlichen Botschaft, in: Neue Zeitschrift für Syst. Theologie und Religionsphilosophie, 151–178.

Obbo, C. (1981): African Women. Their Struggle for Economic Independence, Johannesburg.

Omari, C. K. (1991): God and Worship in Traditional Asu Society. A Study of the concept of God and the way he was worshipped among the Vasu, Erlangen.

Oosthuizen, G. C. (1967): Sielsopvattinge in Afrika, in: Ned. Geref. Theolog. Tydskrif, 95–107.

Parin, P./Morgenthaler F./Parin-Matthèy (1971): Fürchte deinen Nächsten wie Dich selbst. Psychoanalyse und Gesellschaft am Modell der Agni in Westafrika, Frankfurt

(n. d.): Die Wessen denken zuviel. Psychoanalytische Untersuchung in Westafrika, Munich.

Parrinder, G. (1961): West African Religion. A Study of Beliefs and Practices of Akan, Ewe, Yoruba, Ibo and Kindred Peoples, London, 2nd. ed.

(1962): African Traditional Religion, London.

(1963): Witchcraft: European and African, London, 2nd ed.

Pauw, B. A. (1964): Religion in a Tswana Chiefdom, London, 2nd ed.

Pettazoni, R. (1957): Der allwissende Gott. Zur Geschichte der Gottesidee, Frankfurt.

Petzold, L. (Ed.) (1978): Magie und Religion. Beiträge zu einer Theorie der Magie, Darmstadt.

Popp, V. (Hg.) (1969): Initiation, Frankfurt.

Portmann, A. (1950): Vom Urmenschenmythos zur Theorie der Menschwerdung, in: Eranos Jahrbuch, 413ff.

Radcliffe-Brown, A. R. (1952): Structure and Function in Primitive Society, London.

Radin, P. (n. d.): Gott und Mensch in der primitiven Welt, Zurich.

Ranger, T. O., Kimambo, I. (1972): The Historical Study of African Religion, London/Nairobi.

Ratschow, C. H. (1955): Magie und Religion, Gütersloh, 2nd ed.

(1983): Die eine christliche Taufe, Gütersloh, 3rd ed.

Rattray, R. S. (1927): Religion and Art in Ashanti, Oxford.

Raum, O. F. (1967): Chagga Childhood, London 2nd ed.

Raunig, W. (ed.) (1980): Schwarz-Afrikaner, Lebensraum und Weltbild, Innsbruck.

Ray, B. G. (1976): African Religions. Symbol, Ritual and Community, London.

Reisach, Ch. (1981): Das Wort und seine Macht in Afrika, Münsterschwarzach.

Richards, A. I. (1956): Chisungu. A girl's initiation ceremony among the Bemba of Northern Rhodesia, London.

Ricoeur, P. (1971): Symbolik des Bösen, Freiburg/Munich.

Ringwald, W. (1952): Die Religion der Akanstämme und das Problem ihrer Bekehrung, Stuttgart.

Rücker, H. (1985): Afrikanische Theologie. Darstellung und Dialog, Innsbruck.

Samartha, S. J. (ed.) (1977): Faith in the Midst of Faiths, Geneva.

Sawyer, H. (1970): God. Ancestor or Creator? Aspects of traditional belief in Ghana, Nigeria and Sierra Leone, London.

(1972): Persons in Relationship (an examination of three facts of tribal society), in: Les Religions africaines, 189–204.

Shapera, I. (ed.) (1962): The Bantu-Speaking Tribes in South Africa, Cape Town, 7th ed.

(1970): A Handbook of Tswana Law and Custom, London (repr.)

(1971): Married Life in an African Tribe, London (repr.)

Schlosser, K. (1949): Propheten in Afrika, Braunschweig.

Schulz-Weidner, W. (1964): Arbeit und Arbeitsethos im ursprünglichen Schwarz-Afrika, in: Afrikanischer Heimatkalender, Windhoek, 77–93.

Sempebwa, J. W. (1983): African Traditional Moral Norms and their Implications for Christianity. A Case Study of Ganda Ethics, St. Augustin.

(1983a): Schuld und Umkehr in den afrikanischen Naturreligionen, in: M. Sievernich/K. P. Seif (Hg.): Schuld und Umkehr in den Weltreligionen, Mainz, 121–139.

Setiloane, G. M. (1976): The Image of God among the Sotho-Tswana, Rotterdam.

Sidhom, S. (1969): The Theological Estimate of Man, in: K. A. Dickson/P. Ellingworth, 83–115.

Simenauer, E. (1961–62): Ödipus – Konflikt und Neurosenbildung bei den Bantu Ostafrikas, in: Jahrbuch für Psychoanalyse, 41–62.

Smith, E. W. (1946): Knowing the African, London.

(1961): (ed.), African Ideas of God, London, 2nd ed.

Sofola, J. A. (1973): African Culture and the African Personality, Ibadan.

Spiegel, Y. (1973): Der Prozess des Trauerns. Anaylse und Beratung, München.

Spieth, J. (1911): Die Religion der Eweer in Süd-Togo. Göttingen.

Staewen, C./Schönberg, F. (1970): Kulturwandel und Angstentwicklung bei den Yoruba, Westafrika, Munich.

Stayt, H. A. (1968): The Bavenda, London, 2nd ed.

Straube, H. (1955): Die Tierverkleidung der afrikanischen Naturvölker, Wiesbaden.

Sundermeier. T. (1972): Frömmigkeit ist das Streben nach Frieden. Frömmigkeit in den einheimischen Gemeinden im südlichen Afrika, in: Dt. Pfarrblatt, 819–821.

(1973a): Wir aber suchten Gemeinschaft. Kirchwerdung und Kirchentrennung in Südwestafrika, Witten/Erlangen.

(1973b): Unio Analogica. Zum Verständnis afrikanischer dynamistischer Denkformen, in: Ev. Missionszeitschrift, 150–166, 181–192.

(1973c): Ein Ersatz für den Kraal, in: Luth. Monatshefte, 14–16.

(1974): The structures of "people" and the culture and their challenge of the future mission of the Church, in: Missionalia, 167–171.

(1975a): Symbol und Wirklichkeit. Zum Verständnis afrikanischer Symbolik, in: Ev. Missionszeitschrift, 155–176.

(1975b): (ed.) Church and Nationalism in South Africa, Johannesburg.

(1976): Mensch sein heisst Partizipation, in: Luth. Monatshefte, 338–340.

(1977a): Todesriten als Lebenshilfe. Der Trauerprozeß in Afrika, in: Wege zum Menschen, 129–144.

(1977b): Ehrfurcht vor dem Menschen. Bestimmende Elemente der afrikanischen Ethik, in: Luth. Monatshefte, 275–278.

(1977c): Die Mbanderu. Studien zu ihrer Geschichte und Kultur, St. Augustin.

(1981): Afrikanisches Bewusstsein im Wandel, in: Kunst und Kirche, 178–183.

(1983): Christliche Kunst in Südafrika, in: Ordensnachrichten, 256–272.

(1987): Jeder Teil dieser Erde ist meinem Volke heilig, in: G. Rau u. a. (Ed.): Frieden in der Schöpfung, Gütersloh, 20–34.

Sundkler, B. (1964): Bantupropheten in Südafrika, Stuttgart.

Swantz, M.-L. (1979): Ritual und Symbol in Traditional Zaramo Society, Uppsala.

(1985): Women in Development: A Creative Role Denied?, London.

Taylor, J. V./Lehmann, D. (1961): Christians of the Copperbelt. The Growth of the Church in Northern Rhodesia, London.

Taylor, J. V. (1963): The Primal Vision: Christian Presence amid African Religion. London.

(1966): Die Kirche in Buganda, Stuttgart.

Tempels, P. (1959): Bantu Philosophy; translated by C. King, Paris.

Thiel, J. F. (1977): Ahnen – Geister – Höchste Wesen. Religionsethnologische Untersuchungen im Zaire-Kasai-Gebiet, St. Augustin.

Thomas, L. V./Luneau, R. (1975): La terre africaine et ses religions, Paris.

(1977): Les sages dispossédés. Univers magique d'Afrique Noire, Paris.

Thompson, R. F. (1973): An Aesthetic of the Cool. African Arts, Herbst, 40–41, 64–67, 89–92.

Turnbull, C. M. (1973): Das Volk ohne Liebe. Der soziale Untergang der IK, Hamburg.

Turner, H. W. (1967): African Independent Church, vol. I and II: The Church of the Lord (Aladura), London.

(1969): The Place of Independent Religious Movements in the Modernization of Africa, in: Journal of Religion in Africa, 43–63.

(1979): Religious Innovation in Africa. Collected Papers on New Religious Movements, Boston.

Turner, V. W. (1967): The Forest of Symbols. Aspects of Ndembu Ritual, New York.

(1968a): The Waters of Life. Some Reflections on Zionist Water Symbolism, in: J. Neusner (ed.): Religions in Antiquity (Festschrift E. R. Goodenough), Leiden, 506–520.

(1968b): The Drums of Affliction. A Study of Religious Process among the Ndembu of Zambia, Oxford.

Vedder, H. (1923): Die Bergdama, vol. I and II, Hamburg.

Wagner, G. (1939): Die Religion der Bantu von Kavirondo, in: Zeitschrift für Ethnologie, 201–218.

Welbourn, F. B./Ogot, B. A. (1966): A Place to Feel at Home. A Study in Two Independent Churches in Western Kenya, London.

(1968): Some Problems of African Christianity: Guilt and Shame, in: Baeta, 182–199.

(1969): Keyo Initiation, Journal of Religion in Africa, 212–232.

Westermann, D. (1921): Die K`pelle. Ein Negerstamm in Liberia, Göttingen.

(1937): Africa and Christianity, Oxford.

Willoughby, W. C. (1928): Some Conclusions Concerning the Bantu Conception of the Soul, in: Anthropos, 338–347.

Wilson, G./Wilson, M. (1968): The Analysis of Social Change. Based on Observations in Central Africa, Cambridge, 4th ed.

Wilson, M. (1957): Rituals of Kinship among the Nyakyusa, London.

(1959): Communal Rituals of the Nyakyusa, London.

(1963): Good Company. A Study of Nyakyusa Age-Villages, Boston, 2nd ed.

(1971): Religion and the Transformation of Society. A Study in Social Change in Africa, Cambridge.

Whisson, M. G./West, M. (ed.) (1975): Religion and Social Change in Southern Africa (Festschrift M. Wilson), Cape Town.

Winter, E. H. (1969): The Enemy within: Amba Witchcraft and Sociological Theory, in: J. Middleton/E. H. Winter, 277–299.

Zahan, D. (1919): The Religion, Spirituality and Thought of Traditional Africa, Chicago/London.

Subject index

Names of peoples are printed in italics

Akan 26, 136, 169-174, 180, 184, 193
allegory 39
Amba 196
analogy 30, 32-37, 39, 41, 46, 112f, 117,
   199, 206, 211-213, 235
ancestors 5, 11f, 18, 59, 62, 87, 110, 115,
   118f, 124-128, 130, 134-136, 147,
   199, 207, 213, 215
animal 9, 27, 35, 45, 48f, 85f, 98, 100,
   107, 110, 112-115, 119, 133, 137, 146,
   150, 163, 188, 199, 202, 207, 217
anthropology 30f, 39, 51, 53f, 106, 121,
   128, 224
Ashanti 11, 13, 46f, 126, 169, 220
authority 6, 35, 126, 153, 188, 205f, 217
Bakoko 65, 69
Bakossi 122, 130, 197
Bakwiri 111
Bamba 48
Bambara 6, 185
Bantu 6, 14, 20, 25, 30, 32, 39, 47, 56,
   87, 128, 131, 164, 170, 179, 181, 193,
   210f
Basa 131
Bavenda 67, 69, 112, 162
being 11f, 14, 20, 22-24, 30, 39, 52, 68,
   127, 138, 157f, 165, 173, 185
belief 2f, 10, 30, 78, 97, 113f, 120-122,
   125-128, 130f, 134f, 139, 143-149,
   157-159, 164, 172, 174, 186, 190,
   196-198, 207, 213, 216, 223, 226, 236,
   238f
Bemba 214, 223

Bergdama 128
Bete 220
beyond 92, 122, 135, 167f, 221
blessing 21, 23, 75, 90, 145
blood 11, 23, 35, 45-47, 58, 63, 67, 74,
   85, 99, 113, 145, 151, 186, 188, 190,
   208, 214f
Bobeal 111
Bushmen 94, 120
cattle 25, 28f, 33, 44f, 71-73, 76f, 79f,
   101f, 107-110, 131f, 176, 178f, 215
Chagga 23, 144, 233
chaos 26f, 29, 54
Christ 120, 229, 239
Christianity 14, 20, 47, 121f, 125, 131,
   159, 161, 184, 191, 204, 224, 227f,
   237
church 10, 24, 27, 122, 205, 220-223,
   228-231, 233, 238
circumcision 35, 57, 59-67, 76, 213
colour 33, 35, 46-48, 61, 100, 155, 168,
   179, 188, 200, 203, 212
communal 53, 96, 98, 143, 178, 230, 239
communication 5, 35, 38, 90, 109, 135,
   145, 150, 203, 225
community 5, 16-18, 20, 26, 37, 41, 45,
   50, 53, 55, 57-60, 62, 64f, 67-69, 77f,
   87, 92, 97, 113, 115, 126f, 129, 134f,
   154, 175-178, 180, 182f, 189, 192,
   195, 197, 202, 204f, 207, 210, 213,
   219, 221, 225-227, 229f, 234, 238
concept of God 142, 159f, 164, 170, 173,
   240

193, 201, 204, 206, 210f, 223f, 229,
230, 234f, 237, 239
guilt 12, 15, 58, 76, 85, 147, 186, 191-
193, 217, 221
Gwari 216
Hadjerai 183
health 46, 109, 133, 186, 200, 204, 231
heaven 44, 108, 128, 136, 149, 153,
155f, 161, 163-166, 168, 170, 209,
221, 230
Herero 26-29, 33-36, 44, 46, 68, 70, 78,
87, 89, 107-110, 115, 117, 127, 131,
160, 214
Himba 76, 86, 88, 106
history 1-3, 26, 30, 37, 60, 114, 127,
135, 138, 147, 152, 159, 183, 223,
232, 237, 239
human 1, 3f, 9-11, 13f, 18, 20-26, 29,
37-39, 41f, 44f, 47, 50, 52, 55, 68, 81,
86, 91, 98, 104-107, 110-113, 120,
123, 130, 132, 138, 143, 145-148, 151,
162, 164, 166-169, 171-174, 177, 183-
185, 188, 190f, 193, 195f, 202, 210f,
239
Hutu 134
identification 81, 89f, 117, 119, 207, 221
identity 10, 12, 19, 45, 49, 54, 69, 118,
127, 131, 202, 225-227, 232
immanence 167
incarnation 16, 113
incest 189f
independent churches 135, 222f, 228,
230f
indigenisation 233
initiation 59, 63, 64-69, 86, 94, 100f,
183, 202, 206f, 215, 219
inversion 36, 91
Islam 47, 125, 131, 184, 190, 227, 228

Karanga 13, 34, 74, 130
Khoisan 6, 25, 32, 34, 120
Kikuyu 27, 57, 169, 208
Koko 131
Kwanjama 106, 211
language 1, 5, 13, 21f, 39, 41, 66, 80, 89,
99, 122, 145, 155, 160, 171, 205, 234
law 3, 18, 27, 34-37, 39, 46, 49, 55, 71,
74f, 77, 98, 118, 181, 184, 189, 191f,
205, 217, 229f, 239
Lele 18, 93f, 97, 111f
life 4-6, 9, 11-24, 26-30, 34, 36, 38, 40f,
44, 46, 48, 50f, 53-66, 68, 74-76, 80-
83, 86, 88-93, 95, 98f, 101f, 104, 106-
110, 112, 118, 120-123, 126, 128-131,
134-136, 142f, 145, 148, 151, 155f,
158f, 162f, 165f, 169, 172, 175f, 178-
180, 182-184, 187-191, 193, 195, 197,
199f, 202, 204, 206-211, 213-215,
219f, 224-227, 230, 232, 235f, 239
lineage 45, 69, 73, 75, 126, 129, 188
livelihood 27, 58
Lobedu 72, 210f, 214
Lugbara 128, 130, 132, 216
Lunda 211
magic 2f, 30-34, 37, 53, 61, 76, 94, 140,
180, 195, 215
Makonde 146
mana 30, 146
Mbanderu 25, 40, 130
mediator/intermediary 56, 105, 112, 206,
211
medicine 31-34, 36, 42, 47f, 59, 62f, 87,
94-96, 97, 100, 112, 131, 140, 152,
172, 195, 198, 202, 204f, 208, 212
Mende 137, 142f
mission 1, 62, 204, 228f, 231, 233

missionary 6, 14, 24, 30, 40, 110, 120, 156, 160, 174, 178, 190, 230, 236, 239

mother 17, 45f, 57f, 60, 62, 64, 66f, 70f, 73f, 79f, 82, 84f, 88, 90, 99, 113, 126, 149, 151, 156, 165, 178, 184, 186, 189f, 209, 211, 217, 218

mourning 24, 36, 54, 56, 59, 77-79, 82-91, 151, 168, 178, 189, 199, 201, 230, 238, 239

myth 18, 22, 65, 67, 153f, 161-163, 167, 210, 215

name/names 4, 12f, 16, 21-23, 25, 41, 44, 51, 69, 77, 79, 82-84, 91, 94, 101f, 107, 114, 123-126, 129, 137-139, 149, 156, 158-161, 164-167, 170, 173, 187, 197, 210, 213, 220, 234f, 237

Ndebele 218

Ndembu 34f, 42

Nuba 189

Nuer 24, 86, 101f, 110, 115-117, 147, 149, 151f, 169

number 65, 156, 158, 213

Nupe 190, 216

Nyakyusa 85-88, 120, 130, 131, 181, 184, 187, 189

Nyoro 44

Ovambo 73, 107, 170-172, 185, 187

participation 14, 18f, 30, 32, 37f, 41, 49, 55, 61, 64, 68, 98, 101, 111, 130, 157f, 178, 238

peace 23, 47, 51, 61, 75, 98, 102, 111, 123, 134, 144f, 151, 162, 178-180, 185, 192

Pedi 74, 78-82, 85-87, 117, 181

Pondo 143, 197, 215f

power 1, 6, 20, 22f, 26, 30-33, 35, 37, 40, 44, 46-49, 53f, 56, 60f, 73, 82, 90f, 98f, 102, 115, 118, 121, 135, 142, 144,

146f, 153-155, 158, 162, 166f, 173, 183-190, 194f, 197, 202-204, 207, 209, 218, 223, 231, 233

prayer 61, 81, 83, 94, 102, 110, 112, 122-124, 132f, 158, 165, 169, 192, 220, 222, 230

present life 5, 118, 126

priest 40, 156, 233

proverb 23, 78, 115, 148, 163, 170, 177, 183f, 193

reincarnation 91

religion 1-7, 9, 14, 16, 20, 25, 30f, 37, 41, 53, 68, 78, 91-93, 97, 104, 106, 119f, 122, 125, 127, 130f, 135, 144, 146-149, 152, 157-159, 163, 170, 174-176, 187, 190, 192, 194, 198, 207f, 223-227, 231, 233-239

'higher' religion 2

traditional religion 1f, 4, 6, 24, 119f, 122, 135, 146, 160, 174, 205, 220f, 223, 229, 231, 233f, 238-240

world religion 2, 234, 237

religious experience 45, 234-237, 239

rites de passage 57, 106

ritual 6, 10, 12, 23f, 26, 33f, 36f, 40, 42, 46, 53-55, 57-59, 61-65, 67, 70, 76, 78, 82, 86f, 89-94, 98, 100, 111-113, 118, 142, 144f, 166, 169, 178, 182, 195, 203, 205f, 211-215, 217, 219, 229, 233, 235, 240

sacred 13, 29, 42, 55, 65f, 76, 88, 92, 109, 214

sacrifice 42, 45f, 86, 88, 101f, 112, 131, 142f, 147, 151, 158, 169, 188, 207, 214

secular 33, 51, 55, 65, 74, 94, 98, 109, 122, 135, 206, 223, 231, 239

Person index